AF593837

Basic Skills in English

Book 6

Book 5

Book 4

Book 3

Book 2

Book 1

THE McDOUGAL, LITTELL ENGLISH PROGRAM

Basic Skills in English

Book 5

Joy Littell, EDITORIAL DIRECTOR

McDougal, Littell & Company
Evanston, Illinois
Sacramento, California

AUTHORS

Joy Littell, Editorial Director, and
The Editorial Staff of McDougal, Littell & Company

Kraft and Kraft, Developers of Educational Materials

Marilyn M. Sherman, formerly, English teacher,
New Trier Township High School West, Northfield, Illinois

CONSULTANTS

Carolyn McConnell, formerly, English teacher, George C. Marshall High School, Fairfax County, Virginia; and instructor, College of DuPage, Glen Ellyn, Illinois

Rebecca Williams, formerly, English instructor, Kennedy-King College, Chicago, Illinois; and instructor of Special Programs, Indiana University

Editor-in-Chief: Joseph F. Littell
Managing Editor: Kathleen Laya
Senior Editor: Trisha Lorange Taylor
Director of Design: William A. Seabright
Design Associate: Lucy Lesiak
Assistant Editor: Mary Schafer

Acknowledgments: See page 523.

ISBN: 0-88343-790-2

Composition

WRITING SECTION 17

Using a Dictionary 165

WRITING SECTION 18

Using the Library 175

WRITING SECTION 19

Writing a Report Investigating Careers 189

WRITING SECTION 20

Developing Speaking Skills 215

Write Again 227-238

These eleven pages consist of additional writing assignments. There is an exercise for each Part in the twenty Sections. Your teacher may choose to assign each of these exercises as additional practice after each part. The exercises will give you extra practice in improving your writing skills.

Handbook

WRITING SECTION 1

Developing Your Vocabulary

Part 1

Discoveries

Learning Word Meanings from Context

Here's the Idea English has a larger, more varied vocabulary than most other languages. It includes a total of about 600,000 different words. In everyday situations, you usually recognize from 30,000 to 40,000 words. In speaking and writing, you may use 10,000.

One way in which you can continually develop your vocabulary is to examine words in context. **Context** means the words and sentences around a given word. There are context clues that can help you to figure out the meanings of unfamiliar words.

When **definition** is used in context, the meaning of an unfamiliar word is stated directly. Here is an example.

> Jean is taking a *yoga* class at the YWCA. *Yoga* is a system of controlled breathing and exercises.

When **restatement** is used, the meaning of a new word is rephrased. Look for key words like *or*, *that is*, or *which is*.

> The City Council approved a three percent tax *rebate*. That is, taxpayers will receive a return equal to three percent of their taxes.

You may be able to understand the meaning of a word through **examples** given. Look for the key words *especially*, *like*, *other*, *this*, *such as*, *for example*, and *for instance*.

> *Pasta*, especially spaghetti and macaroni, makes a filling and inexpensive meal.

When **comparison** is used, a new word is compared with a similar word that is known to you. Recognize the key words *as*, *like*, *in the same way*, and *similar to*.

Ralph's *astute* answer was as clever as the teacher's question.

When **contrast** is used, a new word is compared with an opposite word that is known to you. Recognize the key words *although*, *but*, *unlike*, *while*, *on the contrary*, and *on the other hand*.

That perfume is *subtle*, but this one has quite a sharp scent.

Check It Out Read the following sentences.

1. I didn't understand the speaker's *dialect*. A dialect is a form of a language with its own vocabulary and pronunciation.
2. Dan's latest *objective*, or goal, is to run two miles every day.
3. Radioactive elements, such as *uranium* and *radium*, must be stored safely.
4. This *minestrone* is similar to Grandma's vegetable soup.
5. Although I was *punctual*, Donna was late for our meeting.

- What is the meaning of each italicized word? What context clue is used in each sentence?

Try Your Skill Choose four of these words: *artist*, *cashier*, *electrician*, *reporter*, *salesperson*, *secretary*. Write a sentence that explains each word. Use key words as context clues.

Keep This in Mind

- Develop your vocabulary by examining unfamiliar words in context. Helpful context clues are definition, restatement, examples, comparison, and contrast.

Now Write Copy five unfamiliar words used in a textbook. Use the context clues to write a definition of each word. Check your meanings in a dictionary. Label your paper **Discoveries,** the title of this lesson. Keep your work in your folder.

Part 2

Drawing Conclusions

Inferring Meaning from Context

Here's the Idea The meaning of an unfamiliar word is not always made clear through direct context clues. However, the surrounding sentences may help you make a good guess at the meaning of an unfamiliar word. You may be able to read between the lines and draw a conclusion about the meaning of the word. This process is called **inference.**

The main idea of a passage or an entire paragraph may be related to the meaning of an unfamiliar word. In the following paragraph, for example, try to *infer* the meaning of the word *serene.*

> Jill has managed to stay *serene* in spite of a trying day. This morning she didn't panic when she discovered that her bicycle had a flat tire. At lunch, she was patient with the freshman who tipped over her soup. She even remained unruffled during our surprize quiz in math this afternoon.

From the clues supplied in this paragraph, you can infer that *serene* means "quiet, calm, undisturbed."

Check It Out Read the following paragraph.

> When I finish high school, I am going to become an *apprentice* in the printing industry. For three years I will work with a master typesetter to learn all the phases of typesetting and printing. I will become familiar with various kinds of presses and with other printing machinery. I will also receive a salary while I learn the business.

- What can you infer about the meaning of *apprentice*?

Try Your Skill As you read these passages, try to infer the meaning of the italicized words. Write definitions for them.

1. My cousin's *dilapidated* car is as unsafe as it looks. The fenders are one color, the roof another, and the trunk a third. The tires are bald. Only one of the brake lights is working. Each visible part of the car is rusty, dented, or worn. It is impossible for me to imagine that this car was ever new.

2. Critics point out that one bad side-effect of watching too much violent TV is increased *irascibility* in young children. Pre-schoolers who watch more than three hours a day are more quick-tempered and irritable than those whose viewing is more limited.

3. The most *prodigious* tides in the world occur in the Bay of Fundy, between Maine and Nova Scotia. In most places, the difference between high and low tide is only a few feet. However, near the narrow mouth of the Bay of Fundy, the tides rise more than fifty feet! Because of these awesome tides and the fog, these waters are considered quite dangerous.

4. Shoveling snow became a *lucrative* activity for me last winter. The heavy snowfalls set records. People in my neighborhood paid me extra money to shovel the large drifts that buried driveways, cars, and sidewalks. In fact, I made more money in one month than I had during the last three winters put together.

Keep This in Mind

- Inference is the process of using clues to draw a conclusion. Inferences about unfamiliar words can be drawn from the main ideas of paragraphs.

Now Write Suppose you want to write a description of a friend who is especially *thoughtful*. Write four or five sentences that suggest this quality without defining it directly. Label your paper **Drawing Conclusions** and put it into your folder.

Part 3
A Word Divided

Recognizing Prefixes

Here's the Idea Another good way to develop your vocabulary is to examine the parts of an unfamiliar word. In English, there are many words that are made up of parts that work together. If you learn some of the most common word parts, you will be able to learn many new words.

A **prefix** is a word part with its own meaning added to the beginning of a base word. For instance, the prefix *sub-* means "under" or "less than." Once you know the meaning of this prefix, you will know that *subsoil* is "a layer of soil beneath the surface soil." You will also see that a *subcompact* is "a car that is smaller than a compact." Notice how the addition of the prefix affects the meanings of the base words *soil* and *compact*.

Study this list of common prefixes, with their meanings and examples. Notice that some prefixes have more than one meaning.

Prefix	Meaning	Example
dis-	"opposite of" or "away"	dishonest, displace
in- (also **il-** **im-** and **ir-**)	"not"	inability, illogical, immature, irreplaceable
mis-	"wrong, bad"	misbehavior
non-	"not"	nonfiction
pre-	"before"	prepay
re-	"again" or "back"	remarry, regain

Do not expect to find prefixes in all words, however. Check a word and its history in a dictionary to determine if the word has a prefix.

Check It Out Examine these words and their definitions.

discomfort—"lack of comfort, distress"
disarm—"to take away weapons; to reduce forces"
inattentive—"not attentive, careless"
illimitable—"not limited, without bounds"
immobile—"not movable, motionless"
irrational—"not reasonable, absurd"
misfortune—"bad luck, trouble"
nonessential—"not essential, unnecessary"
precaution—"care taken beforehand"
rearrange—"to arrange again or differently"
repay—"to pay back"

- What is the prefix in each? What is the base word?

Try Your Skill Twelve of the following words have prefixes. For each word that has a prefix, write the prefix and its meaning, plus the base word. For example, for the word *preview* you would write: pre (before) + view.

1. miscount
2. distrust
3. pressure
4. redecorate
5. incapable
6. nonskid
7. miserable
8. reenlist
9. mispronounce
10. preelection
11. disinterested
12. prepackage
13. irresistible
14. nonrestricted
15. distant

Keep This in Mind

- A prefix is a word part added at the beginning of a base word. A prefix has its own meaning. Learn the meanings of common prefixes.

Now Write Use a dictionary to find six unfamiliar words containing each of the six prefixes you have learned. List these words and define them. Finally, study them. Label your paper **A Word Divided** and keep it in your folder.

Part 4 **On End**

Recognizing Suffixes

Here's the Idea A word part added at the end of a base word is called a **suffix.** Like a prefix, a suffix has a meaning of its own that affects the meaning of the base word. Also like a prefix, a suffix may have more than one meaning or more than one form. For instance, the suffix *-er* or *-or* means "a person or thing that does something." Thus, a *counselor* is "a person who counsels or advises."

Unlike prefixes, however, suffixes usually affect the spelling of the base words. Sometimes the final consonant is doubled. For example, *shop* becomes *shopper*. Sometimes the final letter is dropped. For example, *move* becomes *movable*. Sometimes the final letter of the base word is changed. For example, *penny* becomes *penniless*.

Study this list of common suffixes, with their meanings and examples.

Suffix	Meaning	Example
-able or **-ible**	"can be, having this quality"	lovable, sensible
-less	"without"	thoughtless
-ful	"full of, having"	doubtful
-ous	"full of, having"	courageous
-ist	"a person who does something"	biologist
-ion	"act of, result of, condition of"	correction
-y	"tending to be, characterized by"	foggy

Check It Out Examine these words and their definitions.

sociable—"enjoying the company of others; friendly"
permissible—"that can be permitted; allowable"
artless—"lacking skill or art; simple; natural"
pitiful—"deserving pity because it is sad or pathetic"
spacious—"having more than enough space; large"
naturalist—"a person who studies animals and plants"
formation—"something formed, arranged, or positioned"
faulty—"having faults; imperfect"

- What is the suffix in each ? What is the base word?

Try Your Skill Number your paper from 1 to 15. Find the suffix in each of the following words. Check the spelling of the base word if necessary. Write the base word and the meaning of the suffix for each word. For instance, for the word *typist* you would write: type + a person who does.

1. famous
2. homeless
3. violinist
4. taxable
5. reflection
6. delightful
7. convertible
8. noisy
9. mysterious
10. wavy
11. guitarist
12. priceless
13. cupful
14. reasonable
15. translation

Keep This in Mind

- A suffix is a word part added at the end of a base word. A suffix has its own meaning. Learn the meanings of some of the most common suffixes. Use a dictionary to check the spelling of a word when you add a suffix.

Now Write Use a dictionary to help you find seven words, each containing a different one of the seven suffixes you have learned. List the new words. Define them and study them. Label your paper **On End** and put it into your folder.

Part 5

The Root of the Matter

Using Roots from Latin

Here's the Idea You have been learning about word parts and base words. You have learned that a prefix like *dis-*, meaning "opposite," can be added to a base word such as *loyal*. The word formed, *disloyal*, means "without loyalty; faithless." You have also learned that a suffix, like *-y*, meaning "characterized by," can be added to a base word such as *sleep*. The word formed, *sleepy*, means "likely to fall asleep, drowsy." In these examples, it is clear that base words are separate words with their own meanings. What are the base words in *prearrange*, *weightless*, and *inapplicable?*

There are some words that are formed from a different kind of word part, called a **root.** Usually, a root is not a word by itself. Instead, a root has a particular meaning of its own. Because almost half of the words in English come from Latin, the most common roots also come from Latin.

Study these four common Latin roots given with their meanings and an example. Notice that the forms of some roots may change slightly.

Latin Root	Meaning	Example
cred	"believe"	*credit*, meaning "belief or trust; approval; confidence"
duc, duct, duce	"lead"	*introduction*, meaning "something that leads into or prepares the way for"
fac, fact	"make"	*factory*, meaning "a building in which things are made"
pos, pon	"place or set"	*position*, meaning "the place where a person or thing is, especially in relation to others"

Check It Out Examine these words and their definitions.

creed—"a brief statement of beliefs"
incredible—"unbelievable"
produce—"to lead or bring forth; to create"
deduce—"to figure out by logical reasoning from known facts"
factor—"any of the conditions that makes something happen"
manufacture—"to make goods, especially by machinery"
positive—"definitely set; sure"
impose—"to place something on, such as a burden, tax, or regulation"

- What is the Latin root in each example? How is the meaning of the root related to the meaning of the whole word?

Try Your Skill Copy the following words, circling the Latin root in each. Use the meaning of the root to help you figure out the meaning of the word. Then check the history and the meaning of each word in a dictionary.

creditable	abduct	fact	posture
accredit	aqueduct	facility	postpone

Keep This in Mind

- A root is a part of a word and has a meaning of its own. Many common roots come from Latin. Learn some of the Latin roots, and you will have a clue to the meaning of many unfamiliar words.

Now Write Using a dictionary, find four new words containing each of the four Latin roots you have learned. List and define the new words. Finally, study the roots. Label your paper **The Root of the Matter.** Put it into in your folder.

Part 6

In the Right

Using Words Precisely

Here's the Idea If you use language carelessly, you run two risks. First, your writing may be dull or boring. Second, and more important, your ideas may be misunderstood. Thus, it is important to choose specific words that express the precise meaning you have in mind.

To use words precisely you need to learn to choose among synonyms. **Synonyms** are words with nearly the same meaning. For example, the words *easy*, *effortless*, *smooth*, and *simple* are synonyms. The meanings may be quite similar, but the differences are usually important. These important shades of meaning are often explained in a dictionary. A *synonymy* (si nän′ ə mē) is the list of synonyms and their shades of meaning that is given at the end of some entries in a dictionary.

Synonyms are also given in another helpful reference book called a *thesaurus* (thi sôr′ əs). A thesaurus gives many synonyms for a particular word or idea.

To use words precisely, you also need to learn to use antonyms. **Antonyms** are words with opposite meanings. For example, *find – lose*, *arrive – depart*, and *ancient – modern* are antonyms. Antonyms will help you to show contrasts. For example, you might write, "In Rome the remains of *ancient* buildings are an important part of the *modern* city." You will find antonyms given in some dictionaries as well as in a thesaurus.

Check It Out Look at the synonymy given at the end of the dictionary entry for *sad*.

SYN.—**sad** is the simple, general term, implying anything from a mild unhappiness that is over quickly to a feeling of great, deep grief; **sorrowful** implies a sadness caused by some specific loss, disappointment, etc. [her death left him *sorrowful*]; **melancholy** suggests a more or less continuing mournfulness or gloominess, or, often, merely a deep thoughtfulness [a *melancholy* view of life and its misfortunes]; **dejected** implies discouragement or a sinking of spirits, as because of frustration; **depressed** suggests a mood of worry and hopelessness, as because of feeling tired or useless [the unhappy ending left him feeling *depressed*]; **doleful** implies a mournful, often exaggerated, sadness [the *doleful* look on a lost child's face] —***ANT.*** **happy, cheerful**

- Which synonym for *sad* suggests discouragement?
- What are antonyms for *sad?*

Try Your Skill Choose the synonym that best fits each sentence. Use a dictionary or thesaurus to help you.

1. I couldn't risk driving far on these (bad, wicked, severe, defective) tires.
2. Dr. McKenna hoped her patient would (reply, answer, respond, retort) to the bright light.
3. You can turn to your elders for (intelligent, clever, alert, smart) advice on many practical matters.
4. The youngest children (chuckled, laughed, snickered, guffawed) at the clown's wonderful, silly tricks.

Keep This in Mind

- Use a dictionary or thesaurus to check the meanings of words. Learn to use words precisely.
- Use dictionary or thesaurus to check the meanings of words. Learn to use words precisely.

Now Write Choose two of the synonyms and one antonym for *sad* shown in **Check It Out.** Use each correctly in a sentence that shows its precise meaning. Label your paper **In The Right** and put it into your folder.

Part 7

Special Effects

Building a Vocabulary of the Senses

Here's the Idea Your five senses are constantly giving you specific information. Much of the time you do not pay particular attention to sensory details. However, if you stop and focus on each of your senses, you will realize the variety of impressions you are receiving. When you write, you can use these sensory details to describe an experience and bring it to life.

Through the use of sensory details you can make any experience vivid. For example, suppose you were home alone during a power failure. Can you imagine that experience as you read the following paragraph?

> I felt the sudden silence. The radio stopped. The furnace ceased its steady rumbling. The refrigerator stopped its droning hum. The only sounds were those of the wind whistling and the creaking of the old house. As I sat in the silence I felt a chilly draft. I shivered and moved towards the window. I watched the darkening sky as the storm thundered into the valley.

To learn how to use sensory details effectively, you need to do three things. First, train yourself to be more aware of your senses. Notice the details of your surroundings. Second, build a vocabulary of the senses. Become familiar with sensory words such as those listed on pages 16 and 17 at the end of this lesson. Finally, use your sensory vocabulary effectively. Select sensory words that describe your experience precisely.

Check It Out Look at these examples of sensory words.

Sight	silver, curved, sparkling, massive
Hearing	thud, whine, hiss, rustle, sigh
Touch	lukewarm, spongy, wooly, waxy
Taste	bittersweet, mellow, medicinal, savory
Smell	earthy, pungent, briny, musty

- Which of these sensory words are new to you? What do they mean? Think of an object or place that might be described by each of these words.

Try Your Skill Think of two particular places that fit the general categories below. Name the two places and then list as many sensory words as you can think of that are related to each one. Be specific. Try to use all of your senses.

a museum	a gymnasium
a department store	a classroom
an amusement park	a room
a restaurant	a garage

Keep This in Mind

- Use your senses to learn about your surroundings. Build a vocabulary of the senses. When you write, use vivid sensory details that bring an experience to life.

Now Write Think of a particular place where you go to rest or relax. List as many sensory details about the place as you can. Try to use all of your senses. Choose specific, precise words. You may want to refer to the sample lists on the following pages. Label your paper **Special Effects.** Keep it in your folder.

A List of Sight Words

colorless	round	dotted	tidy
white	flat	freckled	handsome
ivory	curved	wrinkled	tall
yellow	wavy	striped	lean
gold	ruffled	bright	muscular
orange	oval	clear	sturdy
lime	angular	shiny	healthy
green	triangular	sparkling	fragile
turquoise	rectangular	jeweled	pale
blue	square	fiery	sickly
pink	hollow	sheer	small
red	wide	muddy	tiny
maroon	narrow	drab	large
lavender	crooked	dark	massive
purple	lumpy	old	immense
gray	swollen	worn	attractive
silver	long	messy	perky
hazel	wiry	cluttered	showy
brown	lopsided	fresh	lacy
black	shapeless	clean	elegant

A List of Hearing Words

crash	squawk	crackle	chime
thud	whine	buzz	laugh
bump	bark	clink	gurgle
boom	bleat	hiss	giggle
thunder	bray	snort	guffaw
bang	blare	bellow	sing
roar	rumble	growl	hum
scream	grate	whimper	mutter
screech	slam	stammer	murmur
shout	clap	snap	whisper
yell	stomp	rustle	sigh
whistle	jangle	whir	hush

A List of Taste Words

oily	rich	bland	ripe
buttery	hearty	tasteless	medicinal
salty	mellow	sour	fishy
bitter	sugary	vinegary	spicy
bittersweet	crisp	fruity	hot
sweet	savory	tangy	burnt

A List of Smell Words

sweet	piney	acrid	sickly
scented	pungent	burnt	stagnant
fragrant	spicy	gaseous	musty
aromatic	gamy	putrid	moldy
perfumed	fishy	spoiled	dry
fresh	briny	sour	damp
earthy	sharp	rancid	dank

A List of Touch Words

cool	wet	silky	sandy
cold	slippery	velvety	gritty
icy	spongy	smooth	rough
lukewarm	mushy	soft	sharp
tepid	oily	wooly	thick
warm	waxy	furry	dry
hot	fleshy	feathery	dull
steamy	rubbery	fuzzy	thin
sticky	bumpy	hairy	fragile
damp	crisp	leathery	tender

VISE

WRITING SECTION 2

Controlling Your Sentences

Part 1

In the Clear

Using Sentences

Here's the Idea Individual words usually express parts of thoughts. A **sentence** is a group of words that expresses a complete thought.

Good sentences express complete thoughts clearly and directly. A good sentence has something to say. The idea it expresses may be humorous or serious, but it is clear. A good sentence also expresses an idea in a direct and imaginative way.

Read these examples of effective, interesting sentences.

A light heart lives long.—WILLIAM SHAKESPEARE

A wise man will make more opportunities than he finds.
—FRANCIS BACON

Remember, no one can make you feel inferior without your consent.—ELEANOR ROOSEVELT

The language of friendship is not words but meanings.
—HENRY DAVID THOREAU

Please all and you please none.—AESOP

Freedom is the right to be wrong, not the right to do wrong.
—JOHN G. DIEFENBAKER

Each of these sentences has expressed one idea in a clear, direct, and original way. You can see how powerful a single sentence can be. When you write a sentence, use your senses and your imagination to express an idea in an effective way.

Check It Out Read the following sentences.

1. As Nancy raced to the exit, she searched the crowd for a police officer.
2. The patient's room was dark and smelled of antiseptic.

3. Homemade soup makes a light, tasty, and economical supper.

4. All citizens should participate in government by voting in elections.

5. Refugees are people who flee their homes or countries to seek safety during times of war and trouble.

- Does each sentence express a single, complete thought? Is each sentence clear and interesting?

Try Your Skill Write one sentence in response to each of the following directions. Use real or imaginary details to make your sentences clear and effective.

1. Tell one thing you usually do after school.
2. Describe something you own.
3. Explain how to save money.
4. Explain why passengers should wear seat belts in cars.
5. Explain what a basketball is.
6. Describe your favorite meal.
7. Tell one event that happened to your family.
8. Explain what a doctor is.

Keep This in Mind

- A sentence is a group of words that expresses a complete thought. A good sentence is clear and interesting.

Now Write Write five original sentences. One should tell part of a story. One should describe something. One should explain one step of a process. One should explain why something is useful. One should explain what something is.

Before you write, think about each sentence. Decide what point you are trying to make and how you can best make it. Be specific. Label your paper **In the Clear** and put into your folder.

Part 2

Beware of Detours

Keeping to the Point

Here's the Idea A well written sentence expresses one idea as clearly and directly as possible.

The volleyball sailed over our heads.
First prize in the poetry competition was awarded to Sandra.

Sometimes you may want to add details to a sentence to make it more interesting. Related details are those that support the main idea. By adding related details, you can add meaning to a sentence.

The volleyball, hit by Ms. Powers, sailed over our heads.

Here, the added detail is related to the volleyball shot.

First prize in the poetry competition was awarded to Sandra for her poem "Spring."

In this sentence, the added detail is related to the poem.

Whenever you include details in a sentence, be sure they are related to the main idea. Unrelated details will confuse the meaning of the sentence.

The volleyball, which we also use for soccer, sailed over our heads.

The added detail is not related to the volleyball shot.

First prize in the poetry competition was awarded to Sandra Morrison, who is six feet tall.

The added detail is about Sandra. However, the main idea of the sentence is the poetry prize.

Avoid using unrelated details in sentences that you write.

Use only interesting and specific details that are related to the main idea. Be sure to keep to the point.

Check It Out Read the following sentences.

1. My locker, which I share with Dan, is on the third floor.
2. Maria's father, who was born in Mexico, works at city hall.
3. Barrel racing, a sport I've never tried, is popular in many Western states.
4. Open the green door, which used to be brown, at the end of this hallway and you'll see the office.

- In each sentence what unrelated detail should be omitted? Are there any related details you might add?

Try Your Skill Rewrite the following sentences that contain unrelated details. Use related details.

1. Firefighters, who work long shifts, save many lives.
2. Mrs. Collins, our math teacher, gives weekly quizzes.
3. You can park in the lot near the library, one of my favorite places to study.
4. An aunt of mine wrote a book, with her picture on the cover, about how to start a small business.
5. Hundreds of volunteers, mostly local college students, helped rescue birds hurt by the oil spill.

Keep This in Mind

- Use related details that add interest and meaning to the main idea of a sentence. Omit unrelated details that interrupt and confuse the meaning.

Now Write Write four sentences about subjects that interest you. Use related details that support the main idea of each sentence. Be sure that each sentence keeps to the point. Label your paper **Beware of Detours.** Keep it in your folder.

Part 3

Empty-Handed

Avoiding Empty Sentences

Here's the Idea Some sentences do not make a point either clearly or completely. They are called **empty sentences.**

One kind of empty sentence repeats an idea.

The experiment failed because we were unsuccessful with it.

To fail at something means "to be unsuccessful," so the second part of the sentence is a useless repetition. You can see that this kind of sentence goes nowhere.

To improve this kind of empty sentence, you must avoid the repetition. Sometimes you may choose to make the sentence simpler. It is more likely, though, that you will choose to add related information.

The experiment failed.
The experiment failed because we tried to rush it.

There is also another kind of empty sentence. This second kind of empty sentence states a strong opinion. However, the opinion is not supported by facts, reasons, or examples.

Radio talk shows are boring.

You can see that such a strong statement is empty of meaning to a reader unless it is explained. You can improve this kind of empty sentence by adding the supporting evidence necessary to complete the idea. Supporting evidence may be given in the same sentence or in another sentence.

Radio talk shows are boring when their hosts are not well informed about the topics discussed.

Radio talk shows are boring. Often their hosts are not well informed about the topics discussed.

Supporting evidence for such ideas might also be developed in paragraphs or compositions.

Check It Out Read the following empty sentences.

1. Everyone should learn to drive.
2. Roller skating is popular now and many people enjoy it.
3. Hockey is the most exciting sport.
4. I can't do this problem because it's too hard.
5. The team was exhausted, and the players needed rest.
6. The crumbling pavement on Maple Avenue needs repair.

- Which sentences repeat an idea? Which sentences state an unsupported opinion? How would you improve each of these empty sentences?

Try Your Skill Rewrite each of these empty sentences.

1. Keeping wild animals as pets is cruel.
2. The team played so well that they were excellent.
3. People who won't change their opinions are annoying.
4. I find it hard to remember names because I'm forgetful.
5. Outdoor jobs are the most satisfying.

Keep This in Mind

- Sentences that repeat an idea or state an unsupported opinion are empty sentences. Improve a sentence that repeats an idea by simplifying it or by adding related information. Improve a sentence with an unsupported opinion by adding supporting evidence that explains the opinion.

Now Write Label your paper *Empty Sentences*. Write, or find, three examples of each kind of empty sentences. Improve the sentences by avoiding repetition or by supplying facts or reasons. Write the improved sentences.

Part 4

Stay Trim

Avoiding Padded Sentences

Here's the Idea A **padded sentence** contains unnecessary words. The main idea of a padded sentence is smothered by extra words.

There are several unnecessary phrases that usually signal padded sentences and should be avoided.

in my opinion, I think	well
what I mean is that	you see
what I'm saying is	you know
the point is	due to the fact that
the thing is	because of the fact that
the reason is	on account of the fact that

You can usually improve a padded sentence simply by eliminating the useless expressions. Sometimes, however, you may need to revise the sentence totally.

Padded What I mean is that winter is my favorite season.
Improved Winter is my favorite season.

Padded It is becoming easier all the time to take good pictures indoors owing to the fact that color film now available is very sensitive to light.
Improved Since color film is now more sensitive to light, it is easier to take good pictures indoors.

Many groups of words using *who is*, *which is*, or *that is* also pad sentences unnecessarily. Be sure to use such expressions only when they add to the meaning of a sentence.

Padded The auto show, which is being held at the Civic Center, continues through next week.
Improved The auto show at the Civic Center continues through next week.

Check It Out Read the following padded sentences.

1. Have you ever tried halvah, which is a kind of candy made with sesame seeds, nuts, and honey?

2. Well, Bonnie said that what she wanted was only a fair chance to audition for the part.

3. Hang gliding attracts people who like risk on account of the fact that it requires skill and luck.

4. The construction crew had to stop working until spring because of the fact that the ground became frozen.

5. I am going to write about careers in the field of communications, which includes jobs in TV production, you know.

- How would you improve each of these sentences?

Try Your Skill Rewrite the following padded sentences. Improve them by eliminating useless words or by revising a sentence completely.

1. On account of the fact that Saturn has rings, it is one of the most beautiful planets to observe.

2. Brian called Ramon, who is his best friend.

3. What I'm trying to say is what an exciting story you wrote.

4. The reason Dad becomes tired so easily is due to the fact that he has just recovered from the flu.

5. Kate tried on her new sweater, which is red.

Keep This in Mind

- Sentences that include unnecessary words are padded sentences. Improve a padded sentence by eliminating the useless expressions or by revising the sentence totally.

Now Write Label your paper *Padded Sentences*. Write, or find, five examples of padded sentences. Then improve the sentences. Eliminate an unnecessary expression or revise the sentence totally. Keep your paper in your folder.

Part 5

Heavyweights

Avoiding Overloaded Sentences

Here's the Idea There will be times when you need to express a complex idea in writing. However, you should not try to include too many ideas in a single sentence. Sentences having too many ideas are called **overloaded sentences.**

Overloaded sentences usually contain several thoughts loosely joined by *and.* The word *and* is used incorrectly when it is used to connect ideas that are not related.

> Our local radio station has a preference for fire stories, and it seems as if every nightly newscast includes a story about a fire, and I have also noticed that other stations have their own favorite kinds of stories that are repeated often.

From this example, you can see how confusing an overloaded sentence is. Which is the main idea? It is impossible for a reader to know.

You can avoid such confusion. Separate an overloaded sentence into several shorter sentences.

> Our local radio station has a preference for fire stories. It seems as if every nightly newscast includes a story about a fire. I have also noticed that other stations seem to have their own favorite kinds of stories.

Whenever you write, make sure that each sentence contains only one main idea or related ideas.

Check It Out Read this overloaded sentence.

Overloaded Every year when safety inspections are required, I promise to take our car to be inspected early, and every year I promise, and yet I always find that I leave this task until the last possible day, and I have to rush around anxiously trying to have the inspection completed by the deadline.

Improved Every year when safety inspections are required, I promise to take our car to be inspected early. Although I promise, I always find that I leave this task until the last possible day. Then I have to rush around anxiously trying to have the inspection completed by the deadline.

- How has this overloaded sentence been improved?

Try Your Skill Improve these overloaded sentences.

1. It used to be that if you went to the movies you could choose from among many different films, and now there seem to be fewer movies playing, and they play for longer periods of time, and theaters in the same area will be showing the same films.

2. In my opinion, this country's lawmakers should resolve the question of whether an eighteen-year-old is a child or an adult, and the laws should be consistent, so that they are the same from state to state, and they will not be confusing as they are now.

3. As recently as 1979, the town of Kelso in California had no television at all because the mountains around this remote town interfered with TV reception, and it surprises me that no one has studied the 100 people who live there to see if they are different in any way from people who have watched TV.

Keep This in Mind

- Sentences containing too many ideas are overloaded sentences. Improve an overloaded sentence by separating it into shorter sentences.

Now Write Label your paper *Overloaded Sentences*. Write, or find, four examples of overloaded sentences. Improve the sentences by separating the main ideas into several shorter sentences. Keep your work in your folder.

WRITING SECTION 3

Examining the Paragraph

Part 1 **A Good Group**
Defining a Paragraph

Part 2 **Of One Mind**
Recognizing Unity in a Paragraph

Part 3 **I Declare!**
Using a Topic Sentence

Part 4 **From the Ground Up**
Ways of Developing a Paragraph

Part 5 **What's Your Line?**
Recognizing Three Kinds of Paragraphs

Part 1

A Good Group

Defining a Paragraph

Here's the Idea You have examined words and sentences. Now you will examine paragraphs. A **paragraph** is a group of sentences dealing with one main idea. Notice how the sentences in each of these groups work together.

1 Nothing could have kept me there in the house that night. My mind held nothing but the driving desire to follow Shane. I waited, hardly daring to breathe, while Mother watched him go. I waited until she turned to Father, bending over him; then I slipped around the doorpost out to the porch. I thought for a moment she had noticed me, but I could not be sure and she did not call to me. I went softly down the steps and into the freedom of the night.—JACK SCHAEFER

2 There were no shops on the wide street that Billy Weaver was walking along, only a line of tall houses on each side, all of them identical. They had porches and pillars and four or five steps going up to their front doors. It was obvious that once upon a time they had been very elegant residences. Now, however, even in the darkness, Billy could see that the paint was peeling from the woodwork on their doors and windows. All of these handsome white houses were cracked and blotchy from neglect.—ROALD DAHL

3 Years ago, illiteracy was not as serious a handicap to employment as it is today. Society needed many unskilled workers. Today, however, it is very difficult for people who cannot read to find jobs. There are very few jobs that do not require at least some reading ability. For this reason alone, reading must be viewed as a valuable, practical skill.

Check It Out Examine the three groups of sentences. The first group tells part of a story. The second group describes a city street. The third group explains an opinion.

- Are these groups of sentences paragraphs? Does each group of sentences deal with one idea?

Try Your Skill One of the groups below is a paragraph. Two are not. For the paragraph, write the main idea. For the groups that are not paragraphs, explain why they are not.

1 In Lexington, Virginia there is an odd Civil War relic — Stonewall Jackson's horse, which has been stuffed. The horse is displayed on the campus of the Virginia Military Institute. More women are now enrolling in military academies. Little Sorrel, Jackson's horse, still wears a saddle and bridle.

2 Day after day, Luis followed the same routine after school. He took a crosstown bus home, where he worked for two hours on his homework. He cooked dinner, so that it would be ready when his mother returned from work. Later, while she washed the dishes, Luis spread out his paints and materials on the kitchen table. He painted until he was too tired to work any more. Finally he went to bed. He dreamed of the day when his work would hang in a downtown art gallery.

3 Old buildings that once would have been torn down are now being restored. This nationwide trend is partly due to rising interest in the architecture of the past century or so. It is also due to rising building costs and the money saved in renovation. It is becoming more difficult for a family to purchase a new home. People must come up with a big down payment and take a loan at high interest rates.

Keep This in Mind

- A paragraph is a group of sentences dealing with one main idea.

Now Write Rewrite the groups of sentences in **Try Your Skill** that are not paragraphs by changing or omitting sentences that do not belong. Label your paper **A Good Group.**

Part 2

Of One Mind

Recognizing Unity in a Paragraph

Here's the Idea Paragraphs are organized units of ideas. Each paragraph deals with one main idea. Every sentence in a paragraph should be related to that main idea. When all of the sentences work together, a paragraph has **unity.**

A unified paragraph follows a plan. Suppose that a paragraph deals with storms on the surface of the sun. Every sentence in that paragraph should include related information. Sentences about solar energy or sunny days would not belong in such a paragraph. They might be good sentences, but they would belong in other paragraphs.

Notice how these sentences relate to the idea of special contests.

> Sand castle contests are attracting crowds on both the East and West coasts. Contestants use wet sand to build elaborate structures with high walls, towers, and moats. Some contestants use knives or sticks to carve the sand. Others use only their hands. The castles are soon demolished by the wind and waves. These unusual creations can usually be studied only in photographs.

Check It Out Now read the following paragraph.

> When you use yeast in baking, its temperature is very important. Yeast is alive, and cold temperatures stop its growth. Too much heat, on the other hand, kills it completely. Ideally, the liquid ingredients in which yeast is dissolved should be about 110 degrees. At this temperature, the liquid should feel warm but not hot to your touch. If the temperature is correct, you can be reasonably sure that the yeast will do its work.

- Do all of the sentences relate to one main idea? Does the paragraph have unity?

Try Your Skill Read the following paragraphs. Decide if each has unity. If a paragraph does not have unity, write the sentence or sentences that do not belong.

1 ESP is not confined to human beings. There are documented instances in which dogs or cats have shown remarkable psychic powers. Some animals have traveled to find their owners after the owners moved hundreds of miles away. People should not leave pets without first making careful arrangements for them. Other pets have warned humans about earthquakes.

2 There are advantages to driving an older car. For one thing, you will probably worry less about its being damaged or stolen. For another, you will find that many older models are easier for you to repair yourself. Finally, keeping an older car for several years will save you money.

3 It was a terrible sight. The force of the tornado had completely destroyed all major buildings in the downtown area. Uprooted trees blocked the streets. Pieces of glass were scattered everywhere. The results of the damaging storm could be seen for miles. Tornadoes don't last very long. They are short-lived, though powerful.

Keep This in Mind

- All of the sentences in a paragraph should relate to one main idea. Then a paragraph has unity.

Now Write Write the name of someone you admire. Write one sentence that sums up your thoughts about the person. Below that sentence, list five more sentences related to the main idea. Label your paper **Of One Mind.**

Part 3

I Declare!

Using a Topic Sentence

Here's the Idea A **topic sentence** states the main idea of a paragraph in a clear, direct way. A topic sentence is helpful to both readers and writers. It helps readers group related ideas together in their minds. It helps writers keep their ideas organized.

A topic sentence should also state an idea that can be developed by the other sentences in the paragraph. For example, the sentence "February is the second month of the year" is too narrow to be a good topic sentence. It makes a statement of fact that cannot be disputed or developed. Other sentences could have no meaningful purpose. However, suppose you were writing a paragraph about February. A better topic sentence might be "February contains two of my favorite holidays." This topic sentence offers an idea that promises more. It can be supported and developed by other sentences in the paragraph.

The topic sentence is often the first sentence in a paragraph. Used in this position, it prepares a reader for the statements that follow. However, the topic sentence may be used anywhere in a paragraph where it states the main idea most clearly.

Check It Out Read the following paragraph.

> My sister Mary is hard of hearing and needs to wear a hearing aid. Sometimes Mary uses her hearing problem to her own advantage. If we are having a disagreement and she wants to infuriate me, she can. Mischievously, she turns off her hearing aid. I find myself arguing emotionally, but Mary does not hear a word I say.

- Which is the topic sentence? Is it too narrow to be developed? State the main idea of this paragraph.

Try Your Skill Read each paragraph below. Write the topic sentence. If the topic sentence is too narrow, label it *Narrow*. Then rewrite it so that it is a better topic sentence.

1 Ice fishing is not as rugged a sport as it may appear to be. First of all, there are ways to fight the cold. This can be accomplished with warm clothing, portable shelters, and heaters. Second, portable radios and TV's help fishermen pass the time on the ice. Third, a grateful family is likely to show its appreciation to the fishermen who brings home fresh fish during the winter.

2 My birthday is July 12. To celebrate this year I invited five friends to a cookout. Last year my family planned a special day's trip to Jones Beach. When I was younger, my favorite celebration was an afternoon of rides at a carnival.

3 Our dog Duke is an attack dog. Attack dogs are dangerous if not handled properly. Many owners never learn how to handle the animals. As a result, the dogs may cause serious harm to innocent people, including the owners. Owners of attack dogs have a responsibility to learn the proper handling of these animals.

Keep This in Mind

- A topic sentence states the main idea of a paragraph. The sentence should deal with an idea that can be developed in a paragraph in a meaningful way.

Now Write Think of three topics that you might develop in paragraphs. For each paragraph, write a topic sentence that states the main idea you have in mind. Label your paper **I Declare!** and put it into your folder.

Part 4

From the Ground Up

Ways of Developing a Paragraph

Here's the Idea The main idea of a paragraph is stated in the topic sentence. The other sentences in the paragraph should develop and support that idea. One of three basic ways of developing paragraphs will probably be best.

Use **details** that appeal to the senses to describe a subject.

> Late in the afternoon the wet woods had taken on an early gloom. Everything was saturated. Everything was covered by moss. It was growing on the rocks, on the fallen logs, on the trees from top to bottom. It had formed a great sponge filled to capacity. Little waterfalls descended amid the ferns. A thousand tiny rivulets ran down stringy wicks of moss. A wind was rising. We slogged along, slashed by gust-driven sheets of rain.—EDWIN WAY TEALE

Use one or more **examples** to develop a general statement.

> All the Indian tribes in North America learned to make complete use of their surroundings. Deer were used for almost everything. The flesh was used for food, the hide for moccasins and clothes, and the antlers for tool handles. The cords and sinews that connected the muscles of the deer to the bones were used for thread with which to sew clothing. The hooves were made into glue.—ROSEBUD YELLOW ROBE

Use **facts and figures** to make an idea clear or to support an opinion.

> Amelia Earhart was the first woman to fly the Atlantic. In May, 1932, she made the solo flight in a single-engine Lockheed Vega. She was beset by bad weather. The wings of her plane coated with ice, forcing her to fly as close as seventy-five feet above the waves part of the time. Fifteen

hours after her departure from Long Island, she landed in a farmer's pasture in Ireland.
—*The Women's Book of World Records and Achievements*

Check It Out Read the following paragraph.

Second Street was peaceful. There was no traffic at that hour of the morning. Steve stood out in the deserted street looking up at the rows of apartment windows with their shades still drawn. The sky was still dark, but the air was sharp and fresh. Steve began bouncing the basketball he had been carrying. A few minutes later, he heard a shout from an eighth-floor window. "Be right down," Chris hollered.

- Is the topic sentence developed by details, by examples, or by facts and figures?

Try Your Skill Copy the topic sentence in this paragraph. Then write *Details*, *Examples*, or *Facts and Figures* to tell how the main idea is developed.

Ben struggled to climb the muddy trail. The red terrycloth sweatband around his forehead was soaked. His woolen shirt was not heavy enough to protect him from the thorns. His compass and canteen were hung from his belt and banged against his hip. His shoes were caked with mud.

Keep This in Mind

- The main idea of a paragraph may be developed by details, by examples, or by facts and figures.

Now Write Take out the paper you labeled **I Declare!** Choose one of your three topic sentences. List three details, examples, or facts and figures that you might use to develop the main idea stated in the topic sentence. Label your paper **From the Ground Up** and put it into your folder.

Part 5

What's Your Line?

Recognizing Three Kinds of Paragraphs

Here's the Idea Any paragraph you may write fits into one of three main categories. It might be a story, a description, or an explanation. Each kind of paragraph presents a topic in a different way.

A **narrative** paragraph tells a story or relates events. All events, real or imaginary, are usually told in the order in which they happened.

A **descriptive** paragraph is a word picture of an object, a scene, or a person. Its vivid sensory details usually create a particular mood.

An **explanatory** paragraph explains something. It may explain a process, state an opinion, or state a definition.

Check It Out Read the following paragraphs.

1 Willard Farquar felt his weight change the steps under his feet into an escalator. He cursed under his breath, but let them carry him. He was carried up to the tall, blue entrance doors, which silently parted when he was five meters away. The escalator changed to a slideway that carried him into a softly gleaming, high-domed room. "Martian peace to you, Willard Farquar," an invisible voice chanted.—FRITZ LEIBER

2 One summer morning I lay on the sand after swimming in the small lake in the park. The sun beat down—it was almost noon. The water shone like steel. It was motionless except for the feathery curl behind a distant swimmer. From my position I was looking at a rectangle with sun, sand, water, a few solitary people, and around it all a border of dark, rounded oak trees. Ever since I had begun taking painting lessons, I had made small frames with my fingers, to look out at everything.
—EUDORA WELTY

3 The term *checkmate* comes from the game of chess. It describes the situation in which a player attacks the opponent's king so that no defense or escape is possible. This is then the end of the game. The word *checkmate* comes originally from an Arabic word *shāhmāt*, meaning "the king is dead." The word *checkmate* is now also used to mean "to defeat completely."

- Which paragraph is narrative? Which is descriptive? Which is explanatory?

Try Your Skill As you read the following topic sentences decide what kind of paragraph they would most likely be part of. Write *Narrative, Descriptive,* or *Explanatory*.

1. The Golden Gate Bridge glowed in the brilliant orange light of the sunset.
2. One glance told me I had made a terrible mistake.
3. The Jerusalem artichoke is a vegetable that few people recognize.
4. Some old radio shows are still popular.
5. Gilbert seemed to be having a run of bad luck.

Keep This in Mind

- A narrative paragraph tells a story or relates events.
- A descriptive paragraph creates a word picture.
- An explanatory paragraph explains a process, states an opinion, or states a definition.

Now Write Review your work labeled **From the Ground Up.** Write which of the three kinds of paragraphs you would use for this topic. Explain why this choice seems best. Label your paper **What's Your Line?** Keep your work in your folder.

Writing a Paragraph

Part 1

Control Yourself

Narrowing a Topic

Here's the Idea When choosing a topic to develop in a single paragraph, make sure that it is not too broad or general. For example, choosing the topic "winter sports" might lead you to write a vague, dull paragraph.

> Americans enjoy many different winter sports. Skiing is popular. Ice skating is also popular. Other good winter sports are cross-country skiing, ice fishing, and sledding.

However, if you narrow a topic, you can write a lively, informative paragraph. One simple way to narrow a general topic is to ask questions about it. Ask *who*, *what*, *when*, *where*, *why*, and *how* questions and jot down details.

Who? I
What? went ice skating in Texas
When? after we moved to Dallas last winter
Where? Love Field entertainment center
Why? homesick for Oregon
How? indoor rink

Narrowing the general topic "winter sports" might lead you to write a detailed, lively paragraph.

> I went ice skating in Texas. Last year we moved to Dallas from Portland, Oregon. In November, I discovered an indoor skating rink at the Love Field entertainment center. It felt strange to be lacing up my skates on days when the temperature averaged sixty-five degrees, but that's exactly what I did. The rink was smooth and fast, and I was happy to be skating again.

Check It Out Notice how the general topic "flying saucers" has been narrowed.

Who?	Lee Construction company crew
What?	possible local sighting of UFO
When?	in the early evening, last Monday
Where?	Route 31 construction site
Why?	unknown—but causing local arguments!
How?	experts to investigate
Specific Topic:	possible local UFO sighting last Monday on Route 31

- Could this topic lead to a lively paragraph?

Try Your Skill Choose two of these general topics. List *Who? What? When? Where? Why?* and *How?* Narrow each general topic by answering these questions.

hobbies	music
gardening	food
famous women	dreams

Keep This in Mind

- Narrow a general topic by asking *who, what, when, where, why,* and *how* questions. Be sure that your specific topic will lead to a detailed and informative paragraph.

Now Write Now you are ready to write a detailed paragraph on your own. In each lesson in this section, you will be completing one step of the writing process. The first step is to select a topic. Choose two general topics that interest you. Narrow both topics by asking *who, what, when, where, why,* and *how* questions. Write the specific topics. Label your paper **Control Yourself.** Keep your work in your folder.

Part 2

In the Interest of

Writing a Topic Sentence

Here's the Idea A good topic sentence is direct and lively. It states clearly what the subject of the paragraph is. This directness is helpful to a reader, and it helps a writer organize his or her thoughts. A good topic sentence is also interesting. Because it is often the first sentence in the paragraph, a topic sentence should capture a reader's interest.

To make a topic sentence direct, get to the point quickly. Avoid using extra words to introduce the subject. Also avoid using unnecessary phrases that introduce you as the writer. Such rambling or personal statements make dull topic sentences.

> This paragraph will tell about what subways are like for those of us passengers who ride them regularly.
> I want to write about subways, which I like.

Notice how direct a good topic sentence is.

> In 1863, London became the first city to have a subway.
> Several major cities in the United States have subway systems.

To make a topic sentence lively, find an unusual or striking way to express the main idea. Sometimes, when it is appropriate, you may want to express an idea in a humorous way.

> The subway roared through the station in a blur of silver.
> The Sixth Street Subway shakes me up.

Try more than one way to write a topic sentence. You will find several ways to express the same idea. Be sure the topic sentence you use is as direct and lively as you can make it.

Check It Out Read the following topic sentences.

1. My heart was pounding wildly as I crossed the finish line.
2. Dense fog blanketed the city.
3. We were invaded by highway lights, not flying saucers.
4. To win at the card game "I Doubt It" you must be an excellent bluffer.
5. A paramedic is a trained medical worker who provides emergency treatment.

- Which of these sentences are direct? Which sentences state the main idea in a lively way?

Try Your Skill Rewrite these six poorly written topic sentences. Make each one lively and direct. Use real or imaginary details.

1. This paragraph is about movies.
2. I really want to tell you about the poster contest.
3. Now I'll explain surfing.
4. This is my story about Uncle Harry.
5. My paragraph is about a funny mistake.
6. I think I can tell you how to build a box kite.

Keep This in Mind

- Write a topic sentence that states the main idea of a paragraph in a direct and lively way.

Now Write Now you are ready for the next step in the writing of your own paragraph. Take out the topics you narrowed in the last lesson, **Control Yourself.** Write a good topic sentence for each topic. Try to state each idea in several different ways. Write your final topic sentences. Label your paper **In the Interest of** and put it into your folder.

Part 3

A Strong Foundation

Developing a Paragraph

Here's the Idea You have learned how to narrow a topic and to write a good topic sentence. How will you develop this main idea in a paragraph?

In **From the Ground Up** you learned to recognize three basic methods of paragraph development. You saw how the use of vivid, sensory **details** brings an idea to life. You saw how the use of one or more **examples** illustrates a general statement. You also saw how the use of **facts and figures** helps to prove a point or make an idea clear.

Whenever you write a paragraph, you will need to decide how to develop the main idea. Try to select the method of paragraph development that best fits each particular topic.

Check It Out Read these paragraphs.

1 Marvin's closet is filled with treasures. On the floor of the closet is an assortment of boxes and bags containing toy soldiers, model airplanes, baseball cards, and other childhood leftovers. Also neatly stacked are all the school papers that he has written. On the shelf, Marvin has stored his stamp, rock, and matchbook collections. Whatever Marvin treasures is stored here.

2 English has borrowed words from Scotland. The word *macadam*, for example, is one of these words. It comes from the name of a Scottish inventor, J. L. McAdam, who invented the mixture of tar and stones that is used to pave roads. Another example is *macintosh*, a waterproof raincoat made of rubberized cloth. It is also named after a Scottish inventor, Charles Macintosh.

3 Potatoes are one of the most widely grown vegetables in the world. These useful vegetables originated in South America.

More than 400 years ago they were grown by the Incas in the Andes Mountains of Peru and Bolivia. Spanish explorers introduced potatoes to Europe. Today more than eleven million bushels of potatoes are produced every year, with Russia being the world's leading potato-growing country.

- Which paragraph is developed by details? by examples? by facts and figures? Do the choices fit the ideas?

Try Your Skill Here are five possible topic sentences. Decide how each might best be developed in a paragraph. Write *Details, Examples* or *Facts and Figures*. Be prepared to explain your choices.

1. After my brother's birthday party, the house looked like a disaster area.
2. Many types of music are popular today.
3. Philadelphia is our country's birthplace.
4. The colors of the Painted Desert are striking and changeable.
5. There are more than 7,000 kinds of paper.

Keep This in Mind

- You may develop a paragraph by using details, examples, or facts and figures. Choose the method of paragraph development that best fits a particular idea.

Now Write Consider the topic sentences that you wrote in **In the Interest of,** the last lesson. Select your best topic sentence and choose the most fitting method of paragraph development. Write a paragraph that expresses your idea in a clear, interesting way. Label your paper **A Strong Foundation** and put it into your folder.

Part 4

Top It Off

Writing a Good Ending

Here's the Idea An ending sentence serves an important function in a paragraph. It sums up, or ties together, the related ideas of the paragraph. It may also explain the significance of the ideas presented. In this way, an ending helps readers make sense of what they have just read.

An ending sentence should not introduce new information. A good ending makes a clear, final statement that works with the other sentences in the paragraph. In fact, often an ending restates the idea of the topic sentence in a slightly different way.

A good ending should also be interesting. Sometimes the final sentence may even be humorous or surprising. Whenever you write a paragraph, try to express your idea in an ending sentence that is memorable as well as clear.

Check It Out Read the following paragraph.

> Highway lights, not flying saucers, are responsible for a recent wave of UFO sightings. At about the same time that new highway lights were installed on Route 31 in our town, people began reporting UFO sightings. The highway lights are bright orange disks that light up the night sky in an eerie way. However, once a group of residents studied several photographs taken of these lights, they agreed that the lights resembled the UFO's they had reported. Coincidences like these make most people skeptical of all UFO reports—even those without such a simple explanation.

- Does the ending sentence tie together the ideas of the paragraph? Does the ending capture your interest?

Try Your Skill Read these three paragraphs with poorly written ending sentences. Then rewrite or replace the endings. Make your endings clear and interesting.

1 We trudged through the swamp, jars held ready. Each time one of us saw a frog or tadpole, a cry went up. Then all of us would come sloshing to where the sighting had been made, ready to lunge with our jars. Usually, we turned around and around without success. *This was the second field trip for our biology class.*

2 Television news coverage is different from newspaper reporting. The best stories for TV news are those having strong visual elements. Such visible events often deal with violence, death, or disaster. Newspapers, on the other hand, rely more on words than on pictures to tell stories. Therefore, newspapers usually have a better balance of stories than television stations do. *It is better to read a newspaper.*

3 Pike, the superintendent in our building, lets me use the tools in his basement workshop. I go down to the basement whenever I have free time. I gather my tools from the pegboard panel on the prickly cement wall behind the workbench. As I cut, sand, and hammer, time passes quickly. I enjoy the whine of the saw and the smell of freshly cut wood. *I can even taste the sawdust in the air.*

Keep This in Mind

- A good ending sentence should sum up the main idea of a paragraph. It should also be interesting.

Now Write Now you are ready to write a strong ending for your own paragraph. Review what you have written. It is a good idea to read your work aloud, at least to yourself. Then write an ending that sums up your idea in an interesting way. Write your paragraph in a final form and proofread it. Label your paper **Top It Off.** Keep your work in your folder.

A Writer's Choices

Part 1

Who Sees What?

Choosing a Point of View

Here's the Idea Whenever you write, you control what a reader will know. You do this by your choice of a point of view. Point of view means the eyes and mind through which something is perceived.

One point of view you may choose is the **first-person point of view.** When you use this point of view, you must use the pronoun *I*. The character *I* is the narrator who tells what happened. Your reader will know only what the *I* character knows. Therefore, the reader will feel very close to this character.

Another point of view is the **third-person point of view** using the pronouns *he*, *she*, and *they*. Your story is told by an outsider who sees and hears everything that happens. This observer, however, cannot tell what any character is thinking or feeling.

Another choice is the point of view called **omniscient,** meaning "knowing all things." The pronouns *he*, *she*, and *they* are used by a narrator who sees and hears everything. However, this observer also knows what every other character is thinking and feeling.

Check It Out Read the following paragraphs.

1 Once, while I was baby-sitting for Jim and Jenny Lee, I decided to take them shopping. As we entered Filene's, I saw my friend Maria and stopped to say hello. One minute the twins were right next to me, but the next minute they had disappeared. At first, I was frantic. I ran up and down nearby aisles, calling their names. Finally, I had an inspiration—try the toy department!

2 While Steve was talking to Maria near the entrance to Filene's, five-year-old Jim and Jenny wandered off. The twins soon found the toy department. Jim ran to find the trains. Jenny examined a colorful set of building toys. At the same time, Steve was searching for them and calling their names.

3 Steve and Maria were delighted to run into each other in Filene's. As the two chatted, Steve failed to notice that Jim and Jenny had drifted off. When they happened upon the toy department, the children broke into a run. Jim had never seen so many model trains before. Jenny couldn't wait to find out what was inside a huge box of building materials. By then, Steve was frantically searching for the missing twins.

- What is the point of view of each paragraph? What can you see and hear in each?

Try Your Skill Suppose that you arrive home to find that no one is there and you have forgotten your key. While you are trying to find a way in, a stranger appears on the scene. First, write two sentences that relate these events from the first-person point of view. Next, relate the same events from the third-person and omniscient points of view.

Keep This in Mind

- From the first-person point of view, what is written is seen through the eyes of the character *I*.
- From the third-person point of view, the narrator tells whatever can be seen and heard.
- From the omniscient point of view, the narrator tells everything—actions, thoughts, and feelings.

Now Write Think about a situation in which you were involved that might be unclear to an observer. Use two different points of view to write two short paragraphs about the incident. Label each. Label your paper **Who Sees What?**

Part 2

Facts or Fancies?

Writing About Real and Imaginary Ideas

Here's the Idea Another choice you must make as a writer is whether to write about real subjects or imaginary ones. Each time you write you can choose to write about what really exists or about what exists only in your own imagination. You may choose to write narratives about real or imaginary events. You may write descriptions of real or imaginary objects, places, or people. You may write explanations of processes, opinions, and ideas that are either real or imaginary.

The term *nonfiction* is used for pieces of writing about real subjects. When you write about a real subject, you must be accurate. Use **facts** to present your real-life topic. You must make sure that all names, dates, and figures are correct. Use reliable sources to check all information you use.

The term *fiction* is used for pieces of writing based on imaginary subjects. When you write about an imaginary subject, you can invent a world of your own. You have the power to create people, places, or situations. Use vivid, specific **details** to make your personal creations come alive.

Check It Out Compare the following paragraphs.

1 Weather records show that the average annual snowfall has remained about the same since the last half of the 1800's. In some years, it snows only a little, but in others it snows a great deal. Some persons believe that it snows less today than it did years ago, yet new snowfall records are set almost every year. Single snowfalls of over thirty inches (seventy-six centimeters) are not unusual in some places.

—*The World Book Encyclopedia*

2 Snow fell against the high school all day. It was wet big-flaked snow that did not accumulate well. Sharpening two pencils, William looked down on a parking lot. Car tires had cut smooth arcs of black into the white. Wherever a school bus has backed around, it had left a signature of two V's. The snow could not quite bleach these scars away. The temperature must be exactly thirty-two degrees. The window was open a crack, and a slanted pane of glass lifted outdoor air into his face. The draft coated the cedarwood scent of pencil shavings with the transparent odor of the wet window sill.—JOHN UPDIKE

- Which paragraph is based on factual statements? How can they be checked for accuracy?
- Which paragraph is based on imaginary details? What details make the experience come alive?

Try Your Skill Write the name of a real object that you use often. List five facts about it. Then, invent and name an object that you would like to have. List five details that show the imaginary object.

Keep This in Mind

- Use facts to write narratives, descriptions, or explanations about real subjects. Check all information using reliable sources.
- Use details to write narratives, descriptions, or explanations of imaginary subjects. Create vivid, specific details that will bring a subject to life.

Now Write Compare the lists you wrote in **Try Your Skill.** Use each list to write a short paragraph about each object. You may choose to write narrative, descriptive, or explanatory paragraphs. Make final copies of both paragraphs. Label your paper **Facts or Fancies?** and put it into your folder.

Part 3

Word Power

Creating a Mood

Here's the Idea Language can express different feelings, or moods, in much the same way that music can. In music, the use of particular notes and rhythms creates special feelings for listeners. With language, it is the use of specific words that creates special feelings for readers. Whenever you write, you need to choose specific words to help you express an idea exactly. You must also choose words carefully in order to express a particular mood.

First, it is necessary to choose specific verbs. A verb is a word that tells what *happened* or what *is*. Use strong, specific verbs that express an idea precisely. For instance, it is stronger to say, "The whistle *pierced* the night," than "The whistle *was* loud." It is more specific to say, "Linda *tiptoed* into the room," than "Linda *moved* into the room."

Second, it is necessary to choose specific adjectives. An adjective is a word that describes. A voice, for example, might be described as *sweet* or *shrill*. A room might be *cozy* or *cramped*. A gesture might be *gentle* or *rough*. Notice the positive effect created by *sweet*, *cozy*, and *gentle*. In contrast, notice the negative effect of *shrill*, *cramped*, and *rough*.

Choose words carefully to express an idea or create a mood. Try to choose strong, specific words that will *show* what you have in mind and bring the idea to life.

Check It Out Compare the following paragraphs.

1 It was hard for Dale to move or to breathe easily. In the crowded, stuffy room, Dale felt trapped. His head ached and his feet burned and he wanted to leave. Unhappily, he noticed that the exit was blocked by babbling guests. In the midst of these noisy, jostling partygoers, Dale felt alone.

2 Dale turned around and around. In his excitement, he didn't know which old friends to seek out first. All around him he saw smiling faces. Old friends waved or patted him on the back in welcome. Everywhere he heard his name called in greeting. At the center of this noisy, eager crowd, Dale beamed.

- Which strong, specific words help to create the mood of each paragraph?

Try Your Skill Read the following sentences. Write the word or words in the sentence that help to create a specific mood.

1. Janet winced at the horror of the gruesome accident.
2. Jeffrey inched his way up the face of the rock, clinging desperately to the rope.
3. The sleazy material hung limply from the plastic hanger.
4. "Now there's an animal with spirit!" Jack boasted.
5. The candidate droned on.
6. Luckily, the snarling dog was chained to a sturdy doghouse.
7. Jody swaggered up to receive his award.
8. The old man cowered when the police officer commanded him to stop.

Keep This in Mind

- Choose strong, specific verbs and adjectives that will help you to express an idea exactly or to create a particular mood.

Now Write Write a paragraph about a person or a place that you have strong feelings about. Try to express your feelings by choosing strong, specific words. When you are finished, review your paragraph. Perhaps you can be even more specific. If so, revise your work. Label your paper **Word Power** and put it into your folder.

Part 4

Showstoppers

Writing Good Titles

Here's the Idea You have been learning about a writer's choices. Whenever you write, you must choose to write about a real topic or to create an imaginary one. You decide whether to write a narrative, a description, or an explanation. You choose a point of view from which to write. You select a method of paragraph development that is appropriate for a particular idea. You choose strong, specific verbs and adjectives that will express your idea or create a certain mood. Making these decisions will be part of the process of writing whenever you write.

Some forms of writing will require that you make other decisions as well. One decision that you may need to make fairly often is choosing a title. Most short pieces of writing, like paragraphs, do not usually have titles. However, longer pieces of writing, such as compositions and reports, do need titles.

A title should be informative and interesting. Sometimes the best title is a simple one, like "Sixteen," that suggests the main idea of your writing. Straightforward titles will probably work best for pieces of explanatory writing, particularly those about real topics. Sometimes a good title may be unusual or surprising, such as "The Secret Life of Walter Mitty." Unusual titles may work for less formal narratives and descriptions, especially imaginary ones.

Check It Out Read the following titles of stories you may have read.

"Irene, Goodnight"	"The Lottery"
"Fumble"	"A Sense of Shelter"
"The Valentine"	"A Night of Vengeance"
"I Can't Breathe"	"The Open Boat"
"Samuel"	"But Who Can Replace a Man?"

- Are these good titles? Why?

Try Your Skill Choose four of the following possible topics for longer pieces of writing. For each topic, write two titles that might work.

1. a narrative about a childhood adventure
2. a description of a snowy morning
3. a report on careers in business
4. an explanation of how to change a flat tire
5. an explanation of why education is important
6. an explanation of what emotions are
7. a story about a creature from outer space
8. a report on earthquakes

Keep This in Mind

- Use a title for longer pieces of writing. A good title is informative and interesting.

Now Write Review the five paragraphs you have written for **Now Write** in this section. Choose two of these topics and write them on your paper. Suppose that you were going to write compositions or reports on two of those topics. Write three possible titles for each topic. Be sure the titles suggest the main ideas and attract readers' interest. Label your paper **Showstoppers.** Keep your work in your folder.

AFRO
USA

The Process of Writing

The Process of Writing

From this point on, you will be learning, and practicing, the skills of writing. You will be able to write often about what is important to you. You will be able to practice different kinds of writing.

There will be lots of variety in your writing experiences. Whenever you write, however, there will be something that remains the same: **the process of writing.** There are three steps you will follow—**pre-writing, writing,** and **rewriting.** As you follow these steps, you will be learning to write.

On these four pages you can follow the process of writing from beginning to end. First, read about each step in the process. Then look at the example that shows how one person might have followed each step.

Pre-writing Sometimes you write in response to an assignment. Sometimes you choose to write in order to communicate something important to you. Whatever you write, and whenever you write, you will find the beginning steps, called pre-writing, very important.

Before you write, you need to focus on your subject. Take your time at this point in the process of writing. Narrow the topic so that you can handle it in a given length.

Think about your audience. Think about whether you want to use a personal point of view or an outsider's point of view. Use all of your senses to bring your subject clearly into focus.

Make a list of interesting details. Jot down any notes or ideas related to your topic. You don't have to use them all. If you need to learn more about your topic, do that, too.

Pre-writing

You list possible topics.

topics

the Bruins game
spraining my ankle
moving to Denver
my job interview
the music competition

You select a topic.

specifics

City School of Music
112 contestants
six-string guitar
scholarship money
audition panic
five years of practice
Ms. O'Brien, teacher
dark auditorium
wooden chair center
fingers numb
rehearse chords
pacing, waiting
alone on stage
a dream — I won!

You list, in any order, details about your topic.

notes

kind of paragraph — narrative?
develop with details, try to show my feelings
point of view — first-person

You plan what you want to write.

Writing At this point in the process of writing, you are ready to write. Simply put your pencil to paper and write. Don't fuss with the writing. Don't worry about organizing ideas. Don't fret about spelling or punctuation. Don't get trapped by trying to make anything perfect. Just write.

Writing

You write a paragraph about your topic.

It was the day of my audition for a scholarship to the City School of Music. My music teacher had finally persuaded me to enter this competition. As I waited backstage, I flexed my numb fingers. I tried to relax. I had spent so long preparing for this moment. I had practiced so long. Finally my turn came, I sat alone on the empty stage. I forced myself to concentrate only on the music I was playing. When the scholarship winners were announced, my name was among them. What a wonderful moment!

Notice how this paragraph *tells* about the topic.

Rewriting Stop. Read what you have written. At this stage of the process you will need to work more carefully and thoughtfully. You have to check what you have written. Did you include everything you wanted to? Do you like what you've written? Is it interesting? Think about your topic.

At this point, it is possible that you may not like what you've written. It is likely, though, that you generally like your idea. Then you can rewrite whatever you need to change or want to change.

Concentrate on every word. Is your idea clearly expressed? Did you *show* your reader what you want to say? Is your writing organized logically? Is there a beginning, a middle, and an end to the development of your idea? Is the writing lively and direct? Is each word the right word? Take time to read your writing and think about it carefully.

Rewriting

You rewrite. You express your idea in a different way.

It was the day of my audition for a
scholarship to the City School of Music.
Ms. O'Brien,
My music teacher had finally persuaded
test my talent in | citywide | paced nervously
me to ~~enter~~ this competition. As I ~~waited~~
cold, stiff
backstage, I flexed my ~~numb~~ fingers. I
took deep breaths, trying | five years
~~tried~~ to relax. I had spent ~~so long~~ preparing for this moment. I had practiced
for thousands of hours.
~~so long.~~ Finally my turn came. I sat
in a straight-backed chair,
alone on the empty stage. I forced myself
to concentrate only on the music I was play-
Hours later,
ing. When the scholarship winners were
announced, my name was among them.
No music has ever sounded so sweet.
~~What a wonderful moment!~~

Notice how this lively paragraph *shows* your idea clearly.

Now, you need to look at how you have expressed your idea. It is important to make your writing correct as well as clear and lively. Check capitalization and punctuation. Use whatever references you have available to check your work.

Finally, when you are satisfied that your writing is clear and correct, write it in its final form. Write carefully. Make your work as neat as possible.

When you have finished your final copy, proofread your work. Read your writing aloud, to yourself, one final time.

It was the day of my audition for a scholarship to the City School of Music. Ms. O'Brien, my music teacher, had finally persuaded me to test my talent in this citywide competition. As I paced nervously backstage, I flexed my cold, stiff fingers. I took deep breaths, trying to relax. I had spent five years preparing for this moment. I had practiced for thousands of hours. Finally my turn came. I sat in a straight-backed chair, alone on the empty stage. I forced myself to concentrate only on the music I was playing. Hours later, when the scholarship winners were announced, my name was among them. No music has ever sounded so sweet.

You can learn to write only by writing. In each writing section you will be learning an idea about writing, checking your understanding of the idea, practicing your skill, and then writing on your own. Whenever you write, try to follow the steps in the process of writing. Each time you write you will be learning something about writing, and about yourself.

The Narrative Paragraph

Part 1

Time Capsule

Using Chronological Order

Here's the Idea A narrative paragraph tells a story. The events of the narrative, real or imaginary, are usually told in the order in which they happened. This natural time sequence is called **chronological order.** Notice the use of chronological order as you read the following true account.

> When I was free for a few hours, I explored the foothills. I would leave the town and head toward the point of the foothills nearest my home. There I would test my legs and lungs against the hillside. It was hard work. At first, I ran two miles at the fast pace of perhaps five or six miles an hour. Then, I climbed a hillside of five hundred feet or more in elevation. At last, I returned to home and bed, dead tired, every muscle of my legs aching. Time and again I followed this routine.—WILLIAM O. DOUGLAS

In a narrative you may not need to begin with a topic sentence that states the main idea. You may write a strong, interesting sentence that begins the sequence of events. The other events of the narrative should follow in logical order.

There are words and phrases that will help you make the order clear. These words and phrases, called **transitions,** will allow you to show how much time has passed between events in a narrative. Here is a list of useful transitions.

first	now	when	at the same time
then	before	soon	by the time
next	earlier	suddenly	at the beginning
while	after	immediately	in the middle
last	later	finally	at the end

In addition to these general transitions, you may want to use more specific phrases. For example, you may need to say *after ten minutes, at noon,* or *in September.* Use a variety of transitions to make the order of events clear.

Check It Out Now read this imaginary narrative.

> He was an old man who fished alone in a small boat in the Gulf Stream and he had gone eighty-four days now without taking a fish. In the first forty days, a boy had been with him. However, after forty days without a fish the boy's parents had told him that the old man was now definitely and finally unlucky. At their orders, the boy had gone in another boat that caught three good fish the first week. It made the boy sad to see the old man come in each day with his boat empty, and he always went down to help him.—ERNEST HEMINGWAY

- Are the events of this narrative in chronological order?
- Point out the transitions.

Try Your Skill In chronological order, list the events of your normal morning routine on a school day. Add transitions that show the passing of time between events. Use the lists to write a clear, interesting narrative paragraph.

Keep This in Mind

- Organize the events of a narrative paragraph in chronological order.
- Transitions are words and phrases that make a sequence clear. In a narrative, use transitions that show chronological order.

Now Write Write a narrative paragraph based on either real or imaginary events. Follow all the steps in the process of writing. Plan your idea carefully. List events in chronological order. Use clear transitions. Write your narrative. Do any necessary rewriting. Make a final copy of your paragraph. Label your paper **Time Capsule.** Keep it in your folder.

Part 2

Item by Item

Developing a Narrative Paragraph

Here's the Idea A good narrative paragraph is based on a well organized sequence of events. A good narrative is also interesting. What makes a narrative vivid and interesting is the use of **details.** When you write a true account, you will recall details from your memory. When you write an imaginary story, you will invent details by using your imagination.

An effective way to develop a detailed narrative is to ask yourself the questions a reader might ask. Ask *who, what, when, where, why,* and *how* questions. Then answer each question with a specific detail.

You may not find all of these questions appropriate for every topic. You will find it helpful, however, to answer as many as you can. Also, you may not find that you want to use every detail in the final version of a narrative. However, you will find it easier to write a paragraph if you begin by jotting down all the details you can think of. Later, as you write and rewrite, you can select the most suitable and important details for the narrative.

Check It Out Look at this list of details.

Who? Tim
What? had to help rescue his cousin
When? babysitting for four-year-old Jody
Where? at Jody's house
Why? Jody got locked in the closet
How? with the help of two police officers

Now read the narrative about the rescue.

Tim had been babysitting for his four-year-old cousin Jody for two, long hours. He was tired. He was tired of playing rescue squad, so he sent Jody upstairs to find his storybooks. When he heard a long muffled noise overhead, Tim decided that he had better see what Jody was up to. He finally tracked the noise to Jody's closet. After several attempts to open the door, Tim realized that the door lock was jammed. Jody was trapped in the dark closet and he was frightened. Tim tried to calm the crying child and then called the emergency police number. In fifteen minutes, Jody stumbled unharmed out of the darkness. He blinked at the two smiling police officers, his own rescue squad.

- Is this narrative developed by details?
- Does the narrative show *who, what, when, where, why,* and *how*?

Try Your Skill Recall a particular situation in which you were frightened or taken by surprise. On your paper, list *Who? What? When? Where? Why?* and *How?* Recall and list details about the situation.

Keep This in Mind

- Develop a narrative by using vivid details from your memory or your imagination.
- To develop details, answer *who, what, when, where, why,* and *how* questions about your topic.

Now Write Write a lively narrative paragraph. Follow all the steps in the process of writing. Choose either a real or imaginary topic. Organize the events in chronological order, using clear transitions. Develop vivid details by answering *who, what, when, where, why,* and *how* questions. Use your pre-writing notes to write your paragraph. Do any rewriting you feel is necessary. Make a final copy of the paragraph and proofread it carefully. Label your paper **Item by Item.** Keep your narrative in your folder.

WRITING SECTION 8

The Descriptive Paragraph

Part 1 **Uncommon Sense**
Using Your Senses in a Description

Part 2 **Directional Signals**
Using Spatial Order in a Description

Part 1

Uncommon Sense

Using Your Senses in a Description

Here's the Idea A descriptive paragraph is a word picture. When you write a description you can reveal an object, a person, or a scene. Any subject you choose may be either real or imaginary. Through a well written description you will be able to share a vivid experience.

In order to write a good description, you need to include both the details and the feelings related to your experience. First, try to choose details that appeal to all the senses. The five senses—sight, hearing, touch, taste, and smell—tell you about your surroundings. Use your senses to provide the vivid details of a description. Choose specific sensory words that will make an experience come alive. Work from the vocabulary of the senses that you have been building.

Notice the use of sensory details in this description.

> It was dusk. The warm air of the early spring afternoon was edged with an exhilarating chill. In the half-light the dark green turf of the playing field acquired the smooth perfection of a thick rug. This natural carpet spread up to the thin woods lightly brushed with color along one sideline, and down to the river along the other. Across the stream stretched more playing fields. Appearing smoother still in the distance, they sloped gently up to the square gray shape of the gymnasium. Behind it, the towers of the boy's school were etched against the darkening blue sky.—JOHN KNOWLES

Using specific sensory details will also help you to create a special feeling, or mood. As you describe an object, a person, or a scene, you may want to create a particular mood. For example, you may want your readers to feel peaceful, sad, happy, or frightened. Use sensory words and descriptive words carefully. Use them to create the mood or effect you want.

Check It Out Read the following description.

The old man sat on the bench by the shed door and rested in the sunlight. He sat looking at the barn and thinking. Around the corner, blackbirds were rioting in the cherry tree, but he did not have the strength to get up to chase them away. Not that it mattered, for he had given up picking the cherries long ago. Thinking of cherries ought to have made the old man hungry. He did feel a vague notion to go in and eat, but he did not move. Overhead the sun moved past the peak of the house, and the shadow in which he sat lengthened to his feet.—JOYCE CAROL OATES

- What sensory details does this description use?
- What mood does the paragraph create?

Try Your Skill Think of two particular objects, persons, or scenes that fit the following general topics. Think about your feelings for each topic. List sensory details related to each.

a kitchen	a friend	a traffic jam
a garden	a relative	a holiday celebration

Keep This in Mind

- Use sensory details to create a vivid description.
- Choose specific sensory words to create the particular mood you want.

Now Write Write a descriptive paragraph. Choose an object, a person, or a scene that you have strong feelings about. List as many sensory details about your subject as you can. Then select the details that will help you to create a particular mood. Organize the details in a natural order. Write your description. Do as much rewriting as necessary. Make a final copy of your paragraph. Label your description **Uncommon Sense** and put it into your folder.

Part 2

Directional Signals

Using Spatial Order in a Description

Here's the Idea An effective description creates a vivid picture or mood through the use of sensory details. An effective description is also organized clearly.

One way to organize a description is to use **spatial order.** That is, show how the various parts of your subject are related to each other in space. Start from one important part and describe everything else in relation to that part. You may show a subject from top to bottom, from side to side, or in a circle. Choose a pattern suitable for your subject.

Notice the use of spatial order in this description.

> *Bonsai*—the Oriental art of growing miniature trees—is my new hobby. My bonsai tree is a prickly juniper, only eighteen inches high. I have carefully shaped my dwarf tree so that it resembles an umbrella. At the top, the spicy-smelling needles are tightly bunched. Below this cluster of needles, the tiny trunk is twisted and wrinkled. Below that, the roots of the juniper are covered with moss. The base of the bonsai tree is a shallow dish in which the tiny juniper is growing.

Here is a list of **transitions** to help make spatial order clear.

above	beside	in the center	over
against	between	near	side by side
ahead of	by	next to	south
alongside	down	north	throughout
at the end of	east	on	to the left
at the top	facing	on the bottom	to the right
around	in	on the corner	under
below	in back of	on the edge	up
beneath	in front of	outside	west

Check It Out Read this description.

Last weekend I helped my mother turn our once cluttered basement into a well organized workroom for her new upholstery business. At the foot of the stairs we set up a display of fabric selections. Above the fabrics we stapled pictures of finished products. Along the wall to the left of the stairs we arranged samples of a variety of wood stains and varnishes. Beside this display, we set her sewing machine. On the adjoining wall we placed her workbench holding all her tools. Finally, we moved two newly reupholstered chairs against the fourth wall to show customers the end products of my mother's skills.

- How does this description use spatial order?
- Point out the transitions.

Try Your Skill Examine the photograph on page 74. Study the relationship of people and objects. Decide on a logical spatial order that fits the picture. Write a descriptive paragraph about the picture. Use clear transitions.

Keep This in Mind

- Use spatial order to organize a description. Focus on something and describe everything else in relation to it.
- In a description, use transitions that show spatial order.

Now Write Write a descriptive paragraph. Follow all the steps in the process of writing. Choose a real or imaginary subject. List sensory details about the subject. Organize the details in a spatial order. Write your description. Rewrite as necessary. Make a final copy of the paragraph. Label your paper **Directional Signals** and put it into your folder.

The Explanatory Paragraph

Part 1 **Step In**

Writing a Paragraph That Explains a Process

Here's the Idea In addition to narrative and descriptive paragraphs, there are explanatory paragraphs. Some explanatory paragraphs explain a process. Other explanatory paragraphs state an opinion, and still others state a definition. Most explanatory paragraphs are factual, based on real subjects.

A paragraph that explains a process must be detailed and accurate. The explanation may tell how to do something or how to make something. Choose a simple process that you know well. You may want to explain how to wax a floor, sink a foul shot, make waffles, or design your own greeting cards.

You must explain the complete process **step-by-step.** Write each step as a single, specific direction. Organize the steps in the natural time order of the process. Be sure to explain any steps that depend on one another.

> You can make a striking change in your environment by painting a room. Begin by purchasing paint, brushes, and other necessary supplies. Next, move the furniture out of the way and cover it and the floor with plastic. Then, clean all surfaces to be painted. After that, fill any cracks with patching plaster and sand these surfaces. The next step is the painting itself. Paint the ceiling first, then the walls, then the trim. After your cleanup, relax in your new surroundings.

There are **transitions** that will help you to show the step-by-step order. They include such words as *first*, *second*, *next*, *while*, *then*, *until*, and *finally*. They also include such phrases as *at first*, *after that*, *at the same time*, *the next step*, and *the last step*. Any transitions that show the specific time order can be useful in a paragraph that explains a process.

Check It Out Read the following paragraph.

Most dogs enjoy performing tricks. Once your own dog has learned to come to you and to sit, you may want to teach it to shake hands. First, decide what simple command you will use. Second, call your dog by name and make it sit in front of you. Keep its attention through constant eye contact. Next, say the dog's name followed by the command. At the same time, gently nudge the dog's paw. Repeat these steps until the first time your dog correctly responds to your command. Then, immediately reward the dog with a dog biscuit and a great deal of praise. Repeat this training until you and your dog enjoy performing this special trick.

- Does this paragraph explain a process in an accurate way? Which transitions show step-by-step order?

Try Your Skill Write the steps of these jumbled instructions in the correct order. Add clear transitions.

1. Gather a small carton of heavy cream, a teaspoon of vanilla, and a tablespoon of sugar.
2. Put a bowl and an egg beater in the freezer to chill.
3. It's easy to make perfect whipped cream.
4. Beat the mixture until it thickens and stiff peaks form.
5. Put all the ingredients into the chilled bowl.

Keep This in Mind

- An explanatory paragraph may explain the process of doing or making something. Be sure the steps in the process are detailed and accurate. Use transitions that show step-by-step order.

Now Write Write an explanatory paragraph that explains an activity that you do well. Include transitions that show step-by-step order. Write your paragraph in a final form. Label your explanation **Step In** and put it into your folder.

Part 2

Listen to Reason

Writing a Paragraph That States an Opinion

Here's the Idea You hold many opinions on a wide range of subjects. You may want to write an explanatory paragraph that states your opinion. You may want to explain why a certain idea should be accepted or why a certain practice should be changed. Begin your paragraph by expressing your opinion in a direct and specific topic sentence.

In order to be convincing, you need to present strong reasons or facts that support your opinion. For example, you may want to use reasons to explain why television is educational. You may want to use facts to support your opinion about a political candidate. The most effective way to organize supporting evidence is **in order of importance,** from the least important point to the most important point.

There are two kinds of **transitions** that will help you develop your opinion. One group of transitions helps you to state reasons or facts. This group includes *because*, *so*, *since*, *if*, *therefore*, and *as a result*. The other group helps you to put the reasons or facts in order of importance. This group includes *the first reason*, *second*, *more important*, and *finally*.

The concluding sentence of the explanatory paragraph should sum up your argument clearly and convincingly.

Check It Out Look at these notes.

Opinion: Students should work in a local election campaign.
Reasons: to perform a public service, to become familiar with local issues, to understand how government works

In a second pre-writing step, the reasons can be written with the appropriate transitions and arranged in order of importance.

perform community service	*since* candidates need office workers	= *first of all*
learn about issues	*if* involved, you will learn about issues	= *more important*
become informed voter	*as a result*, you will understand government	= *most important*

Now read the completed paragraph.

Every high school student should work for a candidate in a local election campaign. First of all, it is a public service to help candidates by stuffing envelopes and answering phones. More important, by becoming involved, the student will learn firsthand what issues are important to the community and how local government works. As a result, the student will be better prepared to participate as an informed citizen.

- Does the topic sentence state an opinion directly? Is the supporting evidence organized in order of importance? Which transitions are used? Does the concluding sentence sum up the argument?

Try Your Skill Write a topic sentence that expresses an opinion of one of these topics. List three reasons that support your opinion. Write a sentence that sums up your feelings.

sports work women education

Keep This in Mind

- An explanatory paragraph may state an opinion. State the opinion in a topic sentence. Support the opinion with reasons or facts. Use transitions that show the order of importance. Sum up your argument in the concluding sentence.

Now Write Write an explanatory paragraph that states an opinion that is important to you. Follow all the steps in the process of writing. Label your opinion **Listen to Reason.**

Part 3

Come to Terms

Writing a Paragraph That States a Definition

Here's the Idea An explanatory paragraph may also state a definition. What is defined may be an object or something that really exists. What is defined might also be a term or idea. A good definition does three things. First, it gives the word to be defined. Next, it puts a subject in the general class to which it belongs. Then, by giving specific characteristics, it shows how the subject is different from all other members of its class.

Suppose you need to define a canoe. What is a canoe? First, you would state that a canoe is a boat. That is its general class. How is a canoe different from other boats? You would write that a canoe is usually a small boat, ranging from eleven to twenty feet. That shows how a canoe is different from yachts and cabin cruisers. You might add that a canoe is usually paddled. That distinguishes it from rowboats, motorboats, and sailboats. You could add that a canoe is usually an open boat. That shows how it is different from a kayak. Now you have a complete definition. Your complete definition might be stated like this: A canoe is a small, open boat that is paddled.

State your clear, specific definition in the topic sentence of your explanatory paragraph. In the rest of the paragraph, develop that definition as completely as possible using either details or facts and figures.

If you define *herbs*, for example, you will probably choose facts and figures to develop the explanation. You may need to check such information in an encyclopedia or other reference. However, if you define an idea like *success*, you will probably want to use specific details from your own experience to develop your definition. Whatever the subject, be sure that your definition is clear and complete.

Check It Out Read the following paragraph.

An allergy is a medical condition suffered by fifteen percent of all Americans. It is a physical reaction in certain people to a substance that is generally harmless. For example, people can be allergic to anything around them, such as plants, animals, particular foods, types of cloth, or substances in the air. Symptoms of allergies differ. There may be sneezing, as in hay fever, or itching or hives, as with a skin allergy. Once most allergies are discovered, they can be controlled.

- Is the topic sentence a definition? Does the paragraph develop the definition with personal details or with facts and figures?

Try Your Skill Choose three of the following objects, terms, or ideas. For each of your choices, write a good definition. Use a dictionary or encyclopedia if necessary.

moth	atlas	intermission	courage
corporation	corn	GI	loneliness
drum	rain	overtime	love

Keep This in Mind

- An explanatory paragraph may state a definition. The topic sentence should be a definition. The definition should put a subject in its general class and give its specific characteristics. Develop the definition by using details or facts and figures.

Now Write Choose an object, term, or idea that is important to you. Write an explanatory paragraph that states a definition of your choice. Make the topic sentence a good definition. Develop the definition with personal details or with facts and figures. Label your paper **Come to Terms.** Keep your work in your folder.

Examining the Composition

Part 1

Working Together

Defining a Composition

Here's the Idea A **composition** is a group of paragraphs dealing with one main idea. A composition allows you to develop an idea that is too complex for one paragraph. For example, you could describe a drum in a single paragraph. However, you would need to write a composition to tell a story about your first music lesson. Because of its longer length, a composition usually has a title.

A composition is similar in some ways to a paragraph. Like a paragraph, a composition deals with only one main idea. That idea may be real or imaginary. Also like a paragraph, a composition has a logical beginning, middle, and end and is organized by the use of transitions.

Check It Out Read this composition.

I Tamed a Whirlwind

Last summer I arranged my first adoption. However, I didn't adopt a human—I adopted a horse. The United States Government Bureau of Land Management has a program called Adopt-A-Horse. This program gives wild horses to interested people who are qualified to care for the animals. There's one special consideration: these horses are truly wild.

One July morning we went to pick up my horse, a mare I named Whirlwind. She was a reddish-brown color with a stringy mane and tail. Her bones stuck out and her coat was dotted with burrs, scars, and sores. Whirlwind rolled her eyes when she saw me and flattened her ears against her head. It did not seem a promising beginning for our partnership. Finally, however, my father and I coaxed Whirlwind into our trailer and took her home. We put her into the corral and gave her some grain as a welcome.

I had been sure that food and kindness would win her over, but Whirlwind was stubborn. During her first weeks with us, she either ignored me or threatened me. She was eating well and looking better, but she was still easily frightened. In fact, it took almost a month of constant attention before I could walk up close to her. When Whirlwind finally let me approach her, she also let me brush her and put on a halter and a bridle.

After a few more weeks, Whirlwind allowed me to lay a pad on her back and, after that, a light saddle. The weight of the saddle didn't bother Whirlwind, but when I tightened the cinch, which holds the saddle on, she resisted violently. She snorted, bucked, kicked, and ran. However, once she sensed that this activity accomplished nothing, she stopped resisting.

The day I mounted Whirlwind for my first ride I wondered, "Will she buck?" I had spent months working with that horse, for at least two hours each day. As she calmly trotted around the corral with me on her back, I knew it had been worth all the effort. I had tamed a wild horse—a real whirlwind!

- What is the main idea of this composition?

Try Your Skill Read and copy the topics below. Write *P* next to the topic if it could be covered in a paragraph. Write C if the topic requires a composition.

1. how to write a check
2. what first aid is
3. the story of a storm
4. a description of a city
5. how to plan a vacation
6. why TV is popular
7. the causes of inflation
8. how to treat a cold
9. your first job
10. expectations for the 1980's

Keep This in Mind

- A composition is a group of paragraphs dealing with one main idea.

Now Write List six possible composition topics. Label your paper **Working Together.** Keep your list in your folder.

Part 2 **Three-Wheeler**

The Parts of a Composition

Here's the Idea Every composition has three main parts: an introduction, a body, and a conclusion. An **introduction** should state the topic in a clear and interesting way.

The **body** of a composition is the part that develops the main idea. In a narrative, it contains the events of a story. In a description, it contains the sensory details that make up the word picture. In an explanatory composition, the body contains directions that explain a process, reasons that support an opinion, or details that develop a definition.

The **conclusion** is the ending. It may be a summary of the main idea. It may also be surprising or striking. Most importantly, it should clearly signal the end of your idea.

Check It Out Read the following composition.

A Mystery of the Orient

Last year my father went to China on a business trip. He returned home with hundreds of slides, dozens of stories, and many wonderful souvenirs. In fact, Dad brought back small gifts for everyone in the family. For me, he brought the best gift of all—a Happy Harp.

The Happy Harp is a brilliant blue rectangular box about two and a half feet long and six inches wide. It has five strings running lengthwise over a sounding board. When plucked, each string produces a thin, bright tone. Above the strings is a keyboard with twenty-three numbered keys in various shades of pink and yellow. The string arrangement reminds me of a guitar, but the keys look like colored typewriter keys.

The body of the harp is shiny blue enamel, polished so that it feels as smooth as satin. The small wooden panel of the board is covered with decals of red and pink peonies. These flower-filled decals are slightly raised and bumpy. The Happy Harp seems to be a beautiful decorative item rather than a musical instrument.

With the Happy Harp came a diamond-shaped pick, an extra set of strings, and an instruction manual. Unfortunately, the manual is written in Chinese, which I can't read.

In fact, the Happy Harp is a complete mystery to me. I have no idea what it should sound like. I do not understand how it works. However, the mystery is part of its magic. I am hoping that someday soon I will be able to make music with this lovely Happy Harp.

- Point out the introduction, the body, and the conclusion.

Try Your Skill In which part of a composition does this paragraph belong? Write your answer and the reasons for it.

In coastal Peru, scientists have discovered a number of fascinating drawings that cover the land. They are of animals and geometric shapes, and they all are quite large. In fact, these unusual drawings can be seen best not from the ground, but from the air. They were made centuries ago, for reasons that can only be guessed. However, scientists now feel that their guesses are quite close to the truth.

Keep This in Mind

- All compositions have three main parts: an introduction, body, and conclusion.

Now Write Review the topics for compositions that you listed in the last lesson. Choose one topic and write three headings: *Introduction*, *Body*, and *Conclusion*. Then, for each of these parts, write a few sentences that explain what you would include in your composition. Label your paper **Three-Wheeler** and put it into your folder.

Part 3

In Name Only

Recognizing Three Kinds of Compositions

Here's the Idea A composition may tell a story, describe something, or explain something. The form and content of a composition work together to do one of these three things.

A **narrative** composition tells a story. The events of the story may be either real or imaginary. Because the important feature of any narrative is what happened, the events are usually presented in the order in which they occurred.

A **descriptive** composition focuses on sensory details. The details develop a word picture of an object, a place, or a person. Vivid, lively details bring the description to life.

An **explanatory** composition explains something. It may explain how something is done, why something should be believed, or what something is. Steps in a process, reasons, or facts are used to develop the explanation.

Check It Out Now read the following composition.

Pedal Power

Many Americans are trying to find ways to stay fit and save money. The government is trying to save energy and fight pollution. Using bicycles is one good way to make progress towards achieving these goals.

First of all, bicycles can be an asset to physical fitness. They can provide an opportunity for exercise. Even short routine trips to run errands can become practical opportunities to exercise leg muscles and to stimulate the heart.

Secondly, bicycles are inexpensive when compared with cars. There are many reliable models of bicycles that can be bought for a reasonable price. Also, there is a large, used-bicycle market. In addition, police stations auction unclaimed bicycles periodically. Therefore many Americans should be able to find bicycles that are affordable.

More importantly, the bicycle is a potential problem-solver for cities. Every city has its parking problem because spaces are often hard to find. If even one quarter of the drivers switched to bicycles, there would be some relief.

Also, many cities are choking on the pollution that is caused in part by cars. Even a small reduction would be of advantage. However, cities themselves must promote the use of bicycles by providing bicycle paths to accommodate riders safely. Bicycle riders also help save much-needed fuel.

Bicycles can play a more important role in relieving city problems, as they do in parts of Europe and Asia. It would certainly be to the advantage of most cities to promote the use of bicycles by providing safety instruction, parking places, and special riding lanes. Pedal power can be an inexpensive and clean source of energy for cities across America.

- What kind of composition is this? How do you know?

Try Your Skill Examine the compositions shown in this section in **Working Together** and **Three-Wheeler.** Write what kinds of compositions they are and explain your answers.

Keep This in Mind

- There are three kinds of compositions. A narrative composition tells a story. A descriptive composition creates a word picture. An explanatory composition explains a process, states an opinion, or develops a definition.

Now Write Take out the topics you listed for **Working Together.** Now choose one topic that seems suitable for each of the three kinds of compositions. Write your topics under the headings *Narrative*, *Descriptive*, and *Explanatory*. Jot down the notes you would use in each composition. Label your plans **In Name Only** and put the paper into your folder.

The Narrative Composition

Part 1

Head First

Planning a Narrative Composition

Here's the Idea Some narratives are **true accounts** of events that actually happened. Other narratives are **stories** that tell of events that happened in a writer's imagination. When you write a narrative, you must decide whether to write a true account or a story. Before you write, spend time thinking about events that interest you. You may want to use your memory to recall important real-life events. You may decide to use your imagination to create original situations.

Once you choose a topic—real or imaginary—you need to make your pre-writing notes. Plan the three parts of your composition. In the introduction, plan to introduce the most important element of your narrative in an interesting way. In the body of the composition, plan to tell what happened in chronological order. In the conclusion, plan to resolve the main problems of the narrative and tie up any loose ends.

As you list notes for a true account, include details about the people, places, and events that you remember. As you list notes for a story, include details that you invent. Invent details about people in the story, called *characters*; about places, called *setting*; and about events, called *plot*.

Check It Out Examine these notes for a narrative.

Topic: finding a job to earn money for a school trip

Introduction: junior class going on trip to Washington, D.C.
Keith wants to join them
he needs to earn money

Body: Keith answers ad for housekeeper
all other applicants are women
Mrs. Warner not anxious to hire Keith
Keith lists his skills and gets the job

Conclusion Keith works hard for six weeks
he saves enough money for the trip
he proves something to himself

- Does this seem to be a true account or a story?
- What is included in the introduction, the body, and the conclusion? Are there notes about people, places, and events?

Try Your Skill Here are several general topics suitable for narrative compositions. Choose one topic and narrow it to a specific situation that may be either real or imaginary. Make a set of detailed pre-writing notes. Save these notes in your folder. You will need them for an exercise in **Try Your Skill** later in this section.

winning	an argument	saving something
helping someone	a choice	a challenge

Keep This in Mind

- You may decide to write a narrative composition that is a true account or an imaginary story.
- Make a set of pre-writing notes. Plan the introduction, body, and conclusion of the narrative. For a true account, list details about people, places, and events. For an imaginary story, list details about character, setting, and plot.

Now Write Think of a topic suitable for a narrative composition. Choose a situation in which an interesting problem or decision is resolved. The events may be recalled from memory or from your imagination. Plan your narrative by making a set of detailed notes. Label your paper **Head First** and keep it in your folder. You will be using your notes for all of the lessons in this section.

Part 2

What's the Trouble?

Developing a Narrative Composition

Here's the Idea Before you can begin a narrative, you must also select a **point of view** from which to write. If you select the first-person point of view, the narrative will be told by the character you identify as *I*. From the third-person point of view, it will be told by a character who observes the action. From the omniscient point of view, the narrative will be told by a character who knows everything.

Next you are ready to write the **introduction.** In this first paragraph, present the most important element of the narrative. Introduce the person, place, or event that is to be the focus of the story. Prepare the reader for what is to follow.

In the **body** of the narrative you will relate what happened. In a true account, develop the sequence of actual events by using accurate details. In a story, develop the imaginary plot by using details that present the conflict. It is conflict—the major problem affecting the characters—that controls any story. Conflict may result from a force in nature or from trouble between certain characters. Sometimes the conflict is within one character who must make a difficult choice.

As you develop the conflict in the body of a narrative, be sure to include transitions that make the sequence clear.

Check It Out Read the beginning of this narrative.

> Keith Jackson cleaned his way from Georgia to Washington, D.C. His junior class had decided to go on a spring trip to the capital. Keith had never been more than 100 miles from his home so he was anxious to make the trip. His only problem was earning the 250 dollars necessary.
>
> Keith first checked the job placement file at school. However, he discovered that all the fast-food stores, gas stations,

and supermarkets had hired their quota of juniors-saving-for-a-trip. Next Keith read through the help-wanted ads. Nothing seemed to fit either his skills or his hours. The only possibility read "Housekeeper wanted for invalid, five dollars an hour, two days a week." Keith thought that the pay was good, and that he could do the work after school.

Keith arrived at the interview the next day hoping to begin work. He was surprised to find a dozen other applicants there, too—all of them women. How could Keith convince the employer, Mrs. Warner, that he had to be the right person for the job?

- From what point of view is this narrative told?
- What important elements of the story are introduced?
- What conflict is established in the body?
- What transitions make the order clear?

Try Your Skill Use this situation as the basic idea for a narrative: a certain character must struggle against a force in nature. Create details about this character and situation. Select a point of view and write an introduction. Then write one paragraph of the body in which you present the conflict.

Keep This in Mind

- Select a suitable point of view for your narrative.
- In the introduction, present an important element that draws readers into the narrative.
- In the body, develop the action with details. Make sure the action arises from the conflict.
- Include transitions that make the order clear.

Now Write Review your notes labeled **Head First.** Select a point of view and write an introduction. Write the body, developing the conflict. Include transitions. Label your paper **What's the Trouble?** Keep your work in your folder.

Part 3 # Speak Your Mind

Using Dialogue To Reveal Character

Here's the Idea In order to develop a lively narrative composition you may want to use dialogue. A dialogue is simply a conversation. Using dialogue is a good way to bring characters to life by revealing their thoughts and feelings.

Try to make your dialogue realistic. Keep in mind the way people actually talk. Also keep in mind the particular personalities of your characters. Whenever you write dialogue, follow these basic rules.

1. Use quotation marks to show that you are using the exact words of a speaker. This is called a *direct quotation*.
2. Only a speaker's exact words are placed inside the quotation marks. Explaining words, like *Ralph said*, are placed outside.
3. Separate a direct quotation from the explaining words by using a comma or other appropriate punctuation.
4. A direct quotation may be placed at the beginning of a sentence or at the end. It may also be divided into two parts.
5. Use explaining words for each line of dialogue.
6. Begin a new paragraph every time a different person speaks.
7. If you do not use the exact words of a speaker, do not use quotation marks. This is called an *indirect quotation*.

Check It Out Read the following dialogue about Keith.

Mrs. Warner noticed Keith immediately, and with a smile on her face she decided to interview him first.

"As you can see, Keith," said Mrs. Warner, "I have a broken leg, so I need someone to do the housework for me for a couple of months. I must confess that I had not thought about a young man for the job."

Realizing his chances were slim, Keith spoke up in a firm voice, "Consider these advantages, Ma'am. I'm strong, energetic and willing to work. I can do any household job.

Mrs. Warner answered, "I'm sure you're willing, Keith, but I imagine these women are much more experienced. That would save me the time of explaining things."

With the Washington Monument fading from his future, Keith tried even harder.

"Yes, Ma'am," Keith said. "I'm sure they are, but I enjoy working outdoors as well. After I finish in here, I could cut your lawn, trim your hedges, and even mend that broken fence post I noticed on the way in."

Mrs. Warner agreed that Keith's skills would be helpful.

"And after you check my references," Keith continued, "I'll offer you a money-back guarantee. You hire me for one day, and if you're not satisfied, don't pay me. You can't lose."

"You've talked yourself into a job," smiled Mrs. Warner.

- What does the dialogue reveal about these people? Point out at least one example of each of the basic rules for punctuating quotations.

Try Your Skill Write the following dialogue correctly.

My tooth hurts so much moaned Joan who was holding her jaw I know how it must ache said Dr. Goldberg gently this won't hurt a bit is that a promise asked Joan Dr. Goldberg reassured her all right said Joan with a sigh let's get on with it.

Keep This in Mind

- Use dialogue to reveal the thoughts and personalities of the characters in a narrative. Follow the rules for punctuating quotations.

Now Write Review what you have written thus far for your own narrative. Find a place where dialogue would make the characters and the conflict more realistic. Write the dialogue, following the rules for punctuating quotations. Label your paper **Speak Your Mind** and put it into your folder.

Part 4

Grand Finale

Completing a Narrative Composition

Here's the Idea In the **conclusion** of a narrative composition, you need to provide a clear ending to the complex sequence of events you have presented. You must resolve any conflict that the characters have been facing. Tie up all loose ends.

Your conclusion must be consistent with all of the events it follows. For example, if two people have been quarreling throughout a story, they should not suddenly become friends at the end without explanation. The people may, in fact, have changed their feelings during the time span of the story. However, that change should be clearly developed before the conclusion.

Try to make your conclusion interesting. Sometimes, you may want to use humor or surprise to add interest to your conclusion. At other times, you may simply want to sum up a character's reactions after a conflict has been resolved. Try to leave your readers with a final impression that is vivid and memorable.

After you have written a conclusion, review your narrative. Write a title that fits the events and the mood of the composition. Try to appeal to your readers by writing a lively, interesting title.

Check It Out Read the following conclusion and title for the narrative about Keith's job.

> Six weeks and several calluses later, Keith had become an expert at washing windows, cleaning carpets, and waxing floors. He felt ready to take his place in any number of those TV commercials where people separated laundry, tried out dish detergents, and polished their furniture until it gleamed.

He had even painted Mrs. Warner's den for her. More importantly, his bank account totaled 240 dollars, and he would be able to go on the class trip. Keith had helped someone in need and he felt proud of his hard work. Keith had proved to himself and to Mrs. Warner that his willingness and perseverance had made him the right person for the job.

Title: The Cleanup

- Does the conclusion resolve the conflict presented in narrative? Is the conclusion interesting?
- Is the title a good one for this story? Why?

Try Your Skill Review the notes for a narrative composition that you made for the **Try Your Skill** exercise in **Head First** of this section. Using these notes, write a conclusion for the composition you planned. Try to make the conclusion sum up the events of the narrative in an interesting way. Finally, write a title that seems to fit the narrative as planned.

Keep This in Mind

- Write a conclusion that resolves the conflict. Try to tie all the elements of your composition together in a lively way.
- Write an interesting title that fits your narrative.

Now Write From your folder, take the narrative composition you have been writing. Write a conclusion. Resolve the conflict and tie up any loose ends related to the story.

Read over the complete narrative. Is the composition well organized? Is the writing specific and vivid? Is a conflict presented clearly and resolved logically? Make any revisions needed to strengthen your story.

Write a title that is appropriate for the narrative.

Make a final copy of the composition. Label your paper **Grand Finale.** Keep your paper in your folder.

WRITING SECTION 12

The Descriptive Composition

Part 1

Make the Scene

Planning a Descriptive Composition

Here's the Idea A descriptive composition paints a picture with words. The best descriptions appeal to all the senses—sight, hearing, smell, taste, and touch. Whenever you write a description, your first step is to choose a suitable topic. An unusual person or an object or scene that appeals strongly to the senses or arouses feelings makes a good choice.

After you choose a subject, make your pre-writing notes. Use your senses to discover lively and important details. Ask yourself how your subject looks, sounds, smells, tastes, and feels. Then, list the details, using spatial order to organize them. Show how the various features of your subject appear in space. You may want to use such transitions as *under*, *behind*, *beside*, *to the left*, *in front of*, *inside*, or *at the top*.

The last of your pre-writing steps will be to arrange your notes in three parts. First, in the introduction, plan to present your subject. Second, in the body, plan to develop your picture of the subject by using the sensory details you have selected. Third, in the conclusion, plan to summarize your ideas and feelings about your subject.

Check It Out Examine these pre-writing notes.

Topic Haleakala Crater on Maui, Hawaii

Introduction volcanoes are fascinating
  Kilauea, shooting flames and lava
  Surtsey, shooting clouds of dust
  the extinct Haleakala is very different

Body towering Haleakala (top)
  huge crater—2,720 feet deep
  7½ miles long, 2½ miles wide
  bowl-shaped, covered with cones

crater (surface)
  Haleakala means "House of the Sun"
  reddish dust
  hot, dry air

Haleakala is different
  no lava, no flames
  no smoke

Conclusion memorable trip into crater
  unlike violent volcanoes of stories
  peaceful, colorful place

- What will be the main idea of the description?
- What details will describe the volcanic crater? Are the three parts of the composition clearly organized?

Try Your Skill Choose one of these general topics as the subject for a descriptive composition. Narrow the topic to a specific subject that will lead to a vivid description. Make a set of notes, listing main ideas and details. Arrange the notes into an introduction, a body, and a conclusion.

a car a room an outdoor scene a friend

Keep This in Mind

- For a description, choose and narrow a topic that appeals to the senses.
- In your notes, list the main ideas and sensory details that you will use to describe your subject. Organize the notes into an introduction, a body, and a conclusion.

Now Write Select and narrow a vivid topic for a descriptive composition. Make a set of pre-writing notes. List main ideas and sensory details. Organize the notes into three parts. Label your paper **Make the Scene** and put it into your folder.

Part 2

Be Aware

Using Sensory Details

Here's the Idea Begin your descriptive composition by writing the **introduction.** Describe the surroundings of your real or imaginary subject. Set the scene and the mood for your word picture. Try to capture the interest and imagination of your readers. Be sure to state the specific subject of your description in one sentence of the introduction. This sentence serves as a topic sentence for the composition.

Present the complete description of your subject in the **body** of the composition. Use significant sensory details that will create a vivid word picture. Use specific, accurate language rather than general descriptions. For example, you may want to describe something as being *tall* or *bright* or *unusual*. Such general words as these tell about a subject. However, more specific descriptions, such as *twelve feet high* or *purple* or *diamond-studded,* will show a subject more clearly. Use your senses to describe a subject vividly.

Check It Out Read the introduction and body of the description of the Haleakala Crater.

> Volcanoes have always fascinated me. I have seen color photographs of the Hawaiian volcano Kilauea shooting flames and molten, glowing lava. I have seen other pictures showing the volcanic island Surtsey near Iceland with dense clouds of dust pouring from the summit. I thought I knew exactly what it would be like to stare into the crater of a volcano. However, my mental image was changed forever by the surprising appearance of Haleakala Crater on the island of Maui in Hawaii.
>
> The towering Haleakala was much bigger than I had expected. The crater itself, which we were allowed to enter, spread out below us—seven and a half miles long, two and a

half miles wide, and more than two thousand feet deep. We could see that the crater formed a bowl-shaped depression covered with a string of powdery black cones sticking up from its bottom surface. These cones appeared from a distance to be about as tall as a person. As we approached them, though, we realized that they were actually about ten stories tall.

The name *Haleakala* means "House of the Sun," but from its depths, the crater resembled photographs I had seen of the surface of the moon. Everywhere we saw reddish dust and cinders. It was also strangely quiet. The crunching of cinders underfoot was the only sound. The air felt hot and dry, and the gritty dust rose everywhere until I could taste it.

There were no bubbling pools of lava here. There was no billowing smoke or flames. The eerie desert of Haleakala Crater was not like any volcano I had seen in books.

- Is the location of the subject given?
- Point out sensory details. What senses are included?

Try Your Skill Choose three of the following objects. List at least six sensory details that describe each object.

a pine tree	suntan oil	a hamburger	popcorn
a bar of soap	strawberry jam	a jacket	a desk

Keep This in Mind

- In the introduction of a descriptive composition, describe the location of your subject.
- To develop the body of the description, use vivid and specific sensory details.

Now Write Review your notes labeled **Make the Scene.** List any additional sensory details that will make your description more vivid or more accurate. Write the introduction to your description. Then write the body of the composition. Label your paper **Be Aware.** Keep your work in your folder.

Part 3

A Spaceflight

Organizing a Description

Here's the Idea A descriptive composition must be organized in a clear and logical order. Sometimes you may want to organize a description using **spatial order.** You may choose any one of many spatial patterns. For example, you may describe a subject from side to side or from top to bottom. There are certain subjects that can best be described in a circular pattern.

To make any pattern clear, use transitions. Using transitional words and phrases will help you to organize the details within each paragraph. In addition, using transitions between paragraphs will help you to show how the parts of your description are related.

To complete your word picture, write a **conclusion.** Think about the main ideas and details you have presented. How can you summarize your feelings about your particular subject? What impression do you want to leave with readers? Write a clear, strong conclusion that ties your ideas and feelings together.

As a final step, you may want to write an interesting and appropriate title for your descriptive composition.

Check It Out Review the descriptive composition about Haleakala Crater that is shown in the last lesson. Notice how the description is organized. Then read the following conclusion and title.

> After our return climb up one of the trails within the crater, I thought about my previous images of volcanoes. I thought of the stories I had read about Stromboli and Vesuvius and Krakatoa and their violent eruptions. I realized that quiet,

colorful Haleakala had impressed me because it was so different. In fact, Haleakala Crater was so unexpected that I think I shall never forget it.

Title: A Sleeping Giant

- In what order is the description organized? Point out the transitions used.
- Does the conclusion summarize the main idea?
- Is the title interesting?

Try Your Skill Think about the objects listed below. Each one would be a possible topic for a descriptive composition. Decide what is the most logical spatial pattern to describe each object. Write and explain the pattern you would use.

a freight train	a kitchen	a skyscraper
a garden	a dog	a pond

Keep This in Mind

- Use a clear, logical order to organize a descriptive composition. You may want to use transitions that show spatial order.
- In the conclusion, summarize your main ideas and feelings about your subject.
- Write a suitable title.

Now Write Review the composition you have been writing in this section. Is your description organized in a logical order? Have you used clear transitions? Do any rewriting necessary.

Write a strong conclusion for your description. Summarize your main ideas and your feelings. Also, write a title.

Make a final copy of your composition. Label it **A Spaceflight.** Keep it in your folder.

The Explanatory Composition

Explaining a Process

Part 1

Easy Does It

Planning an Explanation

Here's the Idea Everyone has given directions at one time or another. You may have given directions explaining how to make something, such as scrambled eggs or woolen mittens. You may have given directions explaining how to do something, such as lift weights or paint with watercolors.

Writing an explanatory composition that explains a process uses the same skills you have used in everyday situations. You must explain the steps in a process briefly and clearly. Start with the first step and proceed through all the steps in the order in which they must be completed.

Before you can write your explanation, you have to choose and narrow a topic. The best ideas come from your own experience and interests. You may have special skills or talents that you can teach to someone else. Plan your idea in a set of notes. List the major steps in the process. Be sure to include any tools, ingredients, or materials required.

Also, write a title that indicates clearly what the composition will be about. You may want to use the words *How To* as part of the title to announce the process to be explained.

Check It Out Read these pre-writing notes.

How To Take Good Photographs

1. Get to know your camera
   no need for expensive camera
   study manual
   learn use of all knobs, buttons
   practice with camera
2. Learn about types of film
   black and white or color
   indoor, outdoor films

3. Take pictures
   take lots of pictures
   subject must be in focus
   hold camera steady
   press button smoothly

- What process do these steps explain?
- Do the notes clearly list the steps in the process and the materials needed?
- Is the title appropriate?

Try Your Skill Here are jumbled notes for two explanatory compositions that explain processes. Copy the titles on your paper. Below each title, list the steps in the correct order.

How To Wax a Car

Apply wax with damp cloth
Wipe off excess, polishing to a bright shine
Remove any old wax with clean, dry cloth
Wash car
Dry car with chamois or lint-free cloth

How To Splice Electrical Wiring

Strip insulation from ends of wires
Twist ends of wire together tightly
Turn off all electric current
Wrap spliced wires with electrical tape

Keep This in Mind

- Choose a special skill as the topic for an explanatory composition that explains a process.
- In your notes, list the steps in the process and any equipment or ingredients needed.
- Write a title that announces the process clearly.

Now Write Think of five processes you could explain in a composition. List the topics, and a title for each. Label your paper **Easy Does It** and put it into your folder.

Part 2

Think Ahead

Using Step-by-Step Order

Here's the Idea Introduce the topic of your explanatory composition in the first paragraph. One sentence of the **introduction** should serve as the topic sentence for the composition. If your topic is how to take photographs, the topic sentence might say "With practice, you can take memorable photographs of the special times in your life."

In the **body,** give a step-by-step explanation. For example, you might divide the taking of good photographs into learning about your camera, choosing the correct film, and taking pictures. Each of these steps would be discussed in a paragraph. You would develop each paragraph with details from your notes. Be specific, accurate, and complete.

Develop the concluding paragraph from the final step, which is developing the photographs. In your **conclusion,** tie up loose ends and offer any additional advice you have.

Check It Out Read the body of the explanatory composition about the process of taking good photographs.

> Your first step must be to get to know your camera. You certainly do not need an expensive camera to take good pictures. It is far more important to know what your camera can or cannot do. You will probably want to begin by studying the instruction manual. Then practice with the camera itself. Get to know what every knob and button on your camera is used for. Your camera must be so familiar to you and feel so comfortable that you are able to concentrate on your subjects.
>
> A second necessary step is to learn about the different kinds of film available. You may want to ask a clerk at a camera store for help. You may choose black and white film for certain kinds of photographs. You may choose color film,

which is more expensive, for other kinds of pictures. Some films are best for taking pictures outdoors. Other films are best for taking pictures indoors with a flash attachment.

At last, you are ready to take photographs — lots of photographs. Only through constant use of a camera will you develop your skills. Always be sure the subject of your photograph is in focus. Hold the camera as steady as you can. Focus on your subject, and press the shutter-release button smoothly.

- What steps are explained in the body of this explanatory composition?

Try Your Skill Below are jumbled notes for the body of a composition explaining the process of repairing cracks in a wall. Determine the correct order for the steps and write them in that order. Add any necessary details. Save this list for a related exercise in the next lesson.

Force the spackling mixture into damp cracks, smoothing surfaces with putty knife.
First clean loose plaster from cracks and dampen with water.
Let spackling mixture dry until hard; then sand smooth.
Mix spackling compound and water until it looks and feels like toothpaste.
Paint dry patches with final coat.
Paint dry patches first with primer.

Keep This in Mind

- Present your topic in the introduction.
- In the body, give a step-by-step explanation.
- Develop the conclusion from the final step.

Now Write Choose one process you listed in **Easy Does It.** List the steps involved. Using step-by-step order, write the body of a composition that explains the process. Label your paper **Think Ahead** and keep it in your folder.

Part 3

First to Last

Using Transitions

Here's the Idea Transitional words and phrases are important for making clear the step-by-step order of a composition that explains a process. The most helpful transitions are similar to those used for narrative compositions. They indicate the natural time order of a process. You may want to use transitions such as *the first step, the next step, during this time, then, as soon as, at last* or *after one hour.*

Transitions are useful within each paragraph, particularly in the body of a composition as you explain the steps of a process. Transitions are also helpful between paragraphs. They work like bridges to carry the reader from the main idea of one paragraph to the main idea of the next.

Check It Out Note the transitions in the introduction and conclusion of the composition on taking photographs. Review the transitions used in the body of the explanation.

Introduction

What is the best way to recall the most important experiences of our lives? Our memories can hold the details of recent experiences with little difficulty. However, most of us need a little help in remembering details about past experiences. The best reminders of special moments are photographs, which capture them forever. With practice, you can take memorable photographs of the special times in your life.

Conclusion

After you shoot a roll of film, it is important to have it developed as soon as possible. Old film will not produce the clearest pictures. When you receive your developed pictures, store the best of them in a photo album or suitable container.

Arrange the photographs in a logical order for viewing. Be careful not to mar them with fingerprints. As your skill with a camera improves, you will be glad you took the time to take photographs.

- What transitions are used within the introduction and within the conclusion? What transitions link the introduction or the conclusion to the body?

Try Your Skill Read the following explanation of the process of repairing walls. The steps are presented in the correct order, but the paragraph is missing transitions. Rewrite the paragraph and add transitions to make the order clear. Combine steps whenever it makes sense.

Force the spackling mixture into all cracks or holes. Scrape any excess mixture from the surface of the wall. Let the spackling mixture dry. Add more if any spot is not completely filled. Sand the dry spackling mixture. Wipe off dust. Put on one coat of primer. Let it dry. Paint over primer with paint.

Keep This in Mind

- In an explanatory composition that explains a process, use time transitions to make clear the order of the steps in each paragraph. Also use transitions to link paragraphs in all three parts of a composition.

Now Write Review the body of the composition you wrote for **Think Ahead.** Add any transitions necessary to make the order of the steps clear.

Write an introduction and a conclusion for your explanation. Use any transitions necessary to link the paragraphs in all three parts of the composition. Make a final copy. Label your paper **First to Last.** Keep your work in your folder.

The Explanatory Composition

Stating an Opinion

Part 1

In View of

Stating an Opinion

Here's the Idea An explanatory composition may express an opinion and explain why a reader should accept that opinion. For instance, you may explain why most Americans need to change their eating habits. You may argue that human beings should continue to explore outer space. Your opinion may be one shared by many people or only by those in a special group. It may be a controversial idea. Whatever opinions you hold strongly and sincerely are likely to be good topics for your compositions.

As you search for topics, think about your life. Think about your neighborhood, your city, your nation. What do you believe in? What do you believe should be started or stopped or changed? Consider issues you feel strongly about.

Once you have chosen a topic, make your pre-writing notes. Organize your thoughts and feelings. Plan to express your opinion clearly in the introduction. Plan to support your opinion with reasons or facts in the body of the composition. Plan to sum up your argument in the conclusion.

Check It Out Examine these notes for a student's explanatory composition expressing a personal opinion.

Topic Professional athletes deserve to be paid well.

Introduction professional sports—big business
- expensive tickets for professional sports
- athletes earn a great deal
- I think they deserve the money

Body good reasons for high earnings
1. talented athletes work hard
   - men and women train long hours, face tough competition

2. athletes deserve compensation for risks, injuries—head, back, broken bones—which may be a problem for a long time
3. short careers
athletes perform best when young
family life suffers

Conclusion athletes work hard for whatever success they earn
I would not trade places with any of them

- Is the topic suitable for an explanatory composition that states an opinion? Is an opinion clearly expressed?
- Will these notes lead to a strong, lively composition?

Try Your Skill Choose one of these either/or statements and write it so that it expresses your opinion. Write three statements that express other opinions important to you. Be prepared to support your opinions with reasons or facts.

1. Most people (are, are not) honest.
2. The role of women (is, is not) changing in our society.
3. More money (can, cannot) make life happier.
4. It (is, is not) good to be alone.

Keep This in Mind

- Choose a belief that is important to you as the topic for an explanatory composition that states an opinion.
- In your notes, list your opinion and supporting reasons or facts. Organize your notes into the introduction, the body, and the conclusion.

Now Write Write several opinions that you hold. Choose one opinion to be developed in an explanatory composition. List the reasons or facts that support your opinion. Organize your notes into introduction, body, and conclusion. Label your paper **In View of.** Put it into your folder.

Part 2

By Reason of

Supporting an Opinion

Here's the Idea You will want to convince others that your opinion is based on truth and good judgment. To do that you need to present strong, specific reasons or facts in your explanatory composition. Build your argument by organizing supporting evidence **in order of importance** with the weakest reason or fact first and the strongest reason or fact last.

Suppose that your opinion is that your city should create a bikeway. You might list the following reasons.

1. It would provide a good way to tour the city.
2. It would encourage people to commute by bicycle.
3. It would reduce bicycle accidents.

The supporting evidence must be presented in complete detail in the **body** of your composition. Develop each important reason or fact in a separate paragraph of the body.

Check It Out Read the body of the student's composition about professional athletes.

> First of all, hundreds of thousands of fans each season are entertained by outstanding athletes. Talented men and women of every background have earned the opportunity to play through continual tough competition with other athletes. Why should spectators begrudge these hardworking athletes their high salaries? Surely players deserve to be paid well for their demanding performances. In fact, athletes' salaries represent not only their performances in public, but also all their lengthy practice times. Since practice is a professional requirement, athletes should be compensated for it.
>
> More important, athletes need some benefit to compensate for the physical abuse they suffer in certain sports, such as

boxing or hockey. Athletes sometimes risk major physical injuries. They may injure their heads or their backs. They may pull tendons, break bones, or lose teeth. As a result of their careers, they may suffer for the rest of their lives. How many people would face such risks without financial reward?

The most important reason athletes should be paid well is based on simple arithmetic. Most athletes are young and have only a short time to perform at their peak. As a result, athletes must spend a great deal of time away from their families in order to work. In addition, when most other people are firmly settled in their careers, athletes may be out of a job. In fact, money earned early may be needed in leaner years ahead.

- Is an opinion supported by specific reasons or facts? Is the evidence given in order of importance, from the least important to the most important?

Try Your Skill Choose one of these opinions to support. List at least three specific supporting reasons or facts.

1. Everyone should learn basic first aid.
2. Americans should stop buying big, luxury automobiles.
3. A good education is necessary for everyone.
4. Spectators at sports events should be more courteous.

Keep This in Mind

- In the body of an explanatory composition that states an opinion, present specific supporting reasons or facts. Organize supporting evidence in order of importance.

Now Write From your folder, take out your composition notes labeled **In View of.** Review the reasons or facts you have listed to support your opinion and arrange them in order of importance. Write the body of your explanatory composition. Label your paper **By Reason of** and put it into your folder.

Part 3

Famous Last Words

Using Transitions

Here's the Idea You will find transitions helpful as you write an explanatory composition stating an opinion. Using one kind of transition will help you present supporting reasons or facts in their order of importance. This kind of transition includes *the first reason*, *second*, *most important*, and *finally*.

Using the second kind of transition will help you to state reasons or facts. This kind includes such words as *because*, *since*, *if*, *therefore*, and *as a result*.

In your **introduction,** include one sentence that will serve as the topic sentence for the entire composition. In the **conclusion,** summarize your argument effectively. Write a title that presents your topic in an interesting way.

Check It Out Read these parts of the student composition supporting high salaries for athletes.

Introduction

Professional sports is big business. All major sports involve a great deal of money. The public must pay for expensive tickets to sporting events. Many of the athletes involved make huge salaries. All of this moneymaking has led some fans to complain that overpaid athletes are the cause of problems in many sports. These angry fans feel that love of the sport, not money, should be what motivates athletes. However, I believe that professional athletes deserve to be paid well.

Conclusion

Therefore, the next time someone complains about the extraordinary salaries of athletes, consider the prices they pay. Athletes work long hours and risk serious injuries. They must often give up family life. It is easy to sit in the stands and criticize professional athletes. However, would you be willing to be on the field doing what they do? I would not, and I believe professional athletes deserve to be paid well.

Title: The High Cost of Athletes

- Does the introduction clearly state an opinion?
- Does the conclusion summarize the argument?
- Which transitions help to state the reasons or facts?

Try Your Skill Read the groups of sentences below. Each group begins with a topic sentence and is followed by two supporting reasons. Add any details that will strengthen the supporting evidence. Rewrite each group of sentences, adding transitions that state reasons or facts and those that show the order of importance.

1. More jobs should be made available to teenagers.
   Teenagers need to learn how to manage their own money.
   Teenagers need work experience to prepare themselves for graduation from high school.
2. The city is a good place to live.
   Public transportation is better than it is in the suburbs.
   There is more to see and do in the city.

Keep This in Mind

- In the introduction, clearly state your opinion.
- In the conclusion, summarize your argument.
- Use transitions to help state the reasons or facts and to present each bit of supporting evidence in order of its importance.

Now Write Review the explanatory composition that you have been writing. Write an introduction and a conclusion. Include clear transitions. Add a title. Make a final copy. Label your paper **Famous Last Words.** Keep it in your folder.

The Explanatory Composition

Stating a Definition

Part 1

Explain It

Planning a Definition

Here's the Idea As you have learned, an explanatory composition may explain a process or state an opinion. An explanatory composition may also state a definition. For example, you may wonder what *paprika* is, what *progress* is, what a *mime* does, or what the term *liberal arts* means. Any of these subjects could be defined in an explanatory composition. In fact, any object, idea, or special term may be an interesting subject to define.

As you decide on your own topic for an explanatory composition, you will find many possibilities. You may find school situations, for example, in which you are asked to define a *metaphor*, an *equation*, or *freedom of the press*. You may also find real-life situations in which you must explain a *forge*, an *avocado*, or *asbestos*. You may also find a topic related to a sport, a hobby, a household task, or a job. For your definition, choose a topic that interests you and that you can develop in detail.

Plan an explanatory composition that states a definition by making notes. In the introduction, plan to give a specific definition of your topic. In the body, plan to develop the main ideas of your definition with details or with facts and figures. In the conclusion, plan to summarize your definition.

Check It Out Read these pre-writing notes.

Topic bagels

Introduction Americans' new interest in food
 buying woks, crêpe pans, pasta machines
 eating in small, ethnic restaurants
 but overlooking simple food—bread, especially bagels

Body bread
most widely eaten food in the world
quick breads—muffins, biscuits, corn bread
flat breads—*tortillas, pita bread*
yeast breads—white, rye, rolls, bagels

bagels
doughnut-shaped
shiny, crusty outer surface
dense, chewy middle

breakfast food
toasted, warm
good with cream cheese, salmon

Conclusion bagels are simple, delicious
more popular now
found in frozen food sections

- Do these notes include details or facts and figures that will define the subject clearly?

Try Your Skill Imagine that you want to define a sport or game that you like. You might choose basketball or backgammon, for example. Make a detailed set of notes for an explanatory composition.

Keep This in Mind

- Choose an object, term, or idea as the topic for an explanatory composition that states a definition. In your notes, list details or facts and figures that will define your subject clearly.

Now Write Choose a topic for an explanatory composition that states a definition. You may want to define something related to a hobby or a job. Make a detailed set of pre-writing notes. Plan the introduction, the body, and the conclusion of the composition. Label your paper **Explain It**.

Part 2

Precisely Yours

Stating a Definition

Here's the Idea To write any good definition, you must do three things. First, name the word to be defined. Second, name the general class to which the subject belongs. Third, name the particular characteristics of the subject. Through this process of defining a subject, you will be able to present a complete and informative picture of it.

Suppose that you would like to define a violin. You would begin your definition by stating that a violin is a musical instrument. You have named the word and its general class. A musical instrument, however, might be a flute, a tuba, a drum, a piano, or bagpipes. You might add that a violin is a stringed instrument. That one characteristic separates it from woodwind, brass, percussion, keyboard, and other instruments. However, a stringed instrument might be a guitar, a dulcimer, or an aeolian harp. You might add that a violin is played with a bow. That characteristic separates it from stringed instruments in which the strings are plucked or hammered or vibrated by the wind. However, a stringed instrument played with a bow might also be a cello or a viola. You might add that a violin is held under the chin and is the smallest, highest-pitched instrument of those in the violin family. By using all of this specific information, you could write a good definition like this one: A violin is a stringed musical instrument played with a bow. It is the smallest, highest-pitched instrument of the violin family and it is held under the chin to be played.

You should include a good definition as part of the introduction of an explanatory composition. Your definition serves as the topic sentence for the composition. Be sure that your definition is clear and specific.

Check It Out Read the introduction to the explanatory composition that defines bagels.

> Recently, many Americans have become more interested in favorite foods from other lands. Many busy cooks are buying Chinese woks, French crêpe pans, and Italian pasta machines. Many adventurous diners are seeking out small ethnic restaurants that serve tasty homecooked dishes that are traditionally prepared. In their search for specialty foods, however, many people have been overlooking a basic and delicious food—bread. One of the tastiest ethnic varieties of bread is the bagel, a dense, chewy, ring-shaped roll.

- Does this introduction include a good definition? Is the definition a topic sentence that presents a suitable topic for an interesting composition?

Try Your Skill Write a good definition for three of the following objects. Name the word, its general class, and its particular characteristics. If necessary, check a dictionary or encyclopedia for additional facts and figures.

silk	a star	a harmonica	a tractor trailer
snowshoes	tulips	a television	a lion

Keep This in Mind

- To state a definition, name a word, its general class, and its specific characteristics. Include the definition in the introduction as the topic sentence for a composition.

Now Write Review your pre-writing notes labeled **Explain It.** Write a good definition for the subject you have selected. Be sure you have named your subject, its general class, and its particular characteristics. Then write the introduction for your explanatory composition. Label your paper **Precisely Yours** and put it into your folder.

Part 3

Final Appeal

Developing a Definition

Here's the Idea You define a subject in the introduction of an explanatory composition. You need to develop that definition in the **body.** The most informative way to develop a definition is either with details or with facts and figures.

There are certain subjects that you will choose to develop in a factual way. Suppose you were defining *pneumonia* or the *Milky Way*. To define subjects like these you would want to use facts and figures. Use reference books to help you find the most important and most accurate information.

There are other subjects that you will choose to develop in a personal way. Suppose you were defining terms or ideas like *match point*, *standing ovation*, *freedom*, or *courage*. To define subjects like these you would more naturally choose details related to your personal experiences.

Write a **conclusion** that sums up the main idea of your definition. Also, add a title that suggests your main idea.

Check It Out Read the body, conclusion, and title of the explanatory composition about bagels.

> In fact, bread is the most widely eaten food in the world. Combinations of flour and water have existed in some form since the beginning of history. There are quick breads which include an enormous variety of muffins and biscuits, as well as corn bread and gingerbread. There are flat breads, including Mexican *tortillas* and Middle Eastern *pita bread*. Most common in the United States are yeast breads, including many varieties of wheat and rye breads. Bagels are a kind of yeast bread, unique because they are boiled first and then baked.
>
> Bagels are doughnut-shaped, brown, and shiny. Their outer surface looks like smooth, polished wood. Sometimes it is

dotted with tangy black onion flakes. The crust is not entirely crisp, yet not tender either. The inside of a bagel is dense, heavy, and quite chewy. Bagels are like no other bread, because of their unique texture.

Bagels are usually served for breakfast. They are particularly good when they are served warm or toasted. However, bagels may be eaten anytime. They are a perfect companion to cream cheese or smoked salmon.

Bagels are a simple food, but delicious. They can now be bought frozen in some stores. Soon they may turn up on more family breakfast tables. Start your day with a bagel.

Title: Bagels for Breakfast

- Is this definition developed in a factual or in a personal way? What facts and figures or details are used?
- Do the conclusion and title point out the main idea?

Try Your Skill Write definitions for two of these terms or ideas. Then list at least five facts and figures or five personal details that you could use to develop your definition.

soap opera	friendship	harmony	success
jet stream	freedom	chauvinism	family

Keep This in Mind

- Develop the body of an explanatory composition that states a definition by using facts and figures or personal details.
- Summarize the main idea of your definition in the conclusion and in a title.

Now Write Review your notes and the introduction you have written for your explanatory composition. Write the body, using either facts and figures or personal details. Write a conclusion and a title. Make a final copy. Label your paper **Final Appeal.** Keep your work in your folder.

Letters, Applications, and Résumés

Part 1

Keep in Touch

Writing Personal Letters

Here's the Idea The term **personal letter** includes all letters not written to businesses. Writing personal letters is a way of keeping in touch with absent friends or of expressing your feelings in certain social situations. Personal letters, which are usually handwritten, have five main parts.

The **heading** contains three lines: one line for the writer's street address, one for the city, state, and ZIP code, and one for the date. None of this information should be abbreviated. The heading appears at the top right corner of your letter.

The **salutation** is the greeting. Usually beginning with *Dear*, it is written on the next line below the heading. It starts at the left margin of the page and is followed by a comma.

The **body** of the letter is the main part. There you write what you want to say in a detailed and conversational way. The body begins on the line following the salutation. Each paragraph of the body should be indented.

The **closing** is your way of saying "goodbye." You may say *Love*, or *Your friend*, for instance. The closing is written on the line below the last line of the body and is followed by a comma. The first word of the closing should align with the first words of the heading.

Your **signature** is the last part of a letter. Skip a line after the closing and sign your name in line with the first word of the closing. Usually, only your first name is needed.

There are some forms of personal letters written only for special occasions. These social notes include invitations and thank-you notes. The notes also have five main parts, but the heading may be shortened to the date only.

If you send an **invitation,** include all information about the event. If you receive an invitation, reply at once.

Sometimes you will send **thank-you** notes. One kind of thank-you note is written to thank someone for a gift you have received. Another kind of thank-you, called a **bread-and-butter** note, thanks someone for his or her hospitality. You would write this kind of note if you stayed overnight as a guest in someone's house.

Check It Out Read this personal letter.

1315 Albron Drive
St. Paul, Minnesota 55105
April 19, 1980

Dear Susan,

I am sorry to hear about your broken ankle. I know you're as disappointed as I am that we have to postpone our hiking trip. However, resting for two weeks will give you the perfect chance to catch up on all the reading that you said you had to do — not to mention the letter writing!

How about rescheduling your visit for the weekend of June 8? You plan whatever will be best for you. I'm looking forward to seeing you soon.

Love,
Chris

- Identify the five parts of this personal letter.
- Is this a well written letter? Why or why not?

Try Your Skill Arrange the following information in the correct form for a personal letter. Add any other information or details that you think might be included in the letter. Be sure to add capital letters and correct punctuation wherever necessary.

> 31 Forest Street, Fairfield, Iowa 52556, October 23, 1980 dear randy Shortly after you left, I discovered your notebook under the stack of newspapers you had been reading. The notebook is in the mail already, so you should get it in time to finish your English assignment next week. Remember, we have plans to watch more football together on Thanksgiving. until then george

Keep This in Mind

- Write personal letters that are conversational, detailed, and neat. Be sure that the heading, salutation, body, closing, and signature follow the correct form.
- Social notes are short forms of personal letters. Write invitations that are specific and thank-you notes that express your appreciation.

Now Write Write a personal letter to a friend or relative. You may want to write a social note. Use your own address and today's date in the heading. The body of your letter may be based on either real or imaginary events. Make sure that all parts of your letter follow the correct form. Label your paper **Keep in Touch** and put it into your folder. Make a copy of the letter that you could send and save that also.

Part 2

Special Delivery

Preparing Letters for the Mail

Here's the Idea Once you have written a letter, you need to prepare it correctly for mailing. Begin by folding the letter neatly and choosing an envelope that matches the width of the stationery. Insert the folded letter and seal the envelope.

To make sure your letter reaches its destination without delay, take extra care to address the envelope accurately and neatly. Follow these steps.

1. Address the envelope. Add your return address.
2. Double-check all numbers to make sure they are correct.
3. Include the correct ZIP code. To learn the correct use of ZIP codes and state abbreviations, turn to page 145.
4. Put a stamp on the envelope. Be sure you have used enough postage for the letter or package.

Check It Out Look at the envelope below.

Dee Wendell
162 Exeter Street
Kansas City, MO 64108

Jim Shortelle
2178 Broadway
New Haven, CT 06510

- Who wrote the letter? Who will receive it? What state abbreviations are used? How could you check all the information?

Try Your Skill Write each of these jumbled addresses as it should appear on an envelope. Also write a return address. You may need to refer to the list of correct state abbreviations on the next page.

1. Mike Ruddy, 31 Sullivan Street, Livingston, New Jersey 07039

2. 580 Rosewood Avenue, Phoenix, Arizona 85002, Maria Cordova

3. Philadelphia, Pennsylvania 19101, 122 Salem Lane, Robert Bernstein

4. 179 Foster Street, Frankfort, Kentucky 40601, Joe Leone

5. Susan Kim, Des Moines, Iowa 50306, 14 Briar Road

6. Enrico Sanchez, 259 Bennett Road, Falls Church, Virginia 22046

7. Christine Sobel, Atlanta, Georgia 30302, 3871 Beacon Boulevard

8. Whitinsville, Maryland 01588, Dr. Jonathan Schmitt, 644 Eastern Parkway

9. 22 Lyndon Terrace, Chapel Hill, North Carolina 27514, Ellie Johannson

10. Ms. Susan Lindahl, 2002 Oceanview Drive, Santa Monica, California 90405

Keep This in Mind

- Prepare letters for the mail carefully. Check all information for accuracy.

Now Write Find your personal letter labeled **Keep in Touch.** On the other side of the paper, add the title of this lesson **Special Delivery.** Draw a rectangle to represent an envelope. Address it as if you were going to mail it to your friend or relative. Keep this paper in your folder.

Copy your work on a real envelope. Fold the copy of the letter that you can send and put it into the envelope. Put a stamp on your letter and mail it.

ZIP Codes and State Abbreviations

In order to make sure that your letter reaches its destination, check the address, including the ZIP code. The ZIP code is very important today. It enables the postal department to sort your letter for delivery as rapidly as possible. If you don't know a particular ZIP code, call your local post office. Someone will give you the correct ZIP for any address in the United States and the territories.

The United States Postal Service has a list of approved state abbreviations to be used on all envelopes and packages. You must use the ZIP code with these abbreviations.

Abbreviations of State Names

State	Abbreviation
Alabama	AL
Alaska	AK
Arizona	AZ
Arkansas	AR
American Samoa	AS
California	CA
Canal Zone	CZ
Colorado	CO
Connecticut	CT
Delaware	DE
District of Columbia	DC
Florida	FL
Georgia	GA
Guam	GU
Hawaii	HI
Idaho	ID
Illinois	IL
Indiana	IN
Iowa	IA
Kansas	KS
Kentucky	KY
Louisiana	LA
Maine	ME
Maryland	MD
Massachusetts	MA
Michigan	MI
Minnesota	MN
Mississippi	MS
Missouri	MO
Montana	MT
Nebraska	NE
Nevada	NV
New Hampshire	NH
New Jersey	NJ
New Mexico	NM
New York	NY
North Carolina	NC
North Dakota	ND
Ohio	OH
Oklahoma	OK
Oregon	OR
Pennsylvania	PA
Puerto Rico	PR
Rhode Island	RI
South Carolina	SC
South Dakota	SD
Tennessee	TN
Trust Territories	TT
Texas	TX
Utah	UT
Vermont	VT
Virgina	VA
Virgin Islands	VI
Washington	WA
West Virgina	WV
Wisconsin	WI
Wyoming	WY

Part 3 **The World of Business**

Writing Business Letters

Here's the Idea In addition to writing personal letters, you will also be writing **business letters.** Learning to write business letters is a useful, practical skill. There will be times when you need to write to a company regarding its products. There will be times when you will want to write to a school or college. In seeking employment you may need to write letters and résumés and to complete application forms. In all of these situations, you will be likely to meet with more success if you follow the correct form for business letters.

In order to make the best impression, you must make your business letters neat. Plain white paper, 8½x11, is considered standard, and typing is considered an advantage. It is not required that you type any of your business letters. However, most businesses type letters and reports.

Any business letter you write may take one of two forms. One form is the **block** form, which should be used only if you type a letter. In the block form, begin every part of a letter at the left margin. Leave two lines of space between paragraphs and do not indent them. Another form, the **modified block** form, may be used either for handwritten or typewritten letters. In this form, place the heading, closing, and signature at the right side of the page. Indent the paragraphs and do not leave extra space between them.

Every business letter has six parts — the five parts of a personal letter, plus an **inside address.** The inside address is the name and address of the company to which you are writing. Whenever possible, the inside address should include the name of a particular employee or department within the firm. Place an inside address at the left margin below the heading and above the salutation.

More formal language is used in business letters than in personal letters. For the greeting use *Dear Mr.*, *Mrs.*, *Miss*, or *Ms.* before the person's name. Or, use a general greeting like *Dear Sir or Madam*. Place the salutation two lines below the inside address and use a colon (:) after it.

For the more formal closing, write *Sincerely*, *Yours truly*, or *Very truly yours*, followed by a comma. If you type a letter, leave four lines of space between the closing and your typed signature. Then, write your signature in the space.

Always make a business letter polite, specific, and neat. Keep a copy of all business letters you write.

Check It Out Read this business letter.

317 Grantly Boulevard
Los Angeles, California 90017
September 8, 1980

Power Products, Incorporated
1105 Moore Street
Reston, Virginia 22091

Dear Sir or Madam:

Recently I bought a PPI amplifier, Model 217, at The Sound Store in Los Angeles. The package was factory sealed, but when I opened it I found no instructions and no schematic diagrams. The salesperson had assured me that I would find both of them inside the package.

Please send me a copy of each as soon as possible.

Yours truly,

Edward McKenna

Edward McKenna

- What is the purpose of this business letter?
- In what form is this letter?

Try Your Skill Write a letter from Gina Hampton, president of Power Products Incorporated, to Edward McKenna. Have Ms. Hampton apologize to Edward for any inconvenience, and have her assure him that the papers he requested are on their way. For the purpose of this exercise, use the block form, even though your letter will be handwritten.

Keep This in Mind

- You may write a business letter to request information, to order a product, to apply to a school, or to seek employment. Whether you write or type a business letter, be polite, specific, and neat. Keep a copy of every business letter.
- Use either the *block* or *modified block* form for a business letter. Either form has six parts, including an inside address.

Now Write Write or type a letter to a real organization regarding a particular product. Also, draw an envelope and address it. Label your paper **The World of Business** and put it into your folder.

What Do You Need?

Writing Letters of Request

Here's the Idea Often you will write a business letter because you would like something from a company or an organization. You may need information for a report. You may want tourist information about a place you plan to visit. You may want to order a certain product.

Letters of request are business letters. Therefore, they should contain the six parts of a business letter, and they should follow either the *block* or *modified block* form. However, there are two additional points that you need to keep in mind when you write or type a letter of request.

First, be specific. Provide all the information that the other person needs in order to fill your request. If you want information, state exactly what information you need. If you are placing an order, be sure the business knows exactly what you want and where it is to be sent. Also include any necessary details about the size, color, cost, or identification number of the product you want. Most businesses and organizations can fill your request promptly if it is precise and complete.

Second, remember that you are asking another person to take time to fill your request. Therefore, be especially sure that your letter is courteous, clear, and to the point.

Check It Out Read the letter of request on page 150.

28 Plainview Road
Greenfield, Wisconsin 53220
December 3, 1980

Chamber of Commerce
1122 West Main Street
Petersburg, Virginia 23803

Dear Sir or Madam:

I am a junior in high school, and I am working on a report on Tiffany stained glass. Through my research I have discovered that the Blanford Church in Petersburg has windows designed by Louis Tiffany. I need to know the year the windows were installed, the dimensions of the windows, and their original cost. Could you provide me with this information or give me the name of someone in town who can?

I also understand that there are free picture post cards available through your office that feature the windows. May I have a copy of such a post card?

This information, plus any additional facts you might have about the windows, will be very useful for my report and will be greatly appreciated.

Yours truly,

Frances Russell

Frances Russell

- Is this letter of request courteous, specific, and to the point? Which form does this business letter have?

Try Your Skill Write a letter to the United States Soccer Federation, 350 Fifth Avenue, New York, New York 10001, asking for information about where regulation soccer balls may be purchased locally. Use your home address and today's date.

Keep This in Mind

- Write a letter of request that is courteous, specific, and to the point. You may use either the *block* or *modified block* form for this business letter.

Now Write Write to the manufacturer of a particular product that you would like to know more about. You may write to a mail order company that you have seen advertised, or to the manufacturer of a product that is made in your town. Use the phone book or printed advertisements to help you find the address.

Use the modified block form for your handwritten letter. Be sure that you ask for specific information. Write the title of this lesson, **What Do You Need?** on your paper. Put your work into your folder. You may want to make a copy of your letter of request and send it.

To Your Knowledge

Writing Letters to Schools

Here's the Idea You can learn a great deal about various schools and colleges from your guidance department and from the school or public library. Usually, these sources have catalogs for you to look through, as well as some scholarship information. You will also find valuable information about our nation's schools, including their addresses, in such references as *Lovejoy's Career and Vocational School Guide* and *Barron's Profiles of American Colleges.*

However, the best way to get specific information about a particular school that interests you is to write to the school itself. A letter to a vocational school or college is a business letter. Address it to the Admissions Office of the school and follow either of the standard business forms that you have learned. Briefly give the school the information it needs in order to supply you with the information you need.

The school that you might attend will want to know about you. Include information about the name of your school, your grade level, and the date of your graduation. State your main area of interest. Also, you want to know about the school. Include a request for information about entrance requirements, special programs offered, the size and location of the school, tuition costs, and scholarships. Include a request for a catalog. If there is any charge for a catalog, the school will let you know.

Because the cost of education is often high, you may also be interested in information about student loans and scholarships. If so, write directly to the Office of Financial Aid. Ask about financial assistance available for the year you plan to enter. The school will send you information about its programs and the necessary forms to be completed.

Deciding to continue your education is an important decision. You need to compare several schools in order to make the best choice. Writing letters to schools is a good way to learn all you can.

Check It Out Read the following letter.

32 Meyer Road
Galveston, Texas 77550
February 16, 1980

Admissions Office
Texas College of Arts and Industries
Kingsville, Texas 78363

Dear Sir or Madam:

I am a junior and will graduate from Galveston West High School in the spring of 1981. I am interested in continuing my education in the field of data processing, and I am particularly interested in the program you offer. Do you anticipate many openings in your program for the fall of 1981, or will there be a limited enrollment?

I would also like to know what subjects you advise potential students to take during their senior year in high school. Also, is job experience required of applicants? If so, what type of experience is preferred?

Please send me a copy of your catalog so that I may examine the tuition costs, entrance requirements, and the specific courses offered in the data processing program.

Very truly yours,

Jessica Roberts

Jessica Roberts

- What specific information does this business letter include? What specific information does it request?

Try Your Skill Suppose you are a high school senior interested in hospital work. You are considering a career as an emergency medical technician. Write a letter to the Admissions Office of Midwest Vocational Institute, 3527 Western Avenue, Chicago, Illinois 60604. Request a catalog and other important information about the program offered by the school. Include important information about yourself. Invent any necessary details.

Keep This in Mind

- When your write to vocational schools and colleges, use the correct business letter form. Include specific information about yourself and request specific information from the school.

Now Write Write a letter to a real vocational school or college that interests you. Use either correct form for this business letter. Ask about various aspects of a program in the field of your choice. Request a catalog.

Proofread the letter carefully. Label it **To Your Knowledge** and put it into your folder. If you wish, make a copy of your letter and mail it.

Part 6

On the Job

Writing a Letter Seeking Employment

Here's the Idea A letter seeking employment will create the first impression that a possible employer receives of you. A neat, well written letter suggests that you will be an efficient, organized employee. In fact, a well written letter can help you to get the job you want.

When you write a letter seeking employment, you need to be clear and direct. Follow these guidelines.

1. State the title of the job you are seeking.
2. Be specific about the kind of job you are looking for. Indicate whether you are looking for employment full time, part time, or only temporarily—as for the summer or holiday season.
3. Include a brief statement about yourself. Include your age or grade level in school if you are a teenager.
4. Include a brief statement about your qualifications. Be sure to mention any related work experience or courses taken in school.
5. Be specific about your availability for work. Mention particular days or hours you will be available. Always include a starting date.
6. Include a request for an interview if the job is in your area.

If you are sending your letter to a large company, write to the personnel department. If you are writing to a small company, write to the owner or manager. If you answer a newspaper advertisement, look carefully for information telling you how to reply. Many ads will give you a box number to write to in care of the newspaper. Others may contain an address.

Make sure that your letter follows the correct form for business letters. It should be informative, neat, and polite. Also, be sure to proofread your letter carefully. Your attention to detail may lead to a job offer.

Check It Out Read this letter.

257 Walker Road
Memphis, Tennessee 38104
March 18, 1981

Mr. Ralph Owens, Manager
First Federal Food Stores
31 State Street
Memphis, Tennessee 38104

Dear Mr. Owens:

I am interested in working full time this summer as a cashier in any of the First Federal Food Stores. I am currently a junior at Central High School taking a business course. Last summer I worked as a stock clerk and bagger at Dan's Market, 522 Sherman Street. I am working part time on weekends during this school year at the same job. I have had experience at checking stock, operating a cash register, and bagging.

I will be available for full time work on June 6, although I can also be available part-time before that date for any training that is required. I will be able to continue until August 28. I am willing to work any schedule, including weekends.

I will apply in person next week. I will also be available for an interview at your convenience.

Yours truly,

Elizabeth O'Brien

Elizabeth O'Brien

- Does this letter include all the necessary information? Is it courteous and neat?

Try Your Skill Write a letter seeking employment for yourself. Imagine that you are interested in one of the following jobs. For the purpose of this exercise, make up related experience, not necessarily job experience.

1. Wanted: Part-time, year-round help for telephone sales. Good spelling and some typing required. Write Advertising Department, *Suburban Tribune*, 425 Warren Street, Northbrook, Illinois 60062.
2. Wanted: Experienced kitchen help for summer. Write The Summit Inn, Pine Crest Road, Boulder, Colorado 80303.
3. Wanted: Part-time clerks in sales and stock during Christmas season. Write Personnel Manager, Lacy's Department Store, 1890 Grant Avenue, Manchester, Connecticut 06040.

Keep This in Mind

- Write a letter seeking employment that will create a good impression. The letter should be informative, polite, and neat. Include specific information about yourself and the job you want.

Now Write Write a letter seeking employment at a supermarket, restaurant, department store, or other business in your town. Ask to be considered for a particular job. Be sure to include all necessary information. Proofread your letter carefully. Label it **On the Job** and put it into your folder. You may decide to copy your letter and mail it.

Part 7

A Work Sheet

Completing a Job Application

Here's the Idea Whenever you apply for a job, you will probably be asked to complete a job application. The form of the application will vary from company to company. However, there are certain guidelines you should always follow.

1. Be prepared to answer several standard questions. You will be asked to state your address, telephone number, date of birth, social security number, and your citizenship. You will be asked about your education, special skills, and any past work experience. You will also be asked to name references. In other words, you will be asked to name two or three people not related to you who have known you for some time and who would be willing to discuss your strengths and abilities. A reference may be a former employer, a teacher, or a clergyman, for example.

2. Be neat. Print your answers carefully. You are being judged on your ability to follow directions and to work neatly. Use a good pen with blue or black ink. Because there is never enough space for the information requested, plan your answers before you print them. Do not cross out information. If you do make an error, erase it. Read all instructions carefully, especially those in fine print. For example, you may be asked to give your last name first, or your first name last.

3. Complete every item. There may be questions that you cannot answer, such as a question about military service or home ownership. However, you should never leave any space blank on an application. Leaving a blank space only causes confusion. If an item is "not applicable" to you, write N.A. to show that it is not.

4. Be honest. You will be asked to sign your name to a statement that all information is correct.

Check It Out Examine the completed job application on page 159.

FEDERAL FOOD STORES

APPLICATION FOR EMPLOYMENT Date March 25, 1981

Name O'Brien, Elizabeth Ann Tel. No. 555-3650
Last First Middle

Present Address 257 Walker Road, Memphis, Tenn. 38104
Street City State Zip

Do you rent? ☐ Own your home? ☐ Live with parents? ☑

Previous Address N.A.
Street City State Zip

Soc. Sec. No. 986-77-2166 Date of Birth 6/15/64 Are you a citizen? Yes ☑ No ☐

Person to be notified in case of accident or emergency Francis O'Brien

Address same as above Phone same

Position applied for cashier Date available for work? June 16, 1981

RECORD OF EDUCATION

School	Name and Address of School	Years Attended	Circle last year completed			
Elementary	Columbus Elementary School Memphis, Tennessee	1970-1978	5	6	7	(8)
High	Central High School Memphis, Tennessee	1978-Present	1	2	(3)	4
College	N.A.		1	2	3	4

Did you serve in the military? Yes ☐ No ☑ Which branch? N.A.

Rank N.A. Date of discharge N.A.

RECORD OF EMPLOYMENT (List your last two employers, starting with the more recent one)

Dates	Name and Address of Employer	Salary	Position	Reason for Leaving
Sept. 1980	Dan's Market, 522 Sherman, Memphis	$3.50/hr.	cashier	
Summer 1980	Dan's Market, 522 Sherman, Memphis	$3.10/hr.	stockclerk, bagger	

Check the following office operations with which you have had experience

☑ Adding Machine ☐ Switchboard ☐ Shorthand ☐ Addressograph Other cash register
☐ Proof Machine (IBM) ☐ Dictaphone ☐ Typewriter ☐ Bookkeeping Machine

PERSONAL REFERENCES (Not former employers or relatives)

Name and Occupation	Address	Phone No.
Ruth Watson, M.D.	12 Elm Rd., Memphis, Tenn. 38104	555-8611
Michael Simpson (teacher)	Central High, Memphis, Tenn. 38104	555-3274
Rev. John Bucci	St. Mary's Church, Memphis, Tenn. 38104	555-4337

I hereby affirm that my answers to the foregoing questions are true and correct and that I have not knowingly withheld any information which would, if disclosed, be considered sufficient cause for dismissal.

In the event of my employment, I promise to comply faithfully with all the rules and regulations presently in effect, or which may hereafter become effective, relating to the conduct and performance of the employees of Federal Food Stores.

Applicant's Signature Elizabeth Ann O'Brien

- Have all items on the form been completed? How might an employer check that the information is correct?
- Has the application been filled in neatly? Have all of the instructions been followed carefully?

Try Your Skill Suppose that you were applying to First Federal Food Stores for a part-time job as a cashier. You were interested in working after school or on weekends. Refer to the application for employment on page 159. On a separate sheet of paper, list the correct information as you would write it on the application. Your teacher may give you a copy of the actual application to complete.

Keep This in Mind

- Answer all items on an application form honestly, correctly, and completely.
- Fill in the items on the application by printing neatly, using ink. Work carefully. Read all instructions.

Now Write Complete an actual employment application. Use a form given to you by your teacher or one from a business in your community. Complete the form honestly and neatly, following the guidelines you have learned. Label the form **A Work Sheet.** Keep it in your folder.

Part 8

Experience Counts

Writing a Résumé

Here's the Idea Usually you apply for a job by sending a brief letter and a résumé to an employer. A **résumé** (rez′•oo•mā′) is a list that summarizes your life in relation to work. A résumé contains basic information about you, your education, your work experience, and your special skills.

Many employers and schools request that you submit a résumé. In fact, you may be asked for a résumé before you will be given an interview. Using résumés is one way that employers and schools narrow a large number of applicants to a chosen few. Thus, it is important for you to write a résumé that shows who you are in a clear, easy-to-read form.

No two résumés are exactly the same. However, most are one page long and typewritten. All résumés contain brief phrases that summarize information. Use these guidelines.

1. State your name, address, and telephone number, including the area code.
2. State your job objective. What kind of position or general area of work are you seeking?
3. Summarize your education. List your high school, its address, your expected date of graduation, and any special subjects helpful for a particular job. If you have attended more than one school, list the most recent first.
4. Summarize your job experience. State the beginning and ending dates of your employment, the name and address of your employer, the position you held, and your duties. Again, list your most recent jobs first. If you have had any related volunteer experience, also include it here.
5. Mention any meaningful personal achievements. Include special skills, such as computer language, foreign language, office skills, or community work. Also include awards, societies, or clubs, any offices held, hobbies, and related special interests.

6. Mention at least two references. You may list the names of several adults—teachers or employers, for example—who can give you good character or employment references. It is also standard practice to say that you will supply references on request.

As your life and work change so should your résumé. Revise your résumé so that it is accurate and up-to-date.

Check It Out Examine the résumé on page 163.

- Is this résumé well organized and easy-to-read? Does it include all the necessary information?

Try Your Skill Which of the following items should be added to the résumé shown in this lesson? Explain why the information is appropriate for the résumé.

1. broke arm, sophomore year, while ice-skating
2. won school attendance medals for freshman and sophomore years
3. won first-place speed certificate in typing class
4. studied Spanish for two years
5. played lead role in school play

Keep This in Mind

- A résumé summarizes basic information about your life in relation to work. Write a résumé that is well organized, easy-to-read, and up-to-date. Include all information that shows you and your special skills.

Now Write Write your own résumé. Begin by jotting down basic information about yourself. Then organize the information in a way that shows your talents best. Print or type a neat final copy. Label your résumé **Experience Counts.** Keep it in your folder.

	Elizabeth Ann O'Brien
	257 Walker Road Memphis, Tennessee 38104 (901) 555-3650
OBJECTIVE	A summer job as a cashier in a supermarket.
EDUCATION	Central High School Memphis, Tennessee Member of Junior class graduating in June, 1982, with courses in business math and office skills.
WORK EXPERIENCE Present	Cashier Dan's Market 522 Sherman Street Memphis, Tennessee On part-time basis.
Summer, 1980	Stock clerk, bagger Dan's Market Full time.
PERSONAL	Able to operate calculator, adding machine, and cash register. Secretary, Junior Chamber of Commerce, 1978-79. Member of glee club and volleyball team.
REFERENCES	Will be provided upon request.

THE LIVING
SHAKESPEARE

WRITING SECTION 17

Using a Dictionary

Part 1 **Words To Guide You**
Using a Dictionary

Part 2 **In Search of**
Reading a Dictionary Entry

Part 3 **A Fitting Choice**
Finding the Meaning of a Word

Part 1

Words To Guide You

Using a Dictionary

Here's the Idea A dictionary is a useful reference book containing lists of words and information about the words. Whenever you deal with words, you will want to use a dictionary. When you read, you will see unfamiliar words or words used in unfamiliar ways. Using a dictionary will help you to understand the meanings of the words you see. When you write, you will be searching continually for the right words. Using a dictionary will help you to choose the right words and to use them correctly.

There are several kinds of dictionaries you might find helpful. Usually you will be able to find what you need in an abridged, or shortened, dictionary. Sometimes, however, you may need an unabridged dictionary. This contains nearly all of the words in a language, including those that are rare. There are also specialized dictionaries that include only words used with a single subject, such as music.

Become familiar with the dictionaries you use. You will find that every dictionary organizes information in its own way and uses its own symbols and abbreviations. Examine the front of a dictionary for an explanation of its format.

All dictionaries, however, list words in alphabetical order. In addition, all dictionaries have two guide words in large, bold print at the top of each page to help locate words listed on the page. The left guide word is the same as the first word on the page. The right guide word is the same as the last word on the page. When you are looking for a word, flip through the dictionary until you find the page where your word comes alphabetically between the guide words.

Check It Out Look at this top portion of a dictionary page.

Ganymede 391 **garter**

Gan·y·mede (gan′ə mēd) *Gr. Myth.* a beautiful youth who was cupbearer to the gods

gaol (jāl) ***n.*** *Brit. sp. of* JAIL —**gaol′er *n.***

gap (gap) ***n.*** [ON. < *gapa*, to yawn, GAPE] **1.** a hole or opening made by breaking, tearing, etc.; breach **2.** a mountain pass or ravine **3.** an empty space or time; blank **4.** a difference in ideas, natures, etc. **5.** *same as* SPARK GAP —***vi.*** **gapped, gap′ping** to come apart; open

gape (gāp) ***vi.*** **gaped, gap′ing** [< ON. *gapa*, to yawn < IE. base *ghe-*] **1.** to open the mouth wide, as in yawning **2.** to stare with the mouth open, as in wonder **3.** to open wide, as a chasm —***n.*** **1.** an open-mouthed stare **2.** a yawn **3.** a wide opening **4.** *Zool.* the measure of the widest possible opening of a mouth or beak —**the gapes 1.** a disease of poultry and birds, causing them to gape **2.** a fit of yawning —**gap′er *n.*** —**gap′ing·ly *adv.***

☆**gar** (gär) ***n.***, *pl.* **gar, gars:** see PLURAL, II, D, 2 [contr. < GARFISH] any of a group of freshwater ganoid fishes with long, narrow bodies, long, beaklike snouts, and many sharp teeth

GAR
(to 10 ft. long)

G.A.R. Grand Army of the Republic

ga·rage (gə räzh′, -räj′; *Brit.* gar′äzh) ***n.*** [Fr. < *garer*, to GUARD] **1.** a closed shelter for automobiles **2.** a business establishment where automobiles are repaired, stored, etc. —***vt.***

gar·goyle (gär′goil) ***n.*** [< OFr. *gargouille*: see GARGLE] **1.** a waterspout, usually in the form of a carved fantastic creature, sticking out from the gutter of a building **2.** a person with very strange or grotesque features

GARGOYLE

Gar·i·bal·di (gar′ə bôl′dē; *It.* gä rē bäl′dē), **Giu·sep·pe** (jōō zep′pe) 1807–82; It. patriot & general: leader in movement to unify Italy

gar·ish (ger′ish) ***adj.*** [prob. < ME. *gauren*, to stare] too bright or gaudy; showy —see **SYN.** at GAUDY —**gar′ish·ly *adv.*** —**gar′ish·ness *n.***

gar·land (gär′lənd) ***n.*** [< OFr. *garlande*] a wreath of flowers, leaves, etc. —***vt.*** to form into or decorate with a garland or garlands

Gar·land (gär′lənd) [after A. *Garland*, U.S. attorney general (1885–89)] city in NE Tex.: suburb of Dallas: pop. 81,000

gar·lic (gär′lik) ***n.*** [< OE. < *gar*, a spear (see GORE[3]) + *leac*, a leek] **1.** a bulbous plant of the lily family **2.** its strong-smelling bulb, made up of small sections called cloves, used as a seasoning —**gar′lick·y *adj.***

gar·ment (gär′mənt) ***n.*** [< OFr. *garnement* < *garnir*: see GARNISH] **1.** any article of clothing **2.** a covering —***vt.*** to clothe

gar·ner (gär′nər) ***n.*** [< OFr. < L. *granarium* < *granum*, GRAIN] **1.** a place for storing grain; granary **2.** a store of something —***vt.*** **1.** to gather up and store in or as in a granary **2.** to get or earn [*to garner praise*] **3.** to collect or gather [*to garner data*]

- How is each column of words listed? What special symbols are used? What are the guide words? Would you find the word *garden* on this page?

Try Your Skill Look up each word in a dictionary and write the guide·words for that page.

fireworks	synonym	phase	elegant
jackpot	atmosphere	century	limelight
kettle	typical	bouquet	carburetor

Keep This in Mind

- A dictionary is a reference book that lists words alphabetically and explains each word.

Now Write In learning about governments you may see the following words: *aristocracy*, *communism*, *constitution*, *democracy*, *fascism*, *monarchy*, *nation*, and *republic*. Find each word in a dictionary and list the guide words on the page. Use four of the words in sentences. Label your paper **Words To Guide You** and put it into your folder.

Part 2 **In Search of**

Reading a Dictionary Entry

Here's the Idea Each dictionary entry contains much more than the meaning of a word. It also has information to help you understand a word and use it correctly.

The **entry word** itself appears in bold print and is divided into syllables. The word *memorable*, for example, is entered as **mem·o·ra·ble.** Refer to the entry word whenever you need to divide a word at the end of a line of writing.

The **pronunciation** of a word is given in parentheses. Use the symbols and accent marks to help you sound out an unfamiliar word. The word *commercial*, for example, appears as (kə mūr′ shəl). Refer to the explanation of symbols often shown at the bottom of a page. You will usually find the complete explanation at the front of the dictionary.

The **part of speech** of a word is indicated by an abbreviation in bold print. *Noun*, for example, is abbreviated ***n.*** and *adjective* is ***adj.*** Refer to the complete list of abbreviations usually presented in the front of the dictionary. Some words can be used as more than one part of speech. If so, the other parts of speech will be indicated further along in an entry.

If a word has **special forms** or **endings,** they will be included next in the entry. The entry for the irregular verb *see*, for example, includes the forms **saw, seen, seeing.** Plural endings of some nouns are also shown. For the noun *hero*, for example, the plural ending **-oes** is shown.

The **origin,** or **history,** of a word is given next, usually in brackets. The symbol < means "came from." Abbreviations, like *Gr.* and *L.*, stand for the languages from which words came, like Greek and Latin. Refer to a complete list of abbreviations used in a dictionary. This list is also usually given at the front of the dictionary.

Definitions are given next. The most common definition of a word is often given first in a list. When a word has a special meaning within a field, that meaning will be noted. One definition of *return*, for instance, says "*Sports* to hit, run, or throw back a ball."

Sometimes a word may have a special meaning used in conversation and informal writing. This is called a *colloquial* meaning and is usually indicated in the dictionary. For instance, one definition of *character* is "[Colloq.] an odd or peculiar person." Slang—very informal, popular language—is also indicated in the dictionary. For instance, one definition of *charge*, as a noun, is "[Slang] a thrill."

Some dictionaries also list **synonyms** and **antonyms** at the end of certain entries. A *synonymy* may explain a group of synonyms and their shades of meaning. For example, at the end of the entry for *sharp*, its synonyms *keen* and *acute* are also explained. *Dull*, an antonym for *sharp*, is also listed.

From all of these examples, you can see how much useful information is presented in an entry in a good dictionary.

Check It Out Examine the dictionary entry below.

tune (to͞on, tyo͞on) ***n.*** [ME., var. of *tone*, TONE] **1.** a series of musical tones with a regular rhythm; melody; air **2.** the condition of having correct musical pitch, or of being in key; also, harmony; concord: now chiefly in phrases **in tune, out of tune** [a violin that is *in tune;* a person *out of tune* with the times] —***vt.*** **tuned, tun′ing** **1.** to adjust (a musical instrument) to some standard of pitch [to *tune* a piano] **2.** to adapt (music, the voice, etc.) to some pitch, tone, etc. **3.** to adjust (an electronics circuit, a motor, etc.) to the proper or desired performance —***vi.*** to be in tune; harmonize —see ***SYN.*** at MELODY —**call the tune** to be in control —**change one's tune** to change one's attitude or manner: also **sing a different tune** —**to the tune of** [Colloq.] to the amount of —**tune in** **1.** to adjust a radio or television receiver to a given frequency or channel so as to receive (a specified station, program, etc.) ☆**2.** [Slang] to become or make aware, knowing, etc. —**tune out** **1.** to adjust a radio or television receiver so as to get rid of (interference, etc.) **2.** [Slang] to stop paying attention to, showing interest in, etc. —**tune up** **1.** to adjust (musical instruments) to the same pitch **2.** to put (an engine) into good working condition

• How many syllables are there in *tune*? From what language did *tune* come? What parts of speech is *tune*? Which definition is most familiar to you? Where would you find synonyms for *tune*? What informal expressions include *tune*?

Try Your Skill Read this entry and answer the questions.

ice (īs) ***n.*** [OE. *is*] **1.** water frozen solid by cold **2.** a piece, layer, or sheet of this **3.** anything like frozen water in appearance, etc. **4.** coldness in manner or attitude **5.** *a*) a frozen dessert, usually of water, fruit juice, and sugar *b*) [Brit.] ice cream ☆**6.** [Slang] diamonds —***vt.*** **iced, ic′ing** **1.** to change into ice; freeze **2.** to cover with ice **3.** to cool by putting ice on, in, or around [to *ice* a drink] **4.** to cover with icing [to *ice* a cake] **5.** *Ice Hockey* to shoot (the puck) from defensive to offensive territory —***vi.*** to freeze (often with *up* or *over*) —**break the ice** **1.** to make a start by getting over the first problems **2.** to make a start toward getting better acquainted —☆**cut no ice** [Colloq.] to have no effect —☆**on ice** [Slang] **1.** in readiness or reserve **2.** sure to result in victory or success [this game is *on ice*] —**on thin ice** [Colloq.] in a risky situation

1. As what parts of speech can *ice* be used?
2. What endings does the verb *ice* have?
3. From what language does *ice* come?
4. Give a specialized meaning of *ice*.
5. What informal expressions use the word *ice*?

Keep This in Mind

• A dictionary entry contains the meanings of a word and other useful information.

Now Write Use a dictionary to find words with these characteristics. Each word should have one characteristic. Label your paper **In Search of** and put it into your folder.

1. two pronunciations
2. two parts of speech
3. has come from French
4. meaning in a special field
5. an informal meaning
6. an antonym

A Fitting Choice

Finding the Meaning of a Word

Here's the Idea As you look through a dictionary, you will soon notice that many words have more than one meaning. Whenever you need to check a certain word in the dictionary, read through all of its meanings. Find the meaning that fits a particular context.

For instance, the simple word *turn* has a surprising number of meanings. *Webster's New World Dictionary, Students Edition*, gives forty-three meanings for *turn* as a verb. The same entry gives sixteen meanings for *turn* as a noun, and sixteen phrases that include the word. In the following examples, notice how the context helps you determine the correct meaning.

1. It was my *turn* to pitch the ball.
(In this context, *turn* means "the right or chance to do something, especially in regular order.")
2. Marcia *turned* several plans over in her mind.
(Here, *turn* means "to think about, to ponder.")
3. *Turn* your chair away from the window.
(Here, *turn* means "to change the position or direction of.")
4. Hot weather will *turn* milk.
(Here, *turn* means "to make sour.")
5. My sister Barbara just *turned* sixteen.
(Here, *turn* means "to reach or pass.")
6. Grandpa was born at the *turn* of the century.
(Here, *turn* means "the time of change.")
7. Her fall off the ladder gave us quite a *turn*.
(Here, *turn* means "a sudden, brief shock.")

From these few examples, it is clear how many meanings can be contained in a single entry.

There are some words, however, that seem to be repeated

in more than one entry. For instance, you will find the word *lean* entered twice: *lean*[1], a verb, means "to bend from an upright position" or "to depend on for help"; *lean*[2], an adjective, means "thin, containing little or no fat." In each entry, *lean* has a different origin and different meanings. A word like this is called a *homograph*. A homograph has the same spelling, although it may have different pronunciations. Notice that each entry is not a shade of meaning of one word. It is actually a different word. When you notice a word with more than one entry, be sure to read all of the entries to find the meaning you want.

Check It Out Read these dictionary entries.

match[1] (mach) ***n.*** [< OFr. *mesche*, prob. < L. *myxa*, lamp wick < Gr.] **1.** orig., a wick or cord prepared to burn at a uniform rate, used for firing guns or explosives **2.** a slender piece of wood, cardboard, etc. tipped with a composition that catches fire by friction, sometimes only on a specially prepared surface

match[2] (mach) ***n.*** [OE. (*ge*)*mæcca*, a mate < base of *macian*, MAKE] **1.** any person or thing equal or similar to another in some way; specif., *a*) a person, group, or thing able to cope with another as an equal [he met his *match* in chess when he played her] *b*) a counterpart or facsimile **2.** two or more persons or things that go together in appearance, size, etc. [a purse and shoes that are a good *match*] **3.** a contest or game; competition [a tennis *match*] **4.** a marriage or mating **5.** a person regarded as a suitable mate —***vt.*** **1.** to join in marriage; mate **2.** to compete with successfully [he was able to *match* his opponent] **3.** to put in opposition (*with*); pit (*against*) [to *match* one's strength against an enemy] **4.** to be equal, similar, or suitable to [he could never *match* her in an argument] **5.** to make, show, or get a competitor, counterpart, or equivalent to [*match* this cloth] **6.** to suit or fit (one thing) to another **7.** to fit (things) together **8.** to compare ☆**9.** *a*) to flip or reveal (coins) to decide something contested, the winner being determined by the combination of faces thus exposed *b*) to match coins with (another person) —***vi.*** to be equal, similar, suitable, etc. in some way —**match′a·ble** ***adj.*** —**match′er** ***n.***

- Which definition of *match* fits the context of the sentence: My family came to my wrestling *match*?
- From what language is *match*[1]? *match*[2]? Which of the meanings of *match*[2] is most familiar to you?

Try Your Skill Read the following dictionary entries and sentences. Determine which meaning of *pound* fits the context of each sentence and write your answer.

pound[1] (pound) ***n.**, pl.* **pounds,** sometimes **pound** [OE. *pund* < L. *pondo*, abl. of *pondus*, weight, akin to *pendere*: see PENDANT] **1.** a unit of weight, equal to 16 oz. (7,000 grains) avoirdupois or 12 oz. (5,760 grains) troy: abbrev. **lb.** **2.** *a)* the monetary unit of the United Kingdom (in full, **pound sterling**) equal to 100 (new) pennies or, in the earlier system, to 20 shillings: symbol £ *b)* the monetary unit of various other countries, as of Ireland, Israel, etc. See MONETARY UNITS, table

pound[2] (pound) ***vt.*** [OE. *punian*] **1.** to beat to a pulp, powder, etc. [to *pound* corn into meal] **2.** to strike or drive with repeated heavy blows [to *pound* nails into a board] **3.** to make by pounding [he *pounded* a cabinet together] —***vi.*** **1.** to deliver repeated, heavy blows (*at* or *on* a door, etc.) **2.** to move with heavy steps, thumps, etc. [he *pounded* down the hall] **3.** to beat heavily; throb [her heart *pounded* from the exercise] —***n.*** a pounding, or the sound of it —see ***SYN.*** at BEAT —☆**pound one's ear** [Slang] to sleep —**pound out** **1.** to flatten, smooth, etc. by pounding **2.** to produce (musical notes, typed copy, etc.) with a very heavy touch —☆**pound the pavement** [Slang] to walk the streets, as in looking for work —**pound′er** ***n.***

pound[3] (pound) ***n.*** [< OE. *pund-*] **1.** an enclosed place for keeping animals, esp. stray animals [the city dog *pound*] **2.** a place of confinement, as for arrested persons **3.** an enclosed area for catching or keeping fish

1. The almonds must be *pounded* into paste for the cake.
2. They found the lost dog at the city *pound*.
3. The bear *pounded* through the woods.
4. Have you ever seen a British *pound* note?
5. The mysterious noise caused my heart to *pound*.

Keep This in Mind

- When you look up a word in the dictionary, determine which meaning fits the context.
- Sometimes a word has more than one entry, with a different meaning and origin for each.

Now Write Use a dictionary to find one example of a word with many different meanings and one example of a homograph. For each example, copy three definitions. Then write a sentence using each of the meanings you have written. Label your paper **A Fitting Choice** and put it into your folder.

Using the Library

Part 1

Shelf by Shelf

Finding What You Need

Here's the Idea A library serves the needs of people because of the variety of materials and information it has available. You will also find books and magazines that relate unusual imaginary adventures and experiences. To find whatever you need easily, you need to learn how your school or public library is organized.

You will find that all library books are classified into two general groups, fiction and nonfiction. **Fiction** books are arranged alphabetically according to the author's last name. For example, the novel *A Tale of Two Cities*, by Charles Dickens, would be filed under *D*.

Nonfiction books are arranged according to their subjects on a separate section of shelves. Many libraries use a system called the **Dewey Decimal System.** This system groups nonfiction books into ten numbered categories.

000-099	**General Works**	(encyclopedias, almanacs)
100-199	**Philosophy**	(ethics, psychology, occult)
200-299	**Religion**	(the Bible, mythology)
300-399	**Social Science**	(economics, law, education, government)
400-499	**Language**	(languages, grammar, dictionaries)
500-599	**Science**	(mathematics, biology, chemistry)
600-699	**Useful Arts**	(farming, cooking, sewing, television, business)
700-799	**Fine Arts**	(music, photography, dance, sports)
800-899	**Literature**	(poetry, plays)
900-999	**History**	(biography, travel, geography)

Every nonfiction book has a **call number** written on the spine. This call number includes the Dewey Decimal number and other helpful information. A call number identifies a particular book. Some libraries also add the letter *B* to the spine of a biography or the letter *R* to the spine of a reference work such as an encyclopedia.

Look at this example of a nonfiction book.

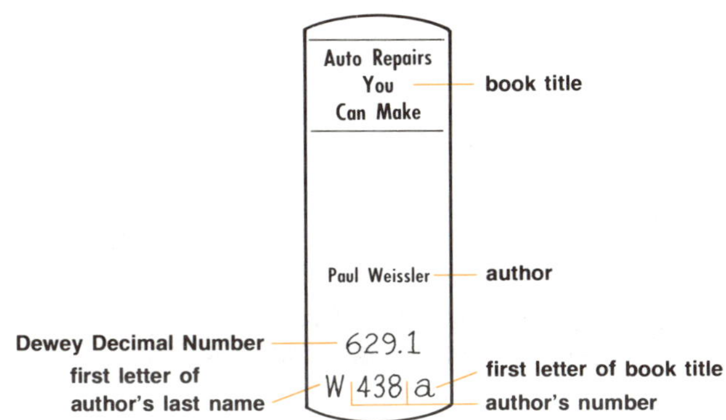

Check It Out Examine the spines of the books represented here.

Better Vacations for Your Money
Michael Frome
917.3
F926b

The Black Pearl
Scott O'Dell

Shape Up for Sports
Ray Slegener
613.71
SLE

Exploring Apprenticeship Careers
Charlotte Lobb
331.55
LOB

Snow Bound
Harry Mazer

Sounder
William H. Armstrong

All Quiet on the Western Front
Erich Maria Remarque

Listening to Jazz
Jerry Coker
781.57
C669.l

- Which books are fiction and which are nonfiction?
- What is the general category of each nonfiction book?

Try Your Skill Write the answers to these questions.

1. Under what letter on the library shelves would you find the following fiction books?

Dragonsinger by Anne McCaffrey
Watership Down by Richard Adams
The Clown by Barbara Corcoran
Incident at Hawk's Hill by Allan W. Eckert
The Good-Luck Bogie Hat by Constance C. Greene

2. In which categories of the Dewey Decimal System would you find information on these subjects?

a play about Thanksgiving
directions for making furniture
a biography of Martin Luther King
teaching pre-school-aged children
the Civil War in the U.S.

Keep This in Mind

- In the library, fiction books are filed alphabetically by the author's last name.
- Nonfiction books may be classified in ten major categories of the Dewey Decimal System. Each nonfiction book has a call number.

Now Write As your teacher directs, learn how materials are arranged in your school or public library. Find out where fiction and nonfiction books are. Find out where reference books, magazines, and special collections are.

Find at least four fiction books and four nonfiction books in the library that you might enjoy reading. You may want to check out one for your own reading. Write the titles and authors of the books you find. Copy the call number or any special marking written on the spine of any of the books. Label your paper **Shelf by Shelf.** Keep it in your folder.

Part 2

On the Track

Using the Card Catalog

Here's the Idea In every library there is a file called the card catalog. This file organizes information about all of the books in that library. Every book is listed in the card catalog three times—by its author, by its title, and by its subject.

Notice that all three cards—author card, title card, and subject card—contain the same information. This information is arranged under different headings so that you will be able to find a book in several ways. All three cards give the call number of a nonfiction book in the upper left corner. This is the same number that appears on the book.

All three cards list the author, title, publisher, date of publication, and the number of pages in the book. There is a notation if the book has illustrations or maps. There may also be a description of the book or a list of related books.

On an **author card,** the author's name is given at the top, last name first. Author cards are filed alphabetically by the author's last name. If there is more than one author, the card is filed by the name of the author whose name is shown first in the book.

On a **title card,** the title appears on the top line, with only the first word of the title capitalized. Title cards are filed alphabetically by the first word of the title. However, if A, An, or *The* appears as the first word in a title, look for the card under the first letter of the second word in the title.

On a **subject card,** the subject appears on the top line. The subject may be written in capital letters or in red. Subject cards are filed alphabetically by the first letter of the subject.

You will find some cards that say *See* or *See also*. These **cross reference cards** refer you to other subject headings that are related to the one you want.

Using the card catalog is simpler if you check the **guide cards.** These blank cards have tabs on which are written general subject headings. These headings will help you to follow the alphabetical arrangement of the card catalog.

author card

650.14 SOU

Souerwine, Andrew H.

Career strategies : planning for personal achievement / Andrew H. Souerwine. — New York : AMACOM, © 1978.

xii, 292 p. : ill. ; 24 cm.

Includes index.
Bibliography: p. 280-284.
ISBN 0-8144-5454-2 : $14.75

title card

650.14 SOU

Career Strategies: Planning for Personal Achievement

Career strategies : planning for personal achievement / Andrew H. Souerwine. — New York : AMACOM, © 1978.

xii, 292 p. : ill. ; 24 cm.

Includes index.
Bibliography: p. 280-284.
ISBN 0-8144-5454-2 : $14.75

subject card

650.14 SOU

JOB SATISFACTION

Career strategies : planning for personal achievement / Andrew H. Souerwine. — New York : AMACOM, © 1978.

xii, 292 p. : ill. ; 24 cm.

includes index.
Bibliography: p. 280-284.
ISBN 0-8144-5454-2 : $14.75

Check It Out Examine the three sample cards.

- Under what letter would each card be filed? Where would you look to find more books by Andrew H. Souerwine? Where would you look to see if there are other books dealing with job satisfaction?

Try Your Skill Here are the authors, titles, and call numbers for three books about careers. Choose one of the books. Draw three rectangles to represent cards in the card catalog. Use the information given about the book you choose to make an author card, title card, and subject card. Make up the other necessary details for the cards. Compare your sample cards with those in the card catalog.

1. Ruth Lembeck, *Teenage Jobs*, 371.425 L542t
2. Joseph L. Norton, *On the Job*, 371.425 N824o
3. Sarah Splaver, *Nontraditional Careers for Women*, 331.702 Sp51n

Keep This in Mind

- Every book in a library is listed in the card catalog on three different cards—author, title, and subject. Each card shows the author, title, publisher, number of pages, and other useful information. Cards for a nonfiction book also list its call number.

Now Write Choose a subject that interests you and that you can research at the library. Using the card catalog, find at least three nonfiction books about your subject. Copy the important information from the author, title, and subject cards. Label your paper **On the Track** and keep it in your folder. Also, select the most interesting book you find and sign it out of the library. Bring the book to class.

Part 3

There's One for You

Using an Encyclopedia

Here's the Idea An encyclopedia is a general reference work that contains information on a great many different subjects. The articles are arranged in alphabetical order by subject, from the first volume through the last. On the spine of each volume is either a single letter or a set of guide letters indicating what is included.

A large library will have several sets of encyclopedias. You will find that they have different reading levels. When you want to use an encyclopedia, be sure to choose one that you can read easily. Select an encyclopedia suitable for your work by skimming through several. You may want to ask a librarian for help with your selection.

Suppose you wanted information about education. You might select *The World Book Encyclopedia*, *Collier's Encyclopedia*, or the *Britannica Junior Encyclopaedia*, for example. Find the appropriate volume and look up "Education." The guide words at the top of the page will help you find the subject quickly.

An encyclopedia article on an important subject, education, for example, is usually presented in several parts with subtitles. The article may include such parts as "Kinds of Education," "Education in the United States," "Education Around the World," "The Educative Process," "History," and "Current Issues in U.S. Education." Depending on your purpose, you may need to read all of the article or only parts of it.

At the end of a major article you will find other helpful information. At the end of an article on education, for example, you may find a list of related articles in the same encyclopedia. These might be about people connected with education, educational institutions, and educational programs and agencies. In addition, you may find an outline of the information in the article, books for further reading on the subject, or a research guide to the subject.

Most encyclopedias also include an index. This is usually the first or last volume of the set. Use the index to find information under related subjects in different articles. Some encyclopedias also publish yearbooks, which contain up-to-date information on continually changing subjects.

Whenever you research a subject, always check more than one source of information. Use several encyclopedias as well as other kinds of reference books. If you find different information in different sources, try to use the most recent or most reliable reference.

You will find many kinds of encyclopedias as you research different subjects. In addition to the general encyclopedias, there are others that deal only with a specific subject. For example, you may find encyclopedias that deal with sports, music, or careers. These encyclopedias will usually be located in the reference room or area of the library.

Check It Out Look at the encyclopedia shown below.

- In what volume, and under what key word, would you find information about canoeing? modern painting? the Panama Canal? William Shakespeare? heredity?

Try Your Skill As your teacher directs, use an encyclopedia to answer the following questions.

1. Who was the first governor of Virginia?
2. What was the birthplace of Sir Winston Churchill?
3. Name an award won by Jane Addams, who founded Hull House.
4. What languages were spoken by the American Algonquin Indians?
5. What are the principal agricultural exports of Colombia, South America?
6. What is the most famous novel by Louisa May Alcott?
7. What is the difference between a crocodile and an alligator?
8. Name two twentieth-century American architects.
9. In Greek mythology, who was the wife of the god Zeus?
10. What was the importance of D-Day to World War II?

Keep This in Mind

- An encyclopedia is a general reference work that contains information on many different subjects. Articles are arranged alphabetically in numbered volumes. Examine a variety of encyclopedias. Select one that is suitable for your purpose.

Now Write Write the name of the subject that you researched in the card catalog in the last lesson. Look up that subject in two encyclopedias. List a few of the most interesting facts that you find in each, and compare them. Also, name which encyclopedia you prefer and briefly explain your answer. Be sure to list all important information about your sources: names of the encyclopedias, numbers of the volumes, page numbers of the articles, and titles of other related articles or books on the subject. Label your paper **There's One for You** and put it into your folder.

Did You Know That?

Using Reference Works

Here's the Idea Usually, a library has an entire room or special section containing reference works. Many of these cannot be taken from the library because they are such useful sources of information for so many people. In addition to general references like dictionaries and encyclopedias, there are other references that deal with particular areas of interest.

Atlases are books of maps. Many atlases contain information about population, weather, and places throughout the world. Among the most widely used atlases are the *National Geographic Atlas of the World*, *The International Atlas from Rand McNally*, and the *Atlas of World History*.

Almanacs and **yearbooks** are published every year. In these references you will find current information about world events, governments, population, and sports. You may want to use the *Guinness Book of World Records*, the *World Almanac and Book of Facts*, the *Information Please Almanac, Atlas, and Yearbook*, or the *Statesman's Yearbook*.

Biographical references contain information about important people. Useful reference books include *The Book of Presidents*, *Current Biography*, *Who's Who*, *Twentieth Century Authors*, and the *Dictionary of American Biography*.

A **vertical file** is the library's collection of pamphlets, handbooks, catalogs, and clippings. Usually kept in a file cabinet, this collection varies from library to library. It often includes special information about local events, travel, and careers.

Magazines are valuable sources of information about a great many subjects. A library may subscribe to any number of the leading magazines published in the United States. In order to find specific information in magazine articles, learn to use the *Readers' Guide to Periodical Literature*. The

The *Readers' Guide* contains the titles of articles, stories, and poems published in more than 100 leading magazines. One hardcover volume of the *Readers' Guide* covers material published during the entire year. Several smaller, paperback volumes cover material over shorter time periods. Once you learn to use the specially abbreviated format, you will find the *Readers' Guide* a useful reference.

Each of these specialized references contains an explanation of how its information is arranged, of the abbreviations that are used, and a sample entry. When you use a reference book for the first time, study these explanations.

Check It Out Examine this portion of a page from the *Readers' Guide to Periodical Literature.*

OTEC (ocean thermal energy conversion) See Ocean thermal power plants

OBESITY

Cracking down on pep pills; ban on prescriptions for weight control. Newsweek 94:66 Jl 30 '79

Obesity. Sat Eve Post 251:107-8 Jl '79

See also

Overeaters Anonymous (organization)

OCCIDENTAL Petroleum Corporation

Fight over ammonia raises a pungent issue; importing anhydrous ammonia. il Bus W p34 Jl 30 '79

OCCUPATIONAL mobility

Career can be satisfying! K. D. Berry. Essence 10:28+ Ag '79

7 rules to follow if you change your job. M. Yarmon. 50 Plus 19:20-1 Ag '79

OCCUPATIONAL prestige, See Prestige

OCCUPATIONS

Job outlook '79. il Glamour 77:74+ Jl '79

OCEAN liners

QE2. M. Kenyon. il Gourmet 39:50-3+ Ag '79

Romance of ships; symposium. il Sat. R 6:22-4+ Ag 4 '79

See also

Steamship lines

Food service

Crossings aboard a calorie express; French Line cuisine. J. Wechsberg and P. Rossi. il Sat R 6:34+ Ag 4 '79

OCEAN thermal power plants

Ocean thermal energy conversion. B. Beorse. il por Humanist 39:12-19 Jl '79

ODORS

Secret language of scent. R. Winter. il Glamour 77:166-7+ Jl '79

OFFENSES against property

Loss of property; impact on blacks. il Ebony 34:44 Ag '79

OFFICE buildings

Heating and ventilation

Why Carter's temperature rule may not work. Bus W p92+ Ag 13 '79

name of magazine
volume number
page numbers
author
title of article
date of magazine
cross reference

- Read through one unmarked listing in this sample and explain all the information given. Where is the *Readers' Guide* located in your school or public library? What other kinds of references are in the reference section of your library?

Try Your Skill Write the name of a reference work in which you would be likely to find an answer to each of the following questions. If magazines would be the best reference, write *Readers' Guide*.

1. Japan consists of how many major islands?
2. What foods might be discussed in a pamphlet called "Eating for Good Health"?
3. What is the present population of California?
4. Name two well known twentieth-century authors.
5. What baseball team won the 1975 World Series?
6. How was President Franklin Roosevelt related to President Theodore Roosevelt?
7. How many countries are members of the United Nations?
8. What was General Custer's full name?
9. What are some arguments for and against nuclear energy?
10. What is the average yearly rainfall in Michigan?

Keep This in Mind

- There are several kinds of useful specialized references. Learn to use those available in your own library.

Now Write Choose a well known person or place that you like. Use several specialized references to find information on your topic. Skim each source and jot down several of the interesting facts. List the titles, call numbers, and volume and page numbers of the sources you find most useful. Label your paper **Did You Know That?** and put it into your folder.

Writing a Report

Investigating Careers

Part 1 **Possibilities**
Starting Research for a Report on Careers

Part 2 **Shortcuts**
Taking Notes for a Report

Part 3 **Pileup**
Organizing Information for a Report

Part 4 **The Bare Essentials**
Making an Outline for a Report

Part 5 **Taking the Plunge**
Writing an Introduction for a Report

Part 6 **Go the Distance**
Writing the Body and Conclusion of a Report

Part 7 **Finishing Touches**
Finishing a Report

A Sample Report

Part 1

Possibilities

Starting Research for a Report on Careers

Here's the Idea A report, like a composition, is a group of paragraphs dealing with one topic. A report, however, usually requires factual information you must learn about from outside sources.

Suppose you are given the subject of careers to report on. This assignment gives you a general subject. You need to find information from which you can select a specific subject.

You know that a career is the pattern of work and job-related activities that develops in a person's lifetime. There are thousands of careers related to many types of work.

Investigate the varieties of careers and choose one for which you will be able to find enough information for a report. Think about and jot down types of work that appeal to you. You might begin by looking through the card catalog for the subject card *Careers*. Look in the nonfiction section that contains books on careers. These would include books with the Dewey Decimal System numbers in the 300's.

Check encyclopedias in the reference section for information on the general subject of careers. Magazines and the pamphlets found in the vertical file are also good sources.

Another valuable source of information about careers is the guidance counselor or vocational guidance department at your school. Your counselor may have on hand the latest information about careers. He or she will be able to tell you where to look or to write to get that information.

Here is a list of possible sources you might check to find general information about careers.

1. *Occupational Outlook Handbook*, from the U.S. Dept. of Labor

2. "Careers" in *The World Book Encyclopedia*, Volume 3, pages 172d-174

3. "Where Tomorrow's Jobs Will Be," *U.S. News and World Report* magazine, November 13, 1978, pages 47-48+

4. "100 Best Careers for the Future," *Ebony* magazine, March, 1977, pages 33-36

5. "Careers," Section 16, *Chicago Tribune*, Sunday, October 14, 1979

After you have read and thought about careers in general, focus on one career. Give some thought to your interests, abilities, likes, and dislikes. You will write your best report on a career that really interests you. At the same time, you may benefit from the information that you will uncover.

Make sure that the career you choose is not too broad to cover in a five-paragraph report. Within this specific length, you want to be able to cover a limited subject thoroughly.

When you have chosen a particular career to investigate, search again for specific information. Check all the sources already mentioned. If possible, talk to someone in the field of your choice. You can also write to the U.S. Department of Labor, Washington, D.C. Record each source of your information in your notebook. Write the titles of books, encyclopedias, pamphlets, and magazine articles in your notebook. Also write the volume and page number of the encyclopedias you may use and the dates of the magazines.

Suppose you decide to write a five-paragraph report on a career in the hotel industry, which is in the general field of personal service jobs. The reading you do on the topic of hotel business is really the beginning of your report.

Check It Out On page 192, look at the list of sources you might use for a report about a career in the hotel industry.

- What general library sources have you looked through?
- Is this a varied and specific list of sources with which to begin a report?

1. *Occupational Outlook Handbook*, 1978-79, U. S. Dept. of Labor
2. *Hotel Keeping and Catering as a Career* a book by John Fuller
3. *Opportunities in the Hotel and Motel Industry*, a book by Shepard Henkin
4. *Encyclopedia of Careers and Vocational Guidance*, Volume I, pages 325-334
5. *Working Woman* magazine, April, 1978, pages 18-19

Try Your Skill As practice for your report, choose one of these groups of careers to research in the library. Narrow the subject to one suitable for a report. List three helpful sources.

manufacturing	health	construction	business
communications	fine arts	public service	recreation

Keep This in Mind

- With a general subject in mind, search through books, magazines, and other reference works to find a specific, limited subject for a report.
- With a specific subject chosen, begin research for a report by examining all possible sources. Keep a list of the sources.

Now Write Choose a career to investigate for a report. Go to the library with a general idea of what you will write about and look for a specific career. Check the reference shelves, the card catalog, the *Readers' Guide*, and the vertical file. Talk to a career counselor and to someone working in the career that interests you. Find at least three kinds of sources in the library. Note the call numbers, the book titles, the magazine issues, or the vertical file references. Write all the information you have gathered and keep it in your folder.

Part 2

Shortcuts

Taking Notes for a Report

Here's the Idea When you write a report, you need to spend time reading and gathering information. In order to complete these steps, you must learn about bibliography cards, note cards, and plagiarism.

Bibliography cards list sources of information.

1. Use one 3x5 note card for each source.
2. Write out each card carefully. You will usually find basic information about a source within its first few pages.
3. As you find and list sources, give each source a number. This number will help you as you take notes. You can identify a note by using the number you have given to its source.

Note cards contain ideas or facts related to your topic.

1. Use a separate 3x5 note card for each fact, idea, or opinion. Use a heading or key phrase that tells the main idea of the note.
2. Label each note card with the source number you have given that source on its bibliography card.
3. Include the exact page reference so that you can check a fact or a quotation.
4. The note itself shall express one idea. This idea must be stated in your own words to avoid plagiarism.

Plagiarism is using someone else's words or ideas as your own. Plagiarism is a serious offense and can result in serious penalties. To avoid plagiarism, follow these steps.

1. Jot down information in your own words as much as possible. Use brief phrases.
2. Check facts, which must be accurate.
3. Use direct quotations only for important or unusual ideas and opinions. Use quotation marks to show that you have copied a statement. Be sure to copy it exactly as given.

Check It Out Look at the sample cards on page 195.

- Which are bibliography cards? What information does each contain?
- Which is a note card? What is its source?
- Is the note card written in the words of a student?

Try Your Skill Read the following information. Make a bibliography card and a note card based on it.

"Personal service jobs are as old as civilization. Some jobs fill essential needs. Others provide luxuries. Some personal service workers keep our lives running smoothly. Others help us to feel better about ourselves or our belongings. Jane Thomas is a rehabilitation counselor. John Glover repairs typewriters. John Glover and Jane Thomas have entirely different jobs, but both perform a personal service. So do barbers, chefs, and interior designers. There are many interesting careers in the field of personal service."

from *Jobs in Personal Services*, by Beatrice and Calvin Criner, Lothrop, Lee & Shepard Company, New York, 1974, on page 13, with public library call number 371.42 S492cr

Keep This in Mind

- Make bibliography cards that contain basic information about all sources for your report.
- Write note cards, containing specific information.
- Take notes in your own words. Avoid plagiarism, which is a serious offense.

Now Write Take your list of sources and a stack of 3x5 note cards to your library. Make bibliography card for all suitable sources. Read through those sources and take notes. Your teacher will want to check your cards before you continue. Keep the cards together as your teacher directs.

Henkin, Shepard (1)
Opportunities in the Hotel and Motel Industry
New York: Universal Publishing and Distributing Corporation, copyright 1967

371.42
H832 he
rev. ed

public library

"Hotel Occupations" (2)
Occupational Outlook Handbook, 1978-79 edition
U.S. Department of Labor
Bureau of Labor Statistics, 1978
Bulletin 1955

guidance counselor

Curran, Ann (3)
"Hotel Industry Makes Room for Women," Working Woman, Volume 3 pages 18-19 April, 1978

school library

women in hotel work (3)

women not new to hotel work, have always been in housekeeping and on support staff
"What is new is their movement into the top spot - manager."

page 18

Part 3 **Pileup**

Organizing Information for a Report

Here's the Idea If you plan a report well, you will be able to write the report much more easily. An important part in your planning must be organizing the information.

The first organizational step is reading through your note cards. Separate them into several piles. Each pile should deal with one general idea. Try to group the cards into four or five main ideas. If you find cards that do not belong with any others, you may decide not to include these ideas in your report. However, save all the cards.

The next step is reading through the piles. In what way are the cards in each pile related? State each main idea in a sentence. You should list only one idea for each group.

If you were writing about a career in the hotel-motel industry, you might find that your information could be organized into four categories: the variety of jobs within this industry, the range of training required, personal traits required, and the benefits of the jobs.

This organizational step requires careful thought. When you read all the cards that contained facts about the variety of jobs, for example, the information might at first have seemed too unrelated to be expressed by one main idea. Some workers are skilled, while some are unskilled. Some jobs involve working with hotel guests, and some do not. After some thought, however, you might be able to write this main idea: Hotel operations are divided into those related to the "front of the house" and those related to the "back of the house." Organize information by following a similar process.

Check It Out If you had organized information about the hotel-motel industry, you might have written this list.

1. The hotel-motel industry consists of a variety of separate operations, those related to the "front of the house" and those related to the "back of the house."

2. Hotel work can be skilled or unskilled so there is a broad range of training required.

3. Certain character traits, such as patience and the ability to get along with people, are also required in this personal service industry.

4. There are many benefits to careers in hotel work.

- Is one main idea stated clearly in each sentence?

Try Your Skill Organize the following careers into five groups. For each group write one sentence that expresses the main idea of the career field represented by the various jobs.

dancer	police officer	railroad conductor
welder	bus driver	licensed practical nurse
printer	X-ray technician	tool and die maker
firefighter	auto mechanic	photographer
musician	mail carrier	medical records clerk

Keep This in Mind

- Organize your note cards. Group cards with the same main idea. Write one sentence stating the main idea of each group.

Now Write Take out your note cards and read them. Organize them into four or five main groups. Make a list of sentences expressing the main idea of each group. Put the paper into your folder, and save the cards as your teacher directs.

The Bare Essentials

Making an Outline for a Report

Here's the Idea Once you have listed the main ideas of your report, make an outline. By making an outline, you will be organizing the ideas of your notes in a more detailed way. You will be deciding where each individual note card with its one idea fits into your report. In this way, the outline will be a plan to follow when you write the report.

Before you begin the actual outline, you need to arrange the main ideas you have written in a logical order. Each main idea will become a main topic in your outline. The related facts on your note cards will become the subtopics and details of the outline. Each main idea, subtopic, and detail will be stated in a word or phrase.

All outlines follow the same form. You must follow the special arrangement of symbols whenever you make an outline. An outline begins with a title. Below that, first in importance, are main ideas shown by Roman numerals. Under main ideas, next in importance, are subtopics, shown by capital letters. Under subtopics, details are shown by Arabic numerals. If more specific details must be shown, small letters are used. In an outline, you must have no fewer than two main topics or subtopics.

Each part of the outline is indented from the one above. However, each symbol is in a straight line with the others like it. Each kind of symbol is followed by a period, although the words of the outline are not to be followed by periods. In a completed outline, the first word and all important words are capitalized in every line, as well as in the title.

Check It Out Examine this outline based on notes about a career in the hotel-motel industry.

I. Introduction
   A. Function of hotel-motel industry
      1. A personal services industry
      2. Provides sleeping rooms and meals
   B. Range of services offered
      1. Small inns with few employees
      2. Large complexes with many services

II. Variety of skilled and unskilled occupations
   A. Front of the house
      1. Management
      2. Uniformed service staff
      3. Front office
      4. Accounting and sales
   B. Back of the house
      1. Housekeeping and laundry
      2. Food preparation
      3. Engineering and security

III. Training for a career in hotel industry
   A. Short on-the-job training
      1. Entry-level positions
      2. Part-time work available
   B. Specialty training
      Long on-the-job training
      2. Vocational education
      3. Leads to advancement

IV. Personal qualifications
   A. Ability to get along with people
   B. Patience and courtesy
   C. Neatness
   D. Attention to detail

V. Benefits of hotel-motel careers
   A. Flexible schedules, many locations
   B. Promotion, personal growth

- What ideas and details explain a career in the hotel-motel industry? Point out how the form for outlining has been followed correctly.

Try Your Skill Make an outline of the following paragraph of information taken from *The Guide to Career Education* by Muriel Lederer.

> "In order to be a computer technician you need to have good vision because you work with small parts. You also need normal color perception because wires are color coded. Normal hearing is also a requirement because machine breakdowns are sometimes detected by sound. A pleasant manner is an asset, as well as the ability to cope with other people, since you will be dealing with customers. Last, but by no means least, you should be resourceful and able to work independently with little or no supervision."

Keep This in Mind

- Use your notes to write an outline of the ideas and details to be presented in your report. Follow the correct form for making an outline.

Now Write Examine the list of main ideas you wrote in the last lesson for your own report on a career. Determine the most logical order for the ideas and number them to show that order.

Take out the note cards that you have grouped into separate main ideas. Make an outline, using your list of main ideas and your note cards. As you read the cards, decide on the order that would be the clearest. Work with the order of the cards until it seems right.

When your outline is written in its final form, arrange the cards in the order in which they appear in the outline. Keep your work together for the next step.

Part 5

Take the Plunge

Writing an Introduction for a Report

Here's the Idea After you have finished the outline for your report, most of your next steps will be familiar. Once you have completed researching a subject and organizing your information, you are ready to begin writing. Writing the report itself is much like writing a composition. Both have three parts—an introduction, a body, and a conclusion. The introduction introduces the main idea of your subject. The body develops the main idea with supporting ideas and details. The conclusion summarizes the important information presented in the report.

However, there is one important difference between compositions and reports. Reports, unlike compositions, must never be written from the first-person point of view. You should not use the words *I*, *me*, or *my*. Your personal opinion has no place in a factual report.

When you write the introduction to a report, be sure to state what the report will be about. Sometimes you will want to present some of your facts in the introduction. At other times you will want to keep the introduction short and general. What you do for any report will depend on your subject and on your choice.

As you write your first draft, refer to your outline and your note cards. Use each of the main topics of your outline as a guide to writing the topic sentence of each paragraph. Use the subtopics of your outline and the facts from your note cards to develop each paragraph in a detailed way.

Keep reading and reviewing your work as you write. Are your ideas clearly expressed? Are they organized logically? Is your writing detailed and interesting? Take time to think about how you can best express your information.

Check It Out Here are the introduction and the first paragraph of the body of the report on a career in hotel work. They are shown as you might have written them after work on a first draft.

¶ Many people choose a career in ^the field of^ personal service^s^. That is, they choose jobs in which they attend to the needs of other individuals. One of the largest ^personal service^ industries is the hotel-motel business. ^Basically,^ The function of this business is to provide sleeping acomodations (sp?) and meals. ^However,^ Hotels and motels range from ~~those~~ ^simple country inns^ with a few rooms and employees to ~~those~~ ^elaborate city skyscrapers^ with more than 1,000 rooms and hundreds of employees. The largest of these businesses offer ^many additional^ conveniences for their guests. ^The services may include gift shops, recreational facilities, and banquet and convention facilities.^

To provide this range of services, the hotel industry employs workers in a ^wide^ variety of ^skilled and unskilled^ occupations. These various occupations can be divided into ^those related to^ the "front of the house" and ^those related to^ the "back of the house." The "front of the house" ~~means~~ ^is a hotel term for^ the operations that deal directly with ^and are seen by^ the guests. These operations are those of management, ^the^ front office, the uniformed service staff, and the accounting and sales departments. The "back of the house" refers to hotel operations that are ~~not~~ ^seldom^ seen by guests. These include housekeeping, food preparation, ^security, laundry,^ and engineering.

- How does this first draft use the information shown in the outline?
- What main idea is presented in the introduction?

Try Your Skill Here is part of an outline for a report on dental assistants. Using the information from the outline, write an introductory paragraph.

I. Nature of the work
  A. Work along with dentist
    1. Prepare patient for treatment
    2. Hand dentist proper instruments and materials
    3. Keep patient's mouth clear
  B. Work independently
    1. Provide oral health instruction
    2. Make casts of teeth and mouth
    3. Order dental supplies

Keep This in Mind

- Use your outline and note cards to write the first draft of a report.
- A report, like a composition, has an introduction, a body, and a conclusion. In an introduction, be sure to state your topic clearly.

Now Write Take out your outline and note cards. Review them and think about whether to introduce the career you have researched in a general or a detailed way. Decide how to state the main idea of your information about this career.

Using both your outline and your note cards, write the introduction to your report. Try to present your ideas clearly. However, in this first draft, don't worry about punctuation, spelling, and grammar. When you have finished the introduction, put all your work back into your folder.

Part 6

Go the Distance

Writing the Body and Conclusion of a Report

Here's the Idea As you write the body of a report, follow your outline. The topic sentence of each paragraph in the body will correspond to a main topic in your outline. The note cards will supply the details. Use those details, examples, and quotations that will add the most to your report.

Be sure to use quotation marks when you use the words of another writer. When you prepare your final copy, you will give that writer credit in the correct way.

A report, like a composition, comes to a logical ending. A report has a clear conclusion in which you tie ideas together naturally. You may include additional facts about the topic, but your most important purpose is to summarize the information presented in the report.

As you complete your first draft, continue the process of writing, reviewing what you have written, and rewriting. Do you like what you have written? Is it interesting as well as accurate? Is there a beginning, a middle, and an end to the development of your idea? Take the time to review your report carefully.

Check It Out On the next page is the rest of the body and the conclusion of the report on a career in the hotel industry. They are shown as you might have written them after working on a first draft.

- Compare this first draft with the outline for the report. What details, examples, or direct quotations are used to develop the body?
- Does the conclusion sum up the information presented in the report?

~~Since~~ Because the hotel industry ~~contains~~ employs such a broad range of occupations, there is ~~not one schedule of preparation~~ no single type of training necessary. Many entry-level positions require only a short period of on-the-job training. ~~Such~~ Entry-level jobs are often available on a part-time basis for students, to aquaint (sp?) them with hotel work. These jobs include waiter, maid, clerk, porter, bellhop, and elevator operator. However, longer on-the-job training or vocational education may lead to other, higher-paying positions. For instance, those who have completed programs in cooking, accounting, or maintenance and repair work may eventually become department heads. "The hotel industry is one of the few wherein a young person can secure a position without too much formal education, and work his way through the various departments to an executive capacity."

To be successful in any position in the hotel business, several basic personal qualifications are required. A person must be able to ~~get along~~ deal with all kinds of people in any situation. Courtesy and patience are ~~necessary~~ essential when serving ~~people~~ guests. In addition to a neat appearance, a pleasant manner is also important. Finally, constant careful attention to detail is called for in all aspects of hotel work.

There are many benefits for those who choose a career in the hotel industry. The first [advantage] is a flexible schedule, since hotels and motels operate [twenty-four hours a day with] three shifts~~ a day~~. Other benefits include ~~a~~ [the] choice of part-time, full-time, or seasonal work, and a wide selection of geographic locations. [At present] The industry is also looking for capable women and members of minority groups [to train as managers]. A career in the hotel industry offers [many] opportunities for [personal and] ~~working and being successful~~ [professional growth].

Try Your Skill As practice for your own report, the **Try Your Skill** exercises in this section have asked you to consider many ideas about careers. Review these exercises. Then write a conclusion.

Keep This in Mind

- Use the ideas, details, examples, and direct quotations from your outline and note cards to develop the body of a report.
- Write a conclusion that summarizes the information presented in the report.

Now Write Review your outline and your notes, and then write the body and conclusion of your report. Keep your writing lively, clear, and direct. Make sure you use quotation marks if you use other writers' words.

Sum up the main ideas in the conclusion.

When you are finished, put your work into your folder.

Finishing Touches

Finishing a Report

Here's the Idea As you rewrite the draft of a report, revise any sentences that are not clear. Check for correct grammar, spelling, capitalization, and punctuation. You are now ready to write footnotes and a bibliography.

A **footnote** gives credit to a writer whose words or ideas you used. A direct quotation requires a footnote, which is usually written on a separate page at the end of the report. The material to be footnoted is followed with a small number that is written slightly above a line like this: [1]. The numbers should match the numbers on the footnote page.

To prepare your footnotes, find each quotation you have used. Locate the note card with the source number that refers you to a bibliography card. That bibliography card should contain all the information you need.

The first line of a footnote should be indented. Each footnote should include the author's first and last names, in that order; the title of the source; the volume number, if applicable; the date, if the reference is a magazine; and the page number. If you have two or more consecutive notes from the same source, use the abbreviation *Ibid.* instead of repeating the same information. *Ibid.* stands for a Latin word meaning "in the same place." *Ibid.* should be followed by a page number if it differs from the previous one.

Finally, prepare your **bibliography,** which is a complete list of sources you used. A bibliography usually appears on a separate, final page. Each entry contains the information from your bibliography cards, except for the source number and library location. The form for a bibliography entry differs slightly for books, magazines, and encyclopedias. The beginning of an entry is not indented, although all lines after the first one are indented. Entries in a bibliography are arranged alphabetically by the last name of the author. If no author is given, use the first main word of the title to determine the order. Page numbers are given if less than the entire work was used as a source.

Check It Out Study the form of a footnote and bibliography for a report on a career in the hotel industry.

Footnote

[1]Shepard Henkin, Opportunities in the Hotel and Motel Industry, page 27.

Bibliography

Curran, Ann. "Hotel Industry Makes Room for Women," Working Woman, Volume 3 (April, 1978), pages 18-19.

Henkin, Shepard. Opportunities in the Hotel and Motel Industry, revised edition. New York: Universal Publishing and Distributing Corporation, 1967.

Occupational Outlook Handbook, 1978-79 edition. U.S. Department of Labor, Bureau of Labor Statistics, 1978, Bulletin 1955

Rush, Ralph A. "The Hotel-Motel Industry," The Encyclopedia of Careers and Vocational Guidance, Volume I (1972), pages 325-334.

- Identify the information listed for each footnote.
- Identify the information given in each entry.

Try Your Skill Read the following quotation about choosing a career and its source. Write a footnote and a bibliography entry based on this information.

"People differ in what they want from a career. Many people desire a high income. Some hope for fame. Others want much leisure time or a life of adventure. Still others want to serve people and help make the world a better place. Before you begin to explore career fields, you should determine (1) your values, or goals in life; (2) your interests; and (3) your abilities. Most people are happiest in occupations that meet their values, interests, and abilities."

from page 172e of an article titled "Careers" by Edwin L. Herr in *The World Book Encyclopedia*, Volume 3 (1979), pages 172d-174

Keep This in Mind

- Use footnotes to give credit to writers whose words or ideas you include in a report.
- Prepare a bibliography to show the sources of information you used in writing your report.

Now Write In your report, make any corrections necessary for clarity, or for correct grammar, capitalization, punctuation, and spelling. Also write a good title.

Insert the numbers for your footnotes into the first draft of your report. Find the information you need for your footnotes on your source cards. Copy it in the correct form on a separate paper labeled *Footnotes*.

Then take out your bibliography cards and write a bibliography entry for each source you used in your report. Copy the entries in alphabetical order onto a separate sheet of paper labeled *Bibliography*, but do not number them.

Neatly copy your report in final form.

For help in preparing the final copy of your report, see **Handbook Section 16, The Correct Form for Writing.**

Also, examine the final copy of the report on a career in the hotel industry shown on the following pages.

Chris Adams

English III

March 8, 1980

Reserve a Future in the Hotel Industry

Many people choose a career in the field of personal services. That is, they choose jobs in which they attend to the needs of other individuals. One of the largest personal service industries is the hotel-motel business. Basically, the function of this business is to provide sleeping accommodations and meals. However, hotels and motels range from simple country inns with a few rooms and employees to elaborate city skyscrapers with more than 1,000 rooms and hundreds of employees. The largest of these businesses offer many additional conveniences for their guests. The services may include gift shops, recreational facilities, and banquet and convention facilities.

To provide this range of services, the hotel industry employs workers in a wide variety of skilled and unskilled occupations. These various occupations can be divided into those related to the "front of the house" and those related to the "back of the house." The "front of the house" is a hotel term for the operations that deal directly with, and are seen by, the guests. These operations are those of management, the front office, the uniformed service staff, and the accounting and sales departments. The "back of the house" refers to hotel operations that are seldom seen by guests. These include housekeeping, food preparation, security, laundry, and engineering.

Because the hotel industry employs such a broad range of occupations, no single type of training is necessary. Many entry-level positions require only a short period of on-the-job training. Entry-level jobs are often available on a part-time basis for students, to acquaint them with hotel work. These jobs include waiter, maid, clerk, porter, bellhop, and elevator operator. However, longer on-the-job training or vocational education may lead to other, higher-paying positions. For instance, those who have completed programs in cooking, accounting, or maintenance and repair work may eventually become department heads. "The hotel industry is one of the few wherein a young person can secure a position without too much formal education, and work his way through the various departments to an executive capacity."[1]

To be successful in any position in the hotel business, several basic personal qualifications are required. A person must be able to deal with all kinds of people in any situation. Courtesy and patience are essential when serving guests. In addition to a pleasant manner, a neat appearance is important. Finally, constant attention to detail is called for in all aspects of hotel work.

There are many benefits for those who choose a career in the hotel industry. The first advantage is a flexible schedule, since hotels and motels operate twenty-four hours a day with three shifts. Other benefits include the choice of part-time, full-time, or seasonal work, and a wide selection of geographic locations. At present, the industry is also looking for capable women and members of minority groups to train as managers. A career in the hotel industry offers many opportunities for personal and professional growth.

Footnote

[1]Shepard Henkin, Opportunities in the Hotel and Motel Industry, page 27.

Bibliography

Curran, Ann. "Hotel Industry Makes Room for Women," Working Woman, Volume 3 (April, 1978), pages 18-19.

Henkin, Shepard. Opportunities in the Hotel and Motel Industry, revised edition. New York: Universal Publishing and Distributing Corporation, 1967.

Occupational Outlook Handbook, 1978-79 edition. U.S. Department of Labor, Bureau of Labor Statistics, 1978, Bulletin 1955.

Rush, Ralph A. "The Hotel-Motel Industry," The Encyclopedia of Careers and Vocational Guidance, Volume 1 (1972), pages 325-334.

WRITING SECTION 20

Developing Speaking Skills

Part 1 **At Ease**
Presenting Yourself

Part 2 **Small Talk**
Relaying Information to Others

Part 3 **Be Prepared**
Preparing for a Job Interview

Part 4 **At Your Best**
Having an Interview

Part 1

At Ease

Presenting Yourself

Here's the Idea Presenting yourself well will make a difference as you look for jobs, meet new people, or persuade others to listen to your point of view. Use the following guidelines to help you to develop good speaking skills.

1. **Posture** Your posture reveals your attitude. A person who slouches looks afraid or indifferent, so stand tall and appear confident.
2. **Eye Contact** Make a point of looking directly at someone as you talk. People listen to speakers who look at them.
3. **Voice** Have you ever had to listen to a speaker who mumbled or one who spoke in a flat, monotonous tone? If so, you probably soon stopped listening. When you talk, speak pleasantly in a voice just loud enough to be heard.
4. **Organization** Think before you speak. You will feel more confident when you are able to plan what you are going to say.
5. **Language** Choose your words carefully. You would probably speak differently to a classmate than you would to an employer. Use correct English when you talk with someone about a job.

A good speaker is sensitive to his or her audience. If you watch your listeners' faces, you can tell whether or not you are getting your message across.

Check It Out Read the following scene.

> Norma had finished her research about careers in electronics and was going to report to her discussion group about what she had learned. Before going to school, Norma dressed carefully and neatly.
>
> When her turn came to talk, Norma sat up straight. She folded her hands on the desk.

Then Norma shifted her eyes to the window. When she spoke, her mind seemed far away. "I know you're not very interested," she said.

Norma's voice was quiet. Only a few people could hear her.

"My report is about jobs in electronics," Norma continued. "I might try to get a job in electronics someday."

- Consider each of the five guidelines for presenting yourself well. What did Norma do right? What mistakes did she make?

Try Your Skill Consider the following situations and explain how you would correct them. Write your answers.

1. Joan needed to leave school early. She had a doctor's appointment at 2:00. She walked up to her teacher. Joan looked at the floor. She murmured, "I have to leave now. OK?"

2. Ray had read a lot about conserving energy. He wanted his parents to recycle aluminum cans. One night he walked into the kitchen and yelled, "Did you know you are wasting resources every day? It wouldn't hurt you to think about the rest of the world!" Then Ray stalked out of the room.

Keep This in Mind

- Whenever you speak, present yourself well. Stand tall, make eye contact with your listeners, and speak in a pleasant voice loud enough to be heard. Plan what you are going to say. Use language that is appropriate for the situation.

Now Speak Prepare to tell others a story about yourself. Your talk should last two or three minutes. Say it out loud several times for practice.

Then divide into small groups. Tell your story to the others in your group. Ask them to tell you what they liked best about your talk and to suggest improvements.

Part 2

Small Talk

Relaying Information to Others

Here's the Idea In many speaking situations, you need to give and receive information. Sometimes, for example, you are called upon to make an **announcement.** In order to be accurate, write out the details of the announcement.

If you are asked for **directions,** you need to explain them clearly. Use landmarks to tell how to get somewhere. Ask the other person to repeat your directions, as you check for accuracy. Sometimes you will need to teach someone how to do something—how to change a tire, for example. Carefully explain the process, one step at a time.

Occasionally, you may be asked to **introduce** a speaker at an assembly or club meeting. It will help you if you can talk with the speaker first. Try to find out a few interesting details to put into your introduction. Your job is to make the audience eager to hear the speaker.

Much of your talking probably takes place on the telephone. You are often asked to deliver a **message** to someone else. Be polite and write down the message.

Check It Out Consider the following situation.

Linda was head of the publicity committee for Careers Day at her school. She had an announcement to make at the Junior Class meeting.

When Linda's turn came to speak, she walked forward, looked at her audience, and paused. Once they were quiet, she spoke in a voice that could be heard everywhere in the room.

"After a lot of talking, we have finally been able to get Careers Day approved by the faculty," Linda said.

The audience cheered. Linda stopped and waited for them to be quiet.

Then she continued, "Careers Day at Pasco High School will be on March 18. We will have speakers come to talk about thirty different careers. Each student may attend five sessions. Please sign up for the sessions you want after today's meeting. The sign-up sheet will be on the table in the hall."

When Linda finished, she paused and then returned to her seat. She could tell by her listeners' faces that they had understood and appreciated her announcement.

- What details did Linda include in her announcement?

Try Your Skill Rewrite the following examples, correcting the errors. Invent any necessary details.

1. Directions from Wilson School to the Court House—"At the main entrance of the school, turn south. Walk four blocks. Then turn right. Walk to the top of the hill. Go several blocks. You'll see the Court House after you cross the street."

2. An Introduction—"This woman on the stage is Mrs. Singer. She is a Licensed Practical Nurse at Reese Hospital. Mrs. Singer is a graduate of Central High School. She now has a son, Mark, who is a freshman here. Please listen to her. Here's the microphone, Mrs. Singer."

Keep This in Mind

- In many speaking situations, you need to give or receive information. Include all important information. Be accurate. Always be courteous.

Now Speak Working in small groups, prepare the following topics. Be sure your group covers all the topics.

1. An announcement about a bus trip to a basketball game.
2. Directions for making or doing something. You may want to choose something related to a hobby or a special skill you have.
3. Directions for going from school to the post office.
4. A phone message that contains several important details. This topic will require two people: a caller and a receiver.

Part 3

Be Prepared

Preparing for a Job Interview

Here's the Idea A job interview is a speaking situation. You must be prepared to talk with a prospective employer.

The first step in your preparation is to be sure your résumé is up-to-date. Sometimes you may want to send it in with a letter seeking employment. At other times, you may want to bring it with you to an interview. In any case, be sure you can talk easily about everything you have included.

It is often helpful to ask yourself some questions about the background information you have included on your résumé. For example, you might practice answering the following questions.

1. What are my strongest assets as an employee?
2. What experience do I have that helps qualify me for this particular job?
3. What personal attributes do I have that will make me valuable to this company?

If your résumé shows a weak area—for example, if you were dismissed from a previous job—be prepared to talk about it. You do not want to stumble if asked a difficult question. Simply explain what happened, emphasizing why you think you will be successful this time.

Before you go to your interview, find out as much as you can about the company and the job you want. Perhaps you can talk to someone who is working there now. If not, try to visit the company. For example, if you want a job as a cashier in a supermarket, shop in the store several times. Watch the cashiers. What seem to be their responsibilities? Of course, you should observe quietly and not talk with employees while they are on the job.

Having done this, you will probably have some questions of your own to ask at the interview. Think about them ahead of time. One or two good questions will show the employer that you are thinking and that you have initiative.

It is also important when you go to an interview to give some thought to your personal appearance. Wear clothes that help you feel good about yourself. It is usually best to dress neatly and tastefully. Anything that calls attention to itself lessens the attention given to you and your job application.

Check It Out Consider the following situation.

> Carrie wanted to apply for a job as an office clerk in a nearby auto parts store. Her résumé was ready, and when she studied it, she discovered this information.

1. My strongest assets are my typing speed and my ability to keep good records.
2. I have two experiences that help qualify me for this job—my work last summer as a clerk in City Hall and my job at school as Ms. Tandy's assistant.
3. My personal attributes include promptness and an ability to get along well with other people in an office.

> Carrie thought of a weakness that could hurt her chances. She was a poor speller. She decided not to mention this problem unless asked. She also planned to explain, if necessary, that her spelling suffered because of a poor beginning in reading. Carrie knew how to use a dictionary, however, and she could promise an employer that she would be careful about looking up words. Carrie had asked Ms. Tandy for a reference, and Ms. Tandy had agreed to write a letter for Carrie to take with her.
>
> On the day of her interview, Carrie dressed in her favorite skirt and blouse, and she wore low-heeled shoes that she had polished that morning.

- What preparations did Carrie make for her interview? What else should Carrie do to get ready?

Try Your Skill Tom wants a job at a service station. He would like to work after school and on weekends. He sent in a résumé and has been offered an interview. Write out and number the steps that Tom should take in getting ready for his interview.

Keep This in Mind

- Before you go to a job interview, review your résumé. Be prepared to talk about yourself. Also, learn as much as you can about the company and the job you want. Think of questions that you might like to ask at the interview. In addition, dress neatly and tastefully.

Now Speak Select a job that interests you. The company and job may be real or imaginary. Next, review a résumé you have prepared. List your strongest skills. Also, jot down something you have learned about the company you want to work for. List questions you might want to ask at your interview. Decide how you will dress for your interview. Jot down your ideas.

Divide into pairs. Hand your résumé to your partner. Review the steps you have been through in preparing for your interview. Ask your partner for suggestions or comments.

Part 4 **At Your Best**

Having an Interview

Here's the Idea A job interview will be much easier for you if you have prepared carefully. Get off to a good start by taking with you everything you might need: several copies of your résumé, a pad of paper, pen or pencil, and identification that includes your social security number. Allow yourself plenty of time in order to be prompt for the interview.

Once you arrive, you will need to introduce yourself. When you meet your interviewer, stand up. It's best to be informal but polite. Perhaps you will say, "Hello, Mr. Logan. I'm Terry Robbins from Jackson High School." Always shake hands if the interviewer extends a hand to you. Look directly at your interviewer.

Be direct and say your name clearly. You should be sure you catch the name of the interviewer. If you don't hear it, ask the interviewer to repeat it.

If you haven't sent in a copy of your résumé earlier, offer it now. While the interviewer reads it, sit quietly. Be thinking about what you are going to say.

Once the interview begins, listen carefully. It's all too easy to be distracted by the office or the view or something unfamiliar to you, especially if you're nervous. Keep your mind on the interview so that you can answer questions well.

If the interviewer asks you a question that is difficult or surprising, remain calm. It is perfectly all right to say, "Let me think about that for a moment." Don't be afraid to pause while you get your ideas together.

In addition, try to avoid some of the common pitfalls in interviewing. For example, if the interviewer asks you a hard question, don't give a negative, dead-end answer, such as, "I don't know." Also, the interview is usually not the time for you to ask about salary or advancement opportunities. If the interviewer offers information on those subjects, you should feel free to discuss them. Otherwise, wait until you get a job offer. Finally, all prospective employers want to see evidence of self-control. Let your hands rest quietly in your lap or on the arms of your chair. Don't smoke or chew gum. Keep your voice at a reasonable pitch and volume.

The interviewer will let you know when the interview is over. Before leaving, show your interest in the job. Ask when you can expect to hear something from the company. As you leave, check to be sure you have all your belongings. It's polite to thank the interviewer. Then shake hands and leave. Don't linger to look around or to talk to employees.

Check It Out Consider the following situation.

> Adam had an interview scheduled for 10:00 Friday morning at a citrus fruit processing plant. He was applying for a summer job in the canning department.
>
> Adam arrived at 10:05. Traffic had been heavy, and he was nervous about being late.
>
> His interviewer greeted him, "Good morning, Adam. I'm John Clark, the foreman."
>
> They shook hands, and Adam said, "Hello, Mr. Clark. I'm Adam Stern. I'm sorry I'm late. The bus was slow."
>
> Adam's interview went well. Here are some of the interviewer's questions and the answers that Adam gave.
>
> Mr. Clark: I see that you worked during the school year. Did you usually get to work on time?
>
> Adam: Yes, I did. I was late only once, and that was the day we had a fire alarm drill at school.
>
> Mr. Clark: What makes you think you could stand the grind of factory work?
>
> Adam: I have a lot of patience. I sometimes spend hours working on wood carvings. My job last year gave me experience, too. I spent most of the time repairing motors on lawnmowers.

Mr. Clark: Why do you want this job?

Adam: I know the plant is good to its employees. I have several friends who have worked here and liked it. There's also the fact that I need the money. My family expects me to earn my own spending money.

- How well did Adam handle this interview? Give specific reasons and details to explain your answer.

Try Your Skill Divide into pairs. Take turns playing the parts of the interviewer and the job applicant. Ask each other these questions. Answer them in terms of your own background and experience. This exercise will give you practice in answering interview questions well.

1. Can you tell me a little about the last job you held?
2. Your school record shows that you are often absent. Can you explain those absences? How do you plan to have a good attendance record on the job?

Keep This in Mind

- Introduce yourself to your interviewer. Answer questions completely and thoughtfully. Let your interviewer see your best assets.

Now Speak For this exercise, work with a partner. Give your partner a copy of a résumé that you have prepared. The partner should study your résumé and think of three good questions to ask you. Then practice the interview. Begin by walking into the room and meeting your prospective employer. Act out the entire interview, including the conclusion. After you have finished, switch roles, and repeat the situation.

Write Again

The more practice you have, the more comfortable you become with writing. The preceding lessons have taught you many writing skills. In the following eleven pages you will find additional practice in improving those skills. As you finish each lesson, your teacher may assign one of these additional exercises. Give them your best effort.

Section 1 Developing Your Vocabulary

Part 1 **Discoveries** In a newspaper, find examples of these context clues: definition, restatement, example, comparison, and contrast. Copy each sentence and circle the word the clue helps to define. Check the definition of each word in a dictionary.

Part 2 **Drawing Conclusions** Write several sentences that hint at the meaning of the word *athletic*. Give information that would help a careful reader infer the meaning.

Part 3 **A Word Divided** In a magazine or book, find five words that contain prefixes. Find the words in a dictionary. List the words and write their meanings.

Part 4 **On End** In a textbook, find five words that contain suffixes. Find the words in a dictionary. List the words and write their meanings.

Part 5 **The Root of the Matter** Look up the words *credence*, *facsimile*, *induct*, and *posit* in a dictionary. Use your knowledge of roots to help you restate each definition in your own words. Write the words and their meanings.

Part 6 **In the Right** Look up the word *easy* in a dictionary. Find two synonyms for the word. Use each synonym correctly in a written sentence that shows its precise meaning. Then write one sentence using an antonym of *easy*.

Part 7 **Special Effects** List sensory words that describe a place where you play or watch a favorite sport. Be specific and try to use every sense.

Section 2 Controlling Your Sentences

Part 1 **In the Clear** Write one sentence describing your favorite city. Write another sentence explaining why you like the city. Write a third sentence telling about something that happened to you while you were in this city. Make your sentences clear and interesting.

Part 2 **Beware of Detours** Write three brief sentences about your school. Rewrite each, adding one related detail that makes the sentence more specific or more interesting.

Part 3 **Empty-Handed** Write one sentence giving an unsupported opinion. Write a second sentence in which an idea is repeated. Then rewrite each empty sentence to improve it.

Part 4 **Stay Trim** Write three padded sentences. Rewrite each sentence, eliminating unnecessary words or revising completely as needed.

Part 5 **Heavyweights** Write two overloaded sentences. Make each contain at least three ideas. Then improve the sentences by breaking each into several shorter sentences.

Examining the Paragraph Section 3

Part 1 **A Good Group** In a newspaper or magazine, find a short paragraph about any form of transportation. Read the paragraph and then decide what the main idea is. Write the main idea in your own words.

Part 2 **Of One Mind** Write one sentence that expresses your feelings about yourself. Then write five sentences related to this idea.

Part 3 **I Declare!** What is your favorite season of the year? Write two good topic sentences for paragraphs about that season. Be sure that your topic sentences are not too narrow and that they could be developed meaningfully.

Part 4 **From the Ground Up** Write three topic sentences. Write one that could best be developed with details, one that could be developed by examples, and one that could be developed by facts and figures.

Part 5 **What's Your Line?** Write a topic that would be suitable for a narrative paragraph. Then write one topic suitable for a descriptive paragraph, and one for an explanatory paragraph. Label each.

Section 4 Writing a Paragraph

Part 1 **Control Yourself** Narrow the general topic "courage" by answering *who, what, when, where, why,* and *how* questions. Write your answers and the specific topic.

Part 2 **In the Interest of** Think of a situation in which you or someone you know showed courage. Write a direct and interesting topic sentence about it.

Part 3 **A Strong Foundation** Write a paragraph about a situation that required courage. Use details, examples, or facts and figures to develop your idea.

Part 4 **Top It Off** Write an ending sentence that sums up the main idea of your paragraph about courage. Make the sentence strong and interesting.

Section 5 A Writer's Choices

Part 1 **Who Sees What?** Imagine that there has been a major storm in your area. Write three paragraphs that tell about it, using the three different points of view.

Part 2 **Facts or Fancies?** Write two short paragraphs about a holiday. Either paragraph may be narrative, descriptive, or explanatory. Make one paragraph about a real experience. Use facts. Make the second paragraph about an imaginary experience. Invent details.

Part 3 **Word Power** Write a paragraph describing a type of transportation that you enjoy using. Write a second paragraph describing a type of transportation that you dislike. Underline the strong, specific words that help you express your feelings.

Part 4 **Showstoppers** Suppose that you are writing a biography of one member of your family. Think about what you find most interesting about the person. Then write three possible titles for the biography.

The Narrative Paragraph

Section 7

Part 1 **Time Capsule** Think about your normal routine when you go shopping for food or clothes. List your actions in chronological order using clear transitions. Then write a paragraph about one shopping trip.

Part 2 **Item by Item** Write a narrative paragraph about a real or imagined race against time. Develop vivid details by asking yourself *who, what, when, where, why,* and *how* questions.

The Descriptive Paragraph

Section 8

Part 1 **Uncommon Sense** Think of the last time you enjoyed a special or unusual meal. Make a list of sensory details that you remember from the experience. Then write a descriptive paragraph using the list.

Part 2 **Directional Signals** Think of a real or imaginary store window display. List the important sensory details and organize them using spatial order. Then write a paragraph of description.

The Explanatory Paragraph

Section 9

Part 1 **Step In** Think of how you would repair some household item if it were broken. Make a list of the steps you would follow, using transitions that will make their order clear. Then write an explanatory paragraph that explains the process.

Part 2 **Listen to Reason** What is your opinion about equal pay for men and women? Write an explanatory paragraph that states your opinion. Include three specific reasons or facts that support your opinion and use clear transitions to show their order of importance.

Part 3 **Come to Terms** Write an explanatory paragraph that defines an object or an idea that is part of your daily life. You may define *school* or *family,* for example. Use details or facts and figures to develop your definition.

Section 10 Examining the Composition

Part 1 **Working Together** Think about the kind of work you enjoy doing. From these kinds of work, write five topics that would be suitable for compositions.

Part 2 **Three-Wheeler** Think about the last time you had to make a quick decision. How would you write a composition about the experience? List three headings: *Introduction*, *Body*, and *Conclusion*. Write notes that tell what you would include in each part of your composition.

Part 3 **In Name Only** As a topic for a composition choose a particular person you would like to meet. You could write a narrative composition telling about meeting the person. You could describe the appearance of the person in a descriptive composition. You could explain why you want to meet the person in an explanatory composition. In a few sentences, write what you would include in each type of composition.

Section 11 The Narrative Composition

Part 1 **Head First** Choose a real or imaginary struggle between two people as your topic. Plan the introduction, body, and conclusion of a narrative composition about this struggle by making pre-writing notes. If you are writing a true account, list details about people, places, and events. For a story, invent and list details about characters, setting, and plot.

Part 2 **What's the Trouble?** Think about a real or imaginary struggle between two people. Think about the struggle from several points of view. Choose one and write an introduction to a narrative about the struggle. Then use your notes to write two or three paragraphs developing the body of the narrative.

Part 3 **Speak Your Mind** Write a dialogue between two people or characters involved in a struggle against each other. Follow the rules for punctuation of quotations.

Part 4 **Grand Finale** Write a conclusion that resolves the conflict of a struggle between two people. Then write a title for the composition.

The Descriptive Composition

Section 12

Part 1 **Make the Scene** Think of a noisy place you have been. It might be a sports arena, an airport, or a factory. Using that place as the topic for a descriptive composition, write and organize pre-writing notes.

Part 2 **Be Aware** Observe or recall a noisy place you know well. List as many sensory details as you can. Use the details to write the introduction and body of a description of the place.

Part 3 **A Spaceflight** Suppose that you are writing a composition about a specific noisy place. Decide what spatial order you would use to describe what you see, and list the transitions you would use. Then write the conclusion. Finally, write a title that is interesting and descriptive.

The Explanatory Composition

Section 13

Explaining a Process

Part 1 **Easy Does It** Make a list of five processes involved in a kind of work that you can do well. Think about how you would explain each process to another person. Write five possible titles for compositions on these skills.

Part 2 **Think Ahead** Choose a process involved in a kind of work that you can do well and list details for each step involved. Write the body of an explanatory composition, giving a step-by-step explanation.

Part 3 **First to Last** Think of a process involved in a kind of work that you can do well. List the steps in the process and add transitions for each step that make the order clear. Then write an introduction and a conclusion to your explanation.

Section 14 The Explanatory Composition
Stating an Opinion

Part 1 **In View of** Review the sample student composition stating that professional athletes deserve high salaries that is shown in Section 14. Plan an explanatory composition that expresses the opposite view. Plan your composition by making pre-writing notes. Include reasons or facts that will support your opinion.

Part 2 **By Reason of** List three specific reasons or facts that support the opinion that athletes do not deserve such high salaries. Arrange the evidence in order of importance, from the least important to the most important. Write the body of your explanatory composition.

Part 3 **Famous Last Words** Review your argument against high salaries for professional athletes. Add transitions that show the reasons and their order of importance. Write an introduction for the composition and a conclusion that sums up your argument. Finally, compare your composition with the student sample. Which one is the more convincing? Why?

Section 15 The Explanatory Composition
Stating a Definition

Part 1 **Explain It** Think of a useful labor-saving gadget that you could define in an explanatory composition. Make pre-writing notes to plan the introduction, body, and conclusion.

Part 2 **Precisely Yours** Write a definition of a useful labor-saving gadget. Be sure you have named the gadget, its general class, and its special characteristics. Then use your definition as part of an introduction to an explanatory composition.

Part 3 **Final Appeal** Think of a useful labor-saving gadget. Decide whether you would develop a definition of it in a factual or personal way. Develop your definition in the body of an explanatory composition. Then write a conclusion in which you summarize your main idea.

Letters, Applications, and Résumés

Section 16

Part 1 **Keep In Touch** Write a personal letter telling about a problem you solved recently. Label each part of the letter.

Part 2 **Special Delivery** Draw a rectangle to represent an envelope. Address it as if it were a letter you were going to send to a relative.

Part 3 **The World of Business** Write to any local business ordering a particular product you have seen advertised. Use the modified block form for this letter.

Part 4 **What Do You Need?** Write a letter to a local organization requesting information about the requirements for becoming a member. Be specific.

Part 5 **To Your Knowledge** Write a letter to a local vocational or technical school asking about courses in television repair. Include specific information about yourself.

Part 6 **On the Job** Write a letter to a business at a nearby recreation area asking for a list of summer jobs that are available.

Part 7 **A Work Sheet** Ask for a job application from your teacher or from a local store. Fill it in completely and honestly.

Part 8 **Experience Counts** What was the job title of your immediate supervisor at the last job you had? Prepare your résumé using that job as your objective.

Using a Dictionary

Section 17

Part 1 **Words To Guide You** If it was to be included in your dictionary, on what page would the name of your town appear? Write the guide words for that page. Then copy five words from that page that are new to you, and use them in sentences.

Part 2 **In Search of** Find the word *clear* in a dictionary. Copy its pronunciation, the language it came from, its possible parts of speech, four meanings, and a synonym.

Part 3 **A Fitting Choice** Look up the word *point* in a dictionary. Copy five different meanings. Write a sentence of your own for each one.

Section 18 Using the Library

Part 1 **Shelf by Shelf** Think of an art form you would like to learn about. Use your school or public library to find at least three nonfiction books related to this art form. Write their titles, authors, and call numbers.

Part 2 **On the Track** In your school or public library, find a title card, an author card, and a subject card for books related to a kind of work that interests you. Copy the information from the cards.

Part 3 **There's One for You** Find an encyclopedia article related to a famous person in history whom you admire. List the name of the encyclopedia, the volume number and letters, the guide words on the page, and names of related articles or books.

Part 4 **Did You Know That?** Write the titles of two different reference books in which you find information related to a country that you would like to visit. Then use the *Readers' Guide to Periodical Literature* to find and write the name of one magazine containing an article related to that country.

Section 19 Investigating Careers

Part 1 **Possibilities** As a subject, choose some type of career in building construction or design. At the library, narrow the subject and find three different sources of information about it. Check the card catalog, indexes, various guides, and the reference shelves. List detailed information about your sources.

Part 2 **Shortcuts** Choose a book, a magazine article, and an encyclopedia article about some aspect of building construction or planning. Make a model bibliography card for each. Then make a note card from one of the sources.

Part 3 **Pileup** Choose a book, a magazine article, or an encyclopedia article about one aspect of building construction or design. From it, choose three related facts and write them. State the main idea of the facts in one sentence.

Part 4 **The Bare Essentials** Find a magazine article about some aspect of building construction or design. On paper, write the first two main ideas in the article. Under each main idea, write the facts or details as subtopics. Finally, write your notes in outline form.

Part 5 **Take the Plunge** As the population increases in the United States, so must the number of available homes and businesses. Write the introduction to a report on careers in building construction or design, including this observation.

Part 6 **Go the Distance** Choose a book or magazine article about one element of building construction or design. Find several interesting facts or figures, and one direct quotation. Write them on your paper and write a statement about them that could be used as a conclusion.

Part 7 **Finishing Touches** Find a magazine article about building construction or design and copy a direct quotation. Write one footnote for the quotation. Then make a bibliography entry for the article.

Developing Speaking Skills

Section 20

Part 1 **At Ease** Write a paragraph in which you discuss your general strengths and weaknesses as a speaker. Discuss your posture, eye contact, voice, organization, and language. For each point that you discuss, try to give a specific example or illustration.

Part 2 **Small Talk** Write a dialogue that shows two people failing to relay information successfully. Your situation should be based on making an announcement, giving directions, introducing a speaker, or taking a phone message. Show a breakdown in communication, and then explain how the situation could be corrected.

Part 3 **Be Prepared** Pretend you are going to an interview for a position requiring you to help out in the main office of your school. The job has these requirements: keeping records, running the ditto machine, and doing errands. Write a paragraph telling how you would prepare for this interview.

Part 4 **At Your Best** With a partner, take turns acting out an interview for a summer job at a local restaurant. Afterwards, write a paragraph discussing each interview. Discuss where each interview was most successful and where each applicant might have done better.

Handbook

A detailed Table of Contents for the Handbook appears in the front of this book.

The Sentence and Its Parts

You may not think of yourself as a mechanic. However, speaking and writing English is somewhat like building an engine. Like a mechanic working on an engine, you combine parts to build the driving force of English, the sentence.

An engine is composed of pistons, shafts, and cylinders. In a similar way, a sentence is made from its separate parts—subjects, verbs, modifiers, objects, and more. When the parts of a motor are put together properly, it runs smoothly. A well put-together sentence also is smooth and efficient.

In this section you will learn about the parts of a sentence and how they are put into working order.

Part 1 The Complete Sentence

Sometimes in conversation, you use only parts of sentences. For example, you might reply to a question with a word or two:

Not now. That one. Yes.

In writing, however, complete sentences are important. With them, your ideas are clear and understandable.

A sentence is a group of words that expresses a complete thought. A sentence makes sense because it is a whole idea, not just part of one.

These groups of words are sentences:

Sean skated down the sidewalk.
That red car is blocking the alley.
The alarm sounded late last night.

Sometimes part of an idea is missing from a sentence. Then the group of words is a sentence fragment. A **sentence fragment** is a group of words that does not express a complete thought. For example, these are sentence fragments:

Skated down the sidewalk. (Who skated?)
That red car. (What about the car?)
Late last night. (What happened?)

Exercise A Number your paper from 1 to 10. For each group of words that is a sentence, write **S.** For each sentence fragment, write **F.**

1. Lost fifteen pounds.
2. The boxers entered the ring.
3. The final score.
4. Opened the top drawer.
5. A photo of the family.
6. This gas station is open.

7. Val planned the route.
8. Vendors at the ballpark.
9. Where was the wedding held?
10. Elston works at a hospital.

Exercise B Follow the directions for Exercise A.

1. Dave Kingman hit a homer.
2. Who is this disc jockey?
3. Dialed the wrong number.
4. A downpour stalled the game.
5. Needs a lot of help.
6. A group of close friends.
7. Smoke from the blaze.
8. A new source of energy.
9. Kim noticed the want ad.
10. The cashier made a mistake.

Part 2 The Subject and the Predicate

Every sentence is made up of two basic parts: the subject and the predicate. The **subject** tells *whom* or *what* the sentence is about. The **predicate** tells something about the subject.

Subject	Predicate
(*Who or what*)	(*What is said about the subject*)
The volcano	erupted again.
A reporter from the paper	relayed the news.
The subway riders	raced for the doors.

Each of these sentences expresses a complete thought. Each of them tells something about a person, place, or thing.

There is an easy way to remember the parts of a sentence. Think of the sentence as telling who did something or what happened. The subject tells *who* or *what*. The predicate tells *did* or *happened*.

Who or What	Did or Happened
The soft mud under my feet	cushioned my toes.
Our lead-off hitter	got a stand-up double.
All four tires	need air.

The subject of the sentence tells *who* or *what* did something, or what the sentence is about.

The predicate of the sentence tells what is done or what happens.

Exercise A Head two columns *Subject* and *Predicate*. Write the proper words from each sentence in the columns.

Example: My cousin needs a part-time job.

Subject	Predicate
My cousin	needs a part-time job.

1. A line of motorcycles zoomed down the freeway.
2. The blaze roared through the forest.
3. Ronald carries his radio with him.
4. Those small cars get good gas mileage.
5. Our career counselor has information on interviews.
6. The new P.E. wing contains two gyms.
7. This year's harvest included soybeans.
8. Those jeans have been washed many times.
9. I need new glasses.
10. Tickets for the Wings concert sold fast.

Exercise B Follow the directions for Exercise A.

1. Cara's friends waited at the corner.
2. The cheapest seats are in the bleachers.

3. Few people remember all of their dreams.
4. The projection booth overlooks the theater.
5. Dancers at the disco rocked with the music.
6. The second semester begins in January.
7. Two friends of mine cut an album.
8. The other people at the party didn't notice Les at first.
9. Frozen yogurt pie is a good dessert.
10. A local woman had quintuplets.

Part 3 Simple Subjects and Verbs

In every sentence a few words are more important than the others. These essential words are the basic framework of the sentence. Look at these examples:

Subject	Predicate
The **volcano**	**erupted** again.
A **reporter** from the paper	**relayed** the news.
The subway **riders**	**raced** for the doors.

All the words in the subject part of the sentence are called the **complete subject.** Within the complete subject is a key word, the **simple subject.** In the last example above, *the subway riders* is the complete subject. *Riders* is the simple subject.

The **complete predicate** is all the words that tell something about the subject. The key word within the complete predicate is the **simple predicate** or **verb.**

In the sentence about the subway riders, the complete predicate is *raced for the doors*. The key word is *raced*.

The key word in the subject of a sentence is called the simple subject. We refer to it as the *subject*.

The key word in the predicate is the simple predicate. The simple predicate is the **verb.** Hereafter we will refer to the simple predicate as the *verb*.

Finding the Verb and the Subject

In any sentence, the verb and the subject are the most important words. The other words only tell more about these key words. To find these key words in any sentence, first find the verb. It shows action or a state of being. Then ask *who* or *what* before the verb. That answer will give you the subject of the verb.

An attendant at the station checked the oil.
Verb: checked
Who checked? attendant
The subject is *attendant*.

The plane glided down the runway.
Verb: glided
What glided? plane
The subject is *plane*.

Diagraming Subjects and Verbs

A sentence diagram is a drawing of the parts of a sentence. It shows how the parts fit together.

A sentence diagram shows the importance of the subject and the verb. These key parts are placed on a horizontal main line. They are separated by a vertical line that crosses the main line. The subject appears before the verb. Later you will learn how every other word in the sentence has its own place in the diagram, too.

In diagraming, only words capitalized in the sentence are capitalized in the diagram. No punctuation is used.

Adam spoke quietly.

Adam | **spoke**

Janelle writes poetry.

Janelle	writes

Exercise A Label two columns *Verb* and *Subject*. Number your paper from 1 to 10. For each sentence, write the verb and its subject.

1. That nursery needs aides.
2. Ten students volunteered.
3. This map of the city indicates bus routes.
4. The eager drivers revved their engines.
5. The network canceled that show.
6. Dana's sister sets high goals for herself.
7. Six different ingredients topped the pizza.
8. A professional stuntman performed the fall.
9. The annual carnival attracted large crowds.
10. Daytime television features soap operas.

Exercise B Follow the directions for Exercise A.

1. Many popular songs are old folk melodies.
2. Clint Eastwood's new film played downtown.
3. A violent tornado destroyed several homes.
4. The radio by my bed wakens me each morning.
5. The crew worked overtime on the highway project.
6. A package arrived in the morning mail.
7. All lockers in the south wing have mirrors.
8. The bridge to Canada crosses the St. Lawrence Seaway.
9. The theater across the street has a sneak preview.
10. Some fans of silent films adore Charlie Chaplin.

Part 4 The Parts of a Verb

A verb may consist of one word, or of several words. The verb may be composed of a **main verb** and one or more **helping verbs.**

Helping Verbs +	Main Verb =	Verb
will	return	will return
would	expect	would expect
is	leaving	is leaving
must have	shown	must have shown

To name the verb in any sentence, you must name all the words that make up the verb.

These words are frequently used as helping verbs:

am	are	have	will	may
is	be	do	would	might
was	has	does	can	shall
were	had	did	could	should

Separated Parts of a Verb

At times you will find words inserted between the parts of a verb. These words are not included in the verb. Look at the following sentences. The parts of the verb are in bold print.

Cassie **had** never **driven** a tractor.
My friends **could** not **offer** any advice.
The artist **will** gladly **show** you her work.

Some verbs are joined with other words to make contractions. In naming verbs that appear in contractions, pick out only the verb. The word *not* and its contraction *n't* are adverbs. They are never verb parts.

Vernon **did**n't **notice** the car. (*Did notice* is the verb.)
The carpenter **had**n't **measured** exactly. (*Had measured* is the verb.)

Exercise A Number your paper from 1 to 10. List the verbs in the following sentences.

1. Bluegrass musicians were gathering for a festival.
2. You haven't ever needed any help before.
3. We could often read his mood.
4. David has never seen an ice hockey game.
5. Yolanda will surely return next week.
6. The umpire didn't respond to the catcalls.
7. That bill hasn't been passed yet.
8. This year I will probably get a paper route.
9. The price does not include delivery.
10. We have never called ourselves experts.

Exercise B Follow the directions for Exercise A.

1. Summer vacation doesn't begin until Tuesday.
2. A relief pitcher will sometimes finish the game.
3. She has already taken her driver's test.
4. A good job will usually require two coats of paint.
5. The birth rate has recently dropped.
6. They are always complaining about homework.
7. Your ideas will certainly help.
8. McDonald's doesn't open until 7:00 A.M.
9. The new clinic on Long Street will soon open.
10. Most players have already signed contracts.

Part 5 Subjects in Unusual Positions

The subject of a sentence usually comes before the verb. In some sentences, however, part or all of the verb comes before the subject.

To find the subject in any sentence, first find the verb. Then ask *who* or *what* before it. The answer will be the subject.

Sentences Beginning with *There*

In sentences beginning with *there*, the verb often comes before the subject.

There is used in two different ways. It may be used to explain the verb. It tells where something is or happens.

> There are your gloves. (*Gloves* is the subject; *are* is the verb. *There* tells where your gloves are.)
>
> There is the exit. (*Exit* is the subject; *is* is the verb. *There* tells where the exit is.)

Sometimes *there* is used simply as an introductory word to help get the sentence started.

> There is a shortage of fuel in this country. (*Shortage* is the subject; *is* is the verb.)
>
> There are jobs available. (*Jobs* is the subject; *are* is the verb.)

To diagram sentences beginning with *there*, you must know if *there* tells *where* or is an introductory word. If *there* tells *where*, it belongs on a slanted line below the verb. If *there* is an introductory word, it belongs on a horizontal line above the subject.

> There stood the manager of the store.

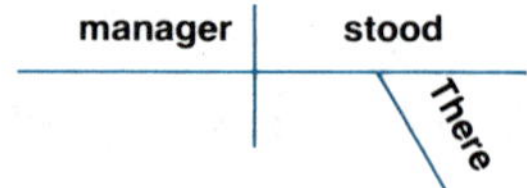

> There has been a mistake.

There

mistake | has been

Exercise A Write the subject and the verb in each sentence. Tell whether *there* is used to tell *where* or as an introductory word.

1. There is the joggers' path.
2. There will be a press conference.
3. There were some questions about the new schedule.
4. There is no excuse.
5. There is the new deadbolt lock.
6. There has been a change of plans.
7. There is the city's civic center.
8. There are the applications.
9. There is the toll booth.
10. There have been many recent medical advances.

Exercise B Follow the directions for Exercise A.

1. There is our canoe.
2. There is a simple solution.
3. There is the factory.
4. There is the pay phone.
5. There are your X-rays.
6. There will be special concerts.
7. There was a junior high reunion.
8. There are two new courses this year.
9. There is the dance floor.
10. There might be another election.

Other Sentences with Unusual Word Order

Sentences beginning with *there* are just one kind of sentence with unusual word order. Here are some others.

1. Sentences beginning with *here*

Here comes the parade. (*Parade* is the subject; *comes* is the verb.)

Here is your wallet. (*Wallet* is the subject; *is* is the verb.)

Unlike *there*, the word *here* always tells *where* about the verb.

2. Questions

Have you finished? (*You* is the subject; *have finished* is the verb.)
Will Kate be joining us? (*Kate* is the subject; *will be joining* is the verb.)

3. Sentences starting with phrases or other words

Slowly came her reply. (*Reply* is the subject; *came* is the verb.)
Around the curve raced the runners. (*Runners* is the subject; *raced* is the verb.)

To find the subject in a sentence with unusual word order, first find the verb. Then ask *who* or *what*.

Here are the scripts.
Verb: are
Who or what are? scripts
Subject: scripts

Unusual word order in a sentence does not change the sentence diagram. The verb and the subject are still placed on the horizontal main line with the subject first and then the verb.

Under the rock slithered the snake.

Sentences Giving Commands

In sentences that give commands, the subject is usually not stated. Since commands are always given to the person spoken to, the subject is *you*. Because *you* is not stated, we say that it is *understood*.

Repeat the question. (*You* is the subject of *repeat.*)
Draw a straight line. (*You* is the subject of *draw.*)

To diagram a sentence giving a command, place the subject *you* in parentheses.

Try again.

Exercise A Label two columns *Subject* and *Verb*. Number your paper from 1 to 10. Write the subject and verb for each sentence.

1. Tell another joke.
2. Here is a good book.
3. Have the plants been watered?
4. Here come the paramedics.
5. Give me that wrench.
6. Will you save a seat for me?
7. Enter through the side door.
8. Into the spotlight danced Marisa.
9. There are too many rules in this game.
10. Underneath my foot lay a dollar bill.

Exercise B Follow the directions for Exercise A.

1. In the distance swam a shark.
2. Have you seen Rod Stewart in concert?
3. Quickly came the answer.
4. Here are my old boots.
5. Here is a quick sketch.
6. Steadily came the drumbeat.
7. Eat a balanced diet.
8. Have you repaid your debt?
9. Do you need glasses?
10. Drive carefully.

Part 6 Objects of Verbs

Some verbs do not need other words to complete their meaning in a sentence. The action they describe is complete.

The players *rested.* The rain finally *stopped.*
Nathan *was worrying.* The T-shirt *will fade.*

Some verbs, though, do not express a complete meaning by themselves. They need other words to complete the meaning of a sentence.

Tony reserved _______. (Reserved what?)
The campers brought _______. (Brought what?)

Direct Objects

Tony reserved a *space.*
The campers brought *firewood.*

One kind of word that completes the action of a verb is called the **direct object.** A direct object receives the action of the verb. In the sentences above, *space* receives the action of *reserved. Firewood* receives the action of *brought.*

Sometimes the direct object tells the *result* of an action.

We drew *pictures.*
Keats composed a *poem.*

To find the direct object, first find the verb. Then ask *whom* or *what* after it.

Steve invited six friends.
Verb: invited
Invited whom: friends
Direct object: friends

Ann repaired the motorcycle.
Verb: repaired
Repaired what: motorcycle
Direct object: motorcycle

A verb that has a direct object is called a **transitive verb.** A verb that does not have a direct object is called an **intransitive verb.** Notice the difference in these sentences:

The sun *was shining.* (*Was shining* is intransitive. It has no direct object.)
Our teacher *gave* a lecture. (*Gave* is transitive. It has a direct object, *lecture.*)

A verb may be transitive in one sentence and intransitive in another.

Intransitive: Your sister called.
Transitive: Your sister called a taxi.

Transitive or Intransitive?

Look at the following sentences. Are the verbs transitive or intransitive?

Louise *left* early.
Louise *left* in the afternoon.
Louise *left* the room.

In the first two examples, the verb *left* has no direct object. In those sentences, *left* is intransitive. However, in the third sentence, if you ask *whom* or *what* after the verb, you find that *room* is the direct object. In that sentence, *left* is a transitive verb.

Louise left the room.
Verb: left
Left what: room
Direct object: room

Exercise A Number your paper from 1 to 10. For each sentence, write the direct object of the verb.

1. The actors studied their lines.
2. Mr. Mendez has opened a new business.

3. The sailors finally reached land.
4. In the morning, the workers will finish the project.
5. Please return my notebook.
6. I enjoyed the performance.
7. The attendant checked the carburetor.
8. Sara quickly smothered the flames.
9. The bus driver had nearly missed the exit.
10. On Saturdays, Keith washes cars.

Exercise B Number your paper from 1 to 10. Decide whether the verb in each sentence is *transitive* or *intransitive*.

1. My cousins visited yesterday.
2. She visited her friends.
3. Amy led an expedition.
4. The general led courageously.
5. Some hedges grow quickly.
6. Miles grows herbs.
7. Some members joined late.
8. A new worker joined the crew.
9. The foreman gives orders.
10. This blood donor gives frequently.

Indirect Objects

In addition to direct objects, some sentences also have **indirect objects** of the verb. Indirect objects sometimes tell *to whom* or *to what* about the verb. At other times they tell *for whom* or *for what* about the verb.

Jeff told **Marla** the *news*. (told *to* Marla)
The clerk sold **us** the wrong *battery*. (sold *to* us)
Carlos made **us** a Mexican *dinner*. (made *for* us)

In the sentences above, the words in bold type are the indirect objects. The words in italics are the direct objects. Indirect objects appear only in sentences with direct objects.

Indirect objects are found between the verb and direct object. Never use the words *to* and *for* with an indirect object.

> Andrew handed the *teller* his deposit. (*Teller* is the indirect object of *handed*.)
> Andrew handed his deposit to the *teller*. (*Teller* is not an indirect object.)

In a diagram, place a direct object on the main line after the verb. The vertical line between the verb and object does not go below the main line.

> Lana bought a hat.

The indirect object belongs on a horizontal line attached below the verb.

> Lana bought her brother a hat.

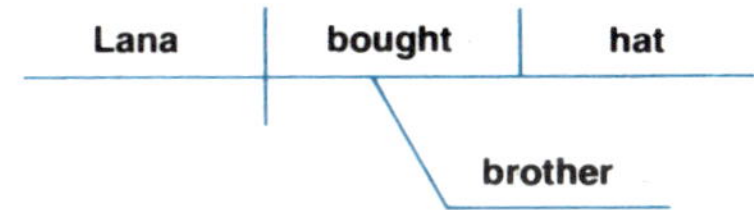

Exercise A Number your paper from 1 to 10. Label three columns *Verb, Indirect Object,* and *Direct Object.* For each sentence below, write down those parts. Not all sentences will have all three parts.

Example: We brought Wendy a gift.

Verb	Indirect Object	Direct Object
brought	Wendy	gift

1. Jonah handed Sarah her ticket.
2. The florist arranged the roses.
3. Diana Nyad told the reporters her story.
4. This store gives customers a discount.

5. Someone asked the boss a question.
6. The neighbors are repairing their porch.
7. Joe left the waitress a tip.
8. Many waitresses earn generous tips.
9. This restaurant has terrific chili.
10. The cook taught me his secret.

Exercise B Follow the directions for Exercise A.

1. Some restaurants serve children smaller portions.
2. The President announced his new policy.
3. The photographer used floodlights.
4. Ms. Orlando gave us more time for the test.
5. We repair engines in the machine shop.
6. The director gave the crew a signal.
7. Tom put sprouts on his salad.
8. The cafeteria serves pancakes for breakfast.
9. We poured syrup on our waffles.
10. That cartoonist drew us some funny portraits.

Part 7 Linking Verbs and Predicate Words

Some verbs do not express action. Instead, they tell of a state of being. These verbs link the subject of a sentence with a word or group of words in the predicate. Because they link the subject with some other word or words, they are often called **linking verbs.**

Jessica *is* a soprano. Thomas *must be* angry.
We *are* the winners. The typists *were* busy.

The verb *to be* is the most commonly used linking verb. *To be* can have many forms. This list will help you to become familiar with them:

be	been	is	was
being	am	are	were

The verbs *be*, *being*, and *been* can also be used with helping verbs. These are examples:

should be	were being	had been
may be	was being	could have been
will be	is being	might have been

The words linked to the subject by linking verbs like *to be* are called **predicate words.** The three kinds of predicate words are **predicate nouns, predicate pronouns,** and **predicate adjectives.** All of them tell something about the subject.

Brad is a *plumber*. (predicate noun)

That was *he*. (predicate pronoun)

Carlotta was *happy*. (predicate adjective)

In the above sentences, the subjects and predicate words are joined by the linking verbs *is* and *was*.

Here are some other common linking verbs.

appear	seem	sound	grow
feel	look	taste	become

Like *be*, these linking verbs have various forms (*grew*, *looked*, or *tastes*). They can be used with helping verbs, as in *will become*, *can seem*, or *might have sounded*.

The chair *looked* comfortable.

The varnish *felt* sticky.

Bruce *has become* an excellent gymnast.

In a sentence diagram, place a predicate word on the main line after the verb. A slanted line above the main line separates the verb from the predicate word. That line, like the predicate word, points back toward the subject.

Ms. Freeman is the new advisor.

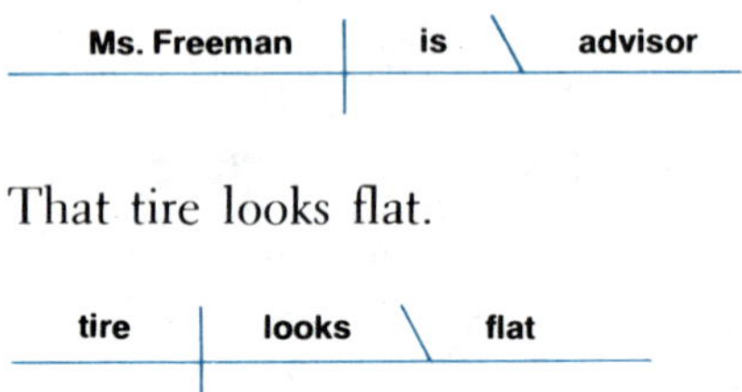

That tire looks flat.

Direct Object or Predicate Word?

A verb may be completed in one of two ways. It may have a direct object. Or it may have a predicate word. How can you tell the difference between a predicate word and a direct object?

The verb is the key word. Decide if the verb is an action verb. If so, the word following it that tells *whom* or *what* is a direct object.

The nurse comforted the patient. (*Comforted* is an action verb. *Patient* is its direct object.)

The ambulance rounded the *corner*. (*Rounded* is an action verb. *Corner* is its direct object.)

Is the verb a linking verb? If so, the word following it that tells about the subject is a predicate word.

David Brenner is a *comedian*. (*Is* is a linking verb. *Comedian* is a predicate word.)

These French fries seem *soggy*. (*Seem* is a linking verb. *Soggy* is a predicate word.)

Look at the following sentences:

Phil Rogers is a *welder*.
Phil Rogers hired a *welder*.

The first sentence has a linking verb, *is*. The word *welder* follows the linking verb and tells about the subject. It is a predicate word. In the second sentence, *hired* is an action verb. In this sentence, *welder* tells *whom* about the action verb. It is a direct object.

Exercise A Label three columns *Subject, Linking Verb,* and *Predicate Word.* Find these parts in the sentences below and place them in the proper columns.

1. Those headlights are dim.
2. The band sounded great.
3. Students were the performers.
4. The skits were hilarious.
5. Curry tastes hot.
6. The sky appeared pink.
7. Kim must feel miserable.
8. The guide is she.
9. Tracy will become president.
10. Roller skates have become popular.

Exercise B Make four columns on your paper. Head the columns *Subject, Verb, Direct Object,* and *Predicate Word.* Find these parts in the sentences below and place them in the right columns. Remember, no sentence can contain both a direct object *and* a predicate word.

1. Janet Gregory is a Congresswoman.
2. Her home is Alaska.
3. First, she was a Congressional aide.
4. That job gave her experience.
5. She ran several unsuccessful campaigns.
6. Finally, she became a legislator.
7. She seems fair.
8. She makes wise decisions.
9. She favors changes in the tax laws.
10. Her district supports her strongly.

Part 8 Compound Parts in a Sentence

The word *compound* means "having two or more parts." Each of the sentence parts described so far in this section can be compound—subjects, verbs, direct objects, indirect objects, and predicate words.

Two parts in a compound form are joined by a conjunction (*and*, *or*, *but*). In a compound form of three or more parts, the conjunction usually comes between the last two parts.

Diagraming Compound Subjects

To diagram compound subjects, split the subject line. Place the conjunction on a dotted line connecting the subjects.

Marshmallows, nuts, and cherries covered the sundae.

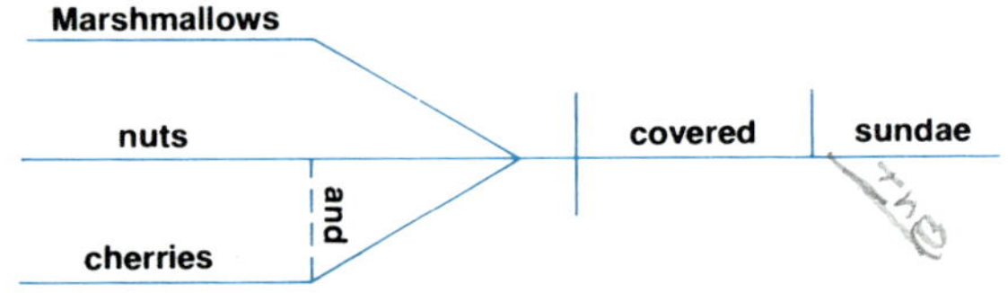

Diagraming Compound Verbs

To diagram compound verbs, split the verb line in the same way.

The crowd booed, hissed, and whistled.

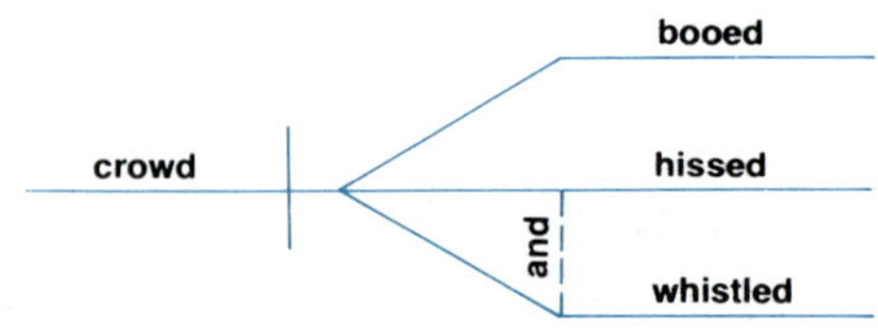

Diagraming Compound Objects

To diagram compound direct objects or indirect objects, split the object line.

Gonzales hit a homer and two singles. (compound direct object)

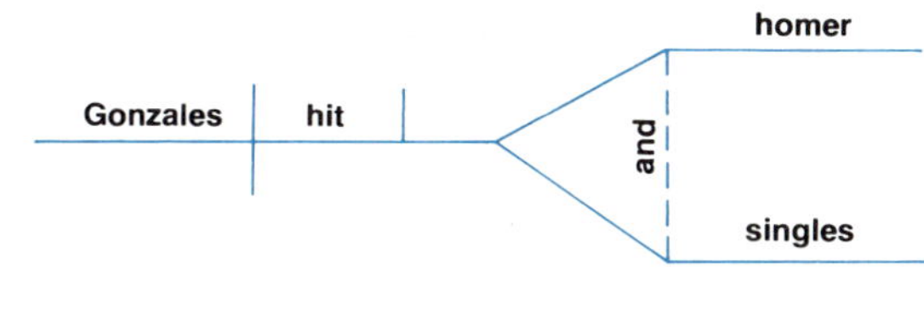

The director gave Brendon and Sandra lead roles. (compound indirect object)

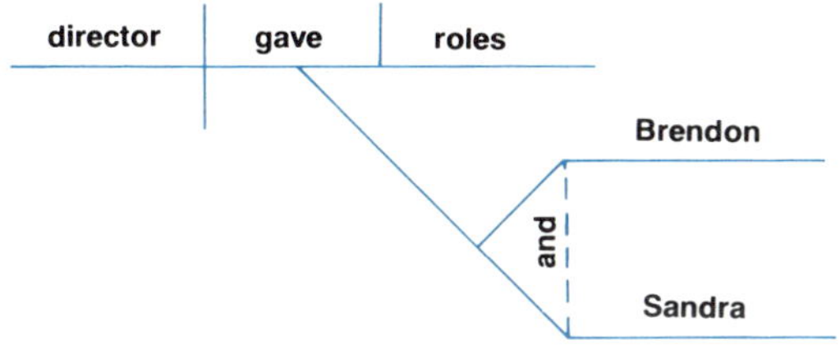

Diagraming Compound Predicate Words

To diagram compound predicate words, split the predicate word line.

The new coaches are Brock and Rudolph. (compound predicate word)

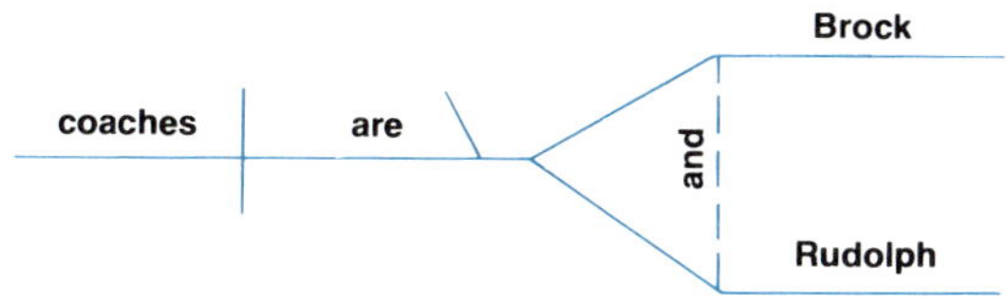

Exercise A As your teacher directs, show the compound parts in the following sentences. Tell whether they are compound subjects, verbs, objects, or predicate words.

1. The Soviet Union and the United States produce the most coal.
2. Coal is plentiful and inexpensive.
3. In strip mines, machines remove earth and rock.
4. In other mines, workers and equipment dig coal underground.
5. Miners cut, drill, and blast.
6. Cars or belts take the coal to the surface.
7. Machines wash and sort the coal at a plant.
8. Two mining problems are ventilation and support.
9. Sometimes walls weaken and collapse.
10. Gases and dust in coal mines may be explosive.

Exercise B For each of the following sentences, make the part noted in parentheses compound. Write the new sentences.

Example: The baby scooted across the floor. (*verb*)
The baby scooted and wriggled across the floor.

1. Sharon wrote several plays. (*direct object*)
2. The audience watched carefully. (*verb*)
3. The chairs were broken. (*subject*)
4. The Coast Guard patrols the lakes. (*direct object*)
5. The owner made a good profit. (*subject*)
6. Our car sputtered down the driveway. (*verb*)
7. Their creative Halloween costumes were colorful. (*predicate word*)
8. The music told a story. (*subject*)
9. The teacher told the parents her goals for the coming year. (*indirect object*)
10. The picnickers brought a grill. (*direct object*)

Part 9 Kinds of Sentences

There are several different reasons for using sentences. Sometimes you want to state something. Sometimes you want to ask a question. At other times, you want to give a command. There are also times when you want to express strong feeling. In each case, you use a different kind of sentence.

A **declarative sentence** is used to make a statement. It ends with a period (.).

> The young woman waited patiently.
> We watched the game on TV.

An **interrogative sentence** asks a question. It ends with a question mark (?).

> Has the wrestling meet begun? What time is it?

An **imperative sentence** gives a command. It ends with a period.

> Wait for the signal. Save me a seat, please.

An **exclamatory sentence** expresses strong emotion. It ends with an exclamation point (!).

> You ruined everything! What a day this has been!

Exercise A For each of the following sentences, write *Declarative, Interrogative, Imperative,* or *Exclamatory* to show what kind each is. Add the proper punctuation mark.

1. Are you going to a trade school
2. Turn off the lights
3. I live on the thirteenth floor
4. Do the elevators work
5. What a long climb that would be
6. Don't leave the windows open

7. This door has four locks
8. Where is the fire escape
9. Pick a card
10. The subway runs on electricity

Exercise B Follow the directions for Exercise A.

1. When is the next game
2. Sheila plays the drums
3. I enjoy club activities
4. Are you avoiding me
5. What a view this is
6. Use the dictionary
7. Where do you go to school
8. What a blaze that was
9. Who is your employer
10. Brian's application was accepted

Part 10 Basic Sentence Patterns

Words can be organized into sentences in an endless number of ways. However, most sentences follow certain basic **sentence patterns.** The five patterns that follow are the most common ones.

Study each sentence pattern carefully. Try to think of an example of your own for each pattern.

Pattern One

This is the basic type of sentence. It has a subject and a verb. The subject is usually a noun or pronoun. In this chart, *N* stands for the noun (or pronoun) in the complete subject. V stands for the verb in the complete predicate.

N	V
Fashions	change.
We	worked hard.
The weekend	goes quickly.
The young man	danced gracefully.

Pattern Two

In this pattern, the noun (or pronoun) that follows the verb is a direct object.

N	V	N
The manager	opened	the store.
Marian	found	her old mitt.
Police	named	a suspect.
The coach	helped	us.

Pattern Three

Two nouns follow the verb in this pattern. The first is an *indirect object*. The second is a *direct object*.

N	V	N	N
Steve	slipped	me	a note.
Nobody	could give	us	directions.
The mayor	told	the reporters	his plans.

Pattern Four

The verb in this pattern is a *linking verb* (LV). The noun that follows it is a *predicate noun* (or predicate pronoun).

N	LV	N
The experiment	was	a success.
Carpentry	is	a trade.
This cap	is	mine.

Pattern Five

In this sentence pattern, a linking verb is followed by a *predicate adjective* (Adj).

N	LV	Adj
Ice hockey	is	rough.
The gears	seem	stiff.
This route	should be	direct.

Exercise A Tell which sentence pattern is used in each sentence.

1. Lopez was the victor.
2. The workers called a strike.
3. Jobs were scarce.
4. The fish are fresh.
5. David works hard.
6. Rhoda gave Leslie a hint.
7. Eric photographed the skyline.
8. K-Mart is a discount store.
9. That request seems unfair.
10. A tornado hit.

Exercise B Follow the directions for Exercise A.

1. The game ended early.
2. That dessert looks rich.
3. We handed the usher our tickets.
4. Meredith delivers pizzas.
5. Beth told Jim her worries.
6. Computers have become necessary.
7. This check is a forgery.
8. Erica slept late.
9. Dense fog is a hazard.
10. The doctor taped Jason's ankle.

REVIEW The Sentence and Its Parts

The Parts of a Sentence Write the subject and verb for each of the following sentences. If there is a direct object, indirect object, or predicate word in any sentence, write that part, too. Identify each part.

1. Truckers from all over gathered at Mel's.
2. The Navy was recruiting here.
3. Tony had recently sold his car.
4. You may certainly react differently.
5. There will be several new courses.
6. Here is a secret compartment.
7. Has Amy proved her point?
8. Beside our house sits a tractor.
9. Fry the eggs for five minutes.
10. The bank gave Lyle a loan.
11. Your teeth are perfectly straight.
12. This station sounds clear.
13. Our truck makes pick-ups and deliveries.
14. Egypt and Israel have held talks.
15. We washed and dried clothes at the laundromat.

Kinds of Sentences Decide whether the following sentences are *Declarative, Interrogative, Imperative,* or *Exclamatory.* Write your answer. Also write what punctuation mark should be used at the end of each sentence.

16. What does this code mean
17. Please fill this order
18. What a gossip he is
19. Plumbers charge an hourly rate
20. Move with the music

Using Complete Sentences

Sentences communicate ideas and feelings. When they are well composed, sentences get your ideas across clearly and completely.

Sometimes, however, people put words together in a confusing way. Then the message gets jumbled or lost.

One cause of confusion is leaving out part of a sentence. The remaining group of words is a **sentence fragment.** Another problem is created when two or more sentences are written as one. This group of words is called a **run-on sentence.**

Both of these writing errors weaken communication. In this section you will learn how to avoid them.

Part 1 What Is a Sentence Fragment?

A group of words that is only part of a sentence is a **sentence fragment.** A sentence fragment does not express a complete thought.

A fragment is confusing because something is missing from the sentence. Sometimes the subject is left out. Then the reader wonders *who* or *what* the sentence is about. At other times the verb is left out. Then the reader wonders *what happened?* or *what about it?*

Fragment: Shifted into fourth gear. (Who shifted? The subject is missing.)

Sentence: The speeding trucker shifted into fourth gear.

Fragment: The quarterback near the ten-yard line. (What happened? The verb is missing.)

Sentence: The quarterback fumbled near the ten-yard line.

Fragments Due to Incomplete Thoughts

Sometimes a writer is in a hurry. He or she jots down only bits of ideas. These ideas are incomplete. The writer's pen doesn't keep up with his or her flow of thoughts.

Maybe the writer understands these pieces of ideas. However, to a reader they will probably seem unclear.

Here is an example of a series of fragments:

> Cars in line for gasoline. On some days are not open. Price of a gallon of gas up sharply.

These complete sentences show what the writer meant:

> Cars wait in line for gasoline at many service stations. On some days no stations are open. The price of a gallon of gas has risen sharply.

Fragments Due to Incorrect Punctuation

All sentences end with punctuation marks. The mark may be a period, a question mark, or an exclamation point. Sometimes a writer uses one of these punctuation marks too soon. The idea is incomplete. A sentence fragment results.

Fragment: Cars with brake problems. Were recalled by General Motors.
Sentence: Cars with brake problems were recalled by General Motors.

Fragment: On a hot July afternoon. Crowds jammed the beaches.
Sentence: On a hot July afternoon crowds jammed the beaches.

Fragment: A diver freed a baby whale. From a fishing net.
Sentence: A diver freed a baby whale from a fishing net.

Exercise A For each group of words that is a sentence, write *S* on your paper. For each sentence fragment, write *F*. Be ready to add words to change the fragments into sentences.

1. A TV show about police work
2. A new series will begin this season
3. Several young actors
4. The director offers advice
5. Scenery, props, and sound effects
6. Will be seen on Monday evenings at 7 P.M.
7. Each episode has a chase scene
8. A stunt person jumps from a building
9. Each scene is filmed several times
10. Usually ends with an arrest

Exercise B Follow the directions for Exercise A.

1. Greg ordered a root beer float
2. His sister worked behind the counter

3. Forty-two flavors of ice cream
4. The movie begins at eight o'clock
5. Teenagers gathered outside
6. Endless rows of bright street lights
7. The police car raced after a speeder
8. Sitting on the porch in the cool evening
9. Potholes in the road
10. Carly Simon writes the lyrics for some of her songs

Part 2 What Is a Run-on Sentence?

A **run-on sentence** is two or more sentences written incorrectly as one.

A run-on confuses the reader. It does not show where the first idea ends and the second one begins. The reader needs a period or other punctuation mark to signal the end of each complete thought. Here are some examples:

Run-on: A motorcycle turned into the alley it skidded on the gravel.
Correct: A motorcycle turned into the alley. It skidded on the gravel.

Run-on: Tom likes disco music Carla likes a Latin beat.
Correct: Tom likes disco music. Carla likes a Latin beat.

Sometimes writers make the mistake of using a comma instead of a period. Again, the result is a run-on.

Run-on: The rookie running back carried the ball, he made a touchdown.
Correct: The rookie running back carried the ball. He made a touchdown.

Run-on: The floats were ready, the parade could begin.
Correct: The floats were ready. The parade could begin.

Exercise A Correct the following run-on sentences.

1. Some radio stations have powerful signals, they can be heard in nearby states.
2. One disc jockey reads letters from listeners he also jokes with callers.
3. Several stations hold contests, prizes are often albums.
4. Tanya won one contest she named a song correctly.
5. The sound equipment is complex, few people could operate it.
6. The Reds won the pennant they will play in the World Series.
7. Rod Carew hit a line drive, the centerfielder caught it.
8. Tony has a set of barbells he lifts weights every day.
9. We saw an old Hitchcock film, it was a classic thriller.
10. Megan hung another poster she has nearly covered her walls.

Exercise B Follow the directions for Exercise A.

1. Lou painted his car, first he sanded it.
2. The racecar driver pulled off the track the pit crew went into action.
3. The expressway is being repaired all lanes are closed.
4. Heavy machinery is blocking the street a worker is directing traffic.
5. Owen works at this station he works four days a week.
6. Gail attached brackets to the wall, she used toggle bolts.
7. The picnic is scheduled for Saturday, sunny weather is predicted.
8. Steve comes from a very large family he has three brothers and four sisters.
9. The hospital staff works on shifts, there are three shifts of eight hours each.
10. A loud noise startled the hikers, a dead tree had fallen.

REVIEW Using Complete Sentences

Sentences, Sentence Fragments, and Run-on Sentences
Number your paper from 1 to 20. Identify each of the following groups of words as a *Fragment, Sentence,* or *Run-on.*

1. Rachel repairs cars in her spare time
2. Ray Simpson was a back-up singer he joined the Village People
3. An overturned truck blocked traffic
4. A nationally known cartoonist
5. Steve types at a fast pace
6. Draws sketches with charcoal
7. The cook grilled two hamburgers
8. Tony tried to skate, he ended up with a sprained arm
9. The apartment on the fourth floor
10. A subway train sped past
11. Led the group in exercises to the music
12. A German neighborhood held a fall festival
13. Larry was trained as a welder, he learned the skills quickly
14. A pipe burst water flooded the basement
15. A part-time job at the grocery store
16. The school district sponsors adult classes, many courses are offered
17. A movie with a surprise ending
18. The horoscope in the daily paper
19. The lights went out everyone lit candles
20. The opening game of the football season

HANDBOOK SECTION 3

Using Nouns

Good, clear sentences are not accidents. They result from understanding how words work.

The words used in sentences fall into certain groups or classes. You can talk and write without knowing these labels. However, skilled speakers and writers understand the different classes of words.

In this section you will learn about one important group of words: nouns.

Part 1 What Are Nouns?

You use words to name the people, places, and things around you. Words that name are called **nouns.**

A noun is a word used to name a person, place, or thing.

Nouns name things that can be seen, like cities, streets, furniture, and books. They name things you cannot see, such as feelings, ideas, and beliefs.

Persons: landlord, Greg, Anne Murray, actor
Places: Wyoming, kitchen, Savannah, hotel
Things: blanket, mirror, energy, concern

Exercise Make three columns on a sheet of paper. Label them *Names of Persons, Names of Places,* and *Names of Things.* Find the nouns in the following paragraph. List each one in the proper column.

Thirty years ago Frisbees began as tin plates from pies. The plates came from the Frisbee Baking Company in Connecticut. People played with the plates. Now the game is not just play. Frisbee has become a sport. The championships are held in Pasadena. Entrants compete in five events. Players even come from other countries.

Proper Nouns and Common Nouns

How do these two italicized nouns differ?

One *sailor, George Ruiz,* jumped from the ship.

The word *sailor* is a general term. It refers to many people. It is a common noun. A common noun is a general name.

The noun *George Ruiz,* on the other hand, refers to only one person. It is a **proper noun.** A proper noun is a specific name.

A common noun is the name of a whole group of persons, places, or things. It is a name that is common to the group.

A proper noun is the name of a particular person, place, or thing. It is capitalized.

Look at the following examples of common nouns and proper nouns. As you can see, some nouns are made up of more than one word.

Common Nouns	Proper Nouns
magazine	*Sports Illustrated*
mountain	Mount Everest
cartoonist	Gary Trudeau
game	Super Bowl
city	Burlington
senator	Senator Hayakawa

Exercise A Make two columns on your paper. Label one column *Common Nouns* and the other *Proper Nouns*. Place each of the following nouns in the correct column. Capitalize all proper nouns.

1. holiday inn, motel, seabreeze motel, shores hotel
2. restaurant, diner, burger king, cafeteria
3. singer, lou rawls, album, willie nelson, ballad
4. allentown, town, village, ridgeville, asheville
5. court, judge, judge ellen rodriguez, jury
6. nation, new zealand, spain, country, canada
7. airlines, trans world airlines, united airlines, airport
8. evanston hospital, hospital, clinic, sheridan dental clinic
9. first national bank, bank, banker, robert abboud, continental bank
10. team, dallas cowboys, manager, cheerleader

Exercise B Write five sentences of your own, using at least one proper noun in each sentence.

Part 2 How Are Nouns Used?

Nouns Used as Subjects

As you learned in **Section 1**, the subject of a sentence tells who or what is being talked about. Nouns are frequently used as subjects.

Scientists can predict earthquakes. (The noun *scientists* is the subject of the verb *can predict*.)

Ace Hardware in Bellwood sponsors our bowling team. (The noun *Ace Hardware* is the subject of the verb *sponsors*. Notice that in this sentence, the subject is not next to the verb.)

Two or more nouns may form a compound subject.

The *divers* and *crew* planned the voyage carefully. (The nouns *divers* and *crew* are the subject of the verb *planned*.)

The *bus* and the *truck* collided in the intersection. (The nouns *bus* and *truck* are the subject of the verb *collided*.)

Exercise A Number your paper from 1 to 10. Write the nouns used as the subjects of these sentences.

1. A factory dumps wastes into this river.
2. The comedian told terrible jokes.
3. The workers organized a car pool.
4. That legend has been told for centuries.
5. The networks and newspapers cover sports events.
6. Many businesses need computers.
7. Vanessa and Nicole have applied for jobs.
8. Sara's wages have gone up each year.
9. Jon has been saving money for a motorcycle.
10. Many families are cutting their expenses.

Exercise B Follow the directions for Exercise A.

1. The cost of movie tickets has risen.
2. Sharon tape-records her friends' albums.
3. Many employees eat in the cafeteria.
4. Shoppers looked for bargains at the sale.
5. The photographer printed her film.
6. A group of soldiers patrolled the shore.
7. The explorers plunged into the wilderness.
8. Ansel Adams is a fine photographer.
9. Lynn and Rice are powerful sluggers.
10. The Russian spacelab returned to earth.

Nouns Used as Direct Objects

A direct object completes the action of a verb. It answers *whom* or *what* about the verb. Nouns are frequently used as direct objects.

The magician fooled the *audience*. (The noun *audience* tells *whom* about the verb *fooled*.)

In the shop class the students wear *goggles*. (The noun *goggles* tells *what* about the verb *wear*.)

Roger shaped *mugs* and a *pitcher* out of clay. (Both the nouns *mugs* and *pitcher* are direct objects. They tell *what* about the verb *shaped*.

Exercise A As your teacher directs, write the nouns used as direct objects in the following sentences.

1. Danielle pounded the ball for a home run.
2. Jim has a short, flat swing.
3. Weight-training built Reed's strength.
4. City folks wear boots, too.
5. Todd reads *Time* every week.

6. That apartment has no heat.
7. Josh piled blankets onto the bed.
8. Will made his own drums.
9. The truckers load crates at the warehouse.
10. Carrie plays softball and basketball.

Exercise B Follow the directions for Exercise A.

1. Britt took a trip to San Francisco.
2. The judge instructed the jury.
3. The company hired a lawyer.
4. Our family has medical insurance.
5. Customers must pay the cashier.
6. That used car has a radio and whitewalls.
7. Kim put radial tires on her car.
8. Bryant tackled the quarterback.
9. The lifeguard rescued two young children.
10. Woods line the coast of Maine.

Nouns Used as Indirect Objects

Another use of the noun is as an **indirect object.** The indirect object tells *to whom* or *for whom* or *to what* or *for what* about the verb.

> The coach showed the *quarterback* a new play. (The noun *quarterback* is the indirect object. It tells *to whom* about the verb *showed*.)

> Sarah gave the *bookcase* and the *shelves* another coat of varnish. (The nouns *bookcase* and *shelves* are the compound indirect object, telling *to what* about the verb *gave*.)

An indirect object is used only with a direct object. The indirect object appears before the direct object in the sentence.

Subject	Verb	Indirect Object(s)	Direct Object
Gail	showed	the cabbie	the route.
Leslie	fed	the dog	its food.
Dairy Queen	offered	Jim and Alice	jobs.

As you have seen, the word *to* or *for* is never used with an indirect object.

Exercise A Find the nouns used as indirect objects in the following sentences.

1. Mr. Scott gave Bonita her paycheck.
2. Police read the suspect his rights.
3. Kent gave the operator the number.
4. The store sent Ms. Alvarez a bill.
5. Sheila handed the teller her deposit.
6. The catcher gave the pitcher a signal.
7. Mark showed Michelle the rabbit's nest.
8. Suzanne gave Les and Maureen her new address.
9. The waiter handed each diner a menu.
10. Andy Kaufman told the audience a joke.

Exercise B Follow the directions for Exercise A.

1. The manager gave Kim a promotion.
2. The coach gave her team a workout.
3. Carolyn handed the conductor her ticket.
4. Debbie made her sister a club sandwich.
5. Cal owes Steve six dollars.
6. Jenny loaned Erin a dress for the dance.
7. Don gives his brother his old clothes.
8. The commander gave Phil his orders.
9. The doctor gave her patient some advice.
10. The interviewer asked the President a tough question about inflation.

Nouns Used as Predicate Words

Sometimes a noun in the predicate part of a sentence is linked to the subject. That noun is called a **predicate noun.** It always follows a linking verb. It means the same thing as the subject.

Carlos was a carpenter's *assistant.*

The counselors were former *teachers.*

Two early autos were the *Model T* and the *Model* A.

The nouns *assistant, teachers, Model T,* and *Model* A are predicate nouns.

Exercise A Find the nouns used as predicate nouns in the following sentences.

1. Canada is the birthplace of ice hockey.
2. The Freeport team is our strongest rival.
3. Saturday is the best day for a party.
4. British coins are shillings and pence.
5. Tyrone's last game was a no-hitter.
6. Pauline is an Olympic contender.
7. Mr. Johnson became the varsity coach.
8. Carl's sister is a bus driver in the city.
9. Gary's construction job is hard work.
10. The running backs were Earl Campbell and Walter Payton.

Exercise B Follow the directions for Exercise A.

1. Many young people will someday become parents.
2. Richard Pryor was the host of the talk show.
3. The Loop is the central area of downtown Chicago.
4. The stars of the movie were Bo Derek, Dudley Moore, and Julie Andrews.

5. Two parts of a brake are the drum and the shoe.
6. Cornelia Street is the subway's last stop.
7. The Marx brothers were comic actors.
8. "Satchmo" was Louis Armstrong's nickname.
9. The Steelers are tough defensive players.
10. *The High and the Mighty* was the late movie last night.

Part 3 The Plurals of Nouns

When a noun names one thing, it is singular. When a noun names more than one thing, it is plural.

Here are some rules for forming the plurals of nouns.

1. To form the plural of most nouns, just add *s*:

prizes dreams circles stations

2. When the singular noun ends in *s, sh, ch, x,* or *z,* add es:

waitresses brushes ditches axes buzzes

3. When the singular noun ends in *o,* add *s*:

solos halos studios photos pianos

For a few words ending in *o*, add *es:*

heroes tomatoes potatoes echoes cargoes

4. When a singular noun ends in *y* with a consonant before it, change the *y* to *i* and add es:

army—armies candy—candies baby—babies

When a vowel (*a*, *e*, *i*, *o*, *u*) comes before the *y*, do not change the *y* to *i*. Just add *s*:

boy—boys way—ways jockey—jockeys

5. For some nouns ending in *f*, add *s* to make the plural:

roofs chiefs reefs beliefs

For many nouns ending in *f* or *fe*, change the *f* to *v* and add *s* or *es*. Since there is no rule to follow, you will have to memorize such words. Here are some examples:

life—lives	calf—calves	knife—knives
thief—thieves	shelf—shelves	loaf—loaves

6. Some nouns have the same form for both singular and plural. They must be memorized.

deer sheep moose salmon trout

7. Some nouns form their plurals in special ways. They, too, must be memorized.

man—men	tooth—teeth	ox—oxen
woman—women	mouse—mice	foot—feet
goose—geese	child—children	louse—lice

Dictionaries show the plural of a word if it is formed in an unusual way. Here is a dictionary entry for the noun *duty*. The entry shows the plural, *duties*.

du·ty (do͞ot′ē, dyo͞ot′ē) ***n.**, pl.* **-ties** [< Anglo-Fr. *dueté*, what is due: see DUE & -TY[1]] **1.** obedience or respect that is due to parents, older people, etc. **2.** something that one ought to do because it is thought to be morally right or necessary [the *duty* of a citizen to vote] **3.** any action required by one's occupation or position [her *duties* include writing the reports] **4.** a sense of obligation [*duty* calls] **5.** service, esp. military service **6.** a payment due to the government, esp. a tax on imports, exports, etc. **7.** service or use: see HEAVY-DUTY —**on** (or **off**) **duty** at (or having time off from) one's work or duty

Use the dictionary if you have a question about plurals.

Exercise A Write the plural of each of these nouns. Then use your dictionary to see if you are right.

1. leaf	6. sky	11. echo	16. spy
2. year	7. knife	12. tomato	17. goose
3. deer	8. tooth	13. bunch	18. hoof
4. holiday	9. radio	14. window	19. wish
5. coach	10. fox	15. moose	20. copy

Exercise B Write each sentence. Correct the errors in plural forms of nouns.

1. The childs were told not to play ball in the alleys.
2. The donkeys carried pouchs of gold.
3. Several tooths from sharkes were found on the beachs.
4. These forkes and knifes are scratched.
5. Basketball hoops are ten foots from the floor.
6. Basketes measure eighteen inchs across.
7. Both halfs of the court have basketes.
8. There are many types of passs and shots in the game.
9. Many large citys have pro teames.
10. Bill Russell and Wilt Chamberlain are my heros.

Part 4 The Possessives of Nouns

Nouns can indicate possession or ownership.

Mr. Lowe's car   a farmer's land   Betty's keys

Nouns can show that something is part of a person.

Meg's sense of humor   Harold's concern

The 's makes the above nouns show ownership. Words like *farmer's*, *Meg's*, and *Harold's* are called **possessive nouns.**

Usually, people and animals possess things. Sometimes, however, things are also used in the possessive. We speak of a *week's wages*, *a day's work*, or *a city's growth*.

Forming Possessives

There are three rules for forming the possessive of nouns.

1. If the noun is singular, add an apostrophe (') and s.

Amanda—Amanda's arm
Ross—Ross's desk

2. If the noun is plural and ends in s, add just the apostrophe.

artists—artists' studios   Spencers—Spencers' home

3. If the noun is plural but does not end in s, add an apostrophe and s.

women—women's discussion   people—people's choice

Exercise A Write the possessive form of each of these nouns.

1. mayor	6. ranch	11. car	16. admiral
2. Meg	7. child	12. Charles	17. Jenny
3. country	8. player	13. runner	18. salesperson
4. senator	9. Penny	14. store	19. boss
5. today	10. host	15. secretary	20. Linda

Exercise B Follow the directions for Exercise A.

1. people	6. guests	11. mice	16. families
2. fans	7. friends	12. wives	17. men
3. brothers	8. women	13. workers	18. clerks
4. hours	9. doctors	14. sheep	19. islands
5. experts	10. teachers	15. Jacksons	20. bodies

Exercise C Write the possessive form for each italicized word.

1. The *Bears* lineup looks strong.
2. *Jerry* car needs new shock absorbers.
3. *Tuesday* game features the Steelers and the Cowboys.
4. The *voters* choice is Ms. Marie Tonelli.
5. Reynolds beat the other *racers* times.
6. *Louis* pass landed in the end zone.
7. The assistant *state* attorney met with the reporters.
8. The *children* zoo has baby animals.
9. Everyone watched the *astronauts* splashdown.
10. *Donna* neighborhood has a softball league.

REVIEW Using Nouns

Recognizing Nouns List the nouns in each of the following sentences. Be sure to capitalize each proper noun that you list.

1. The hurricane tore through cuba and haiti.
2. The ship docked in milwaukee after a tour of lake michigan.
3. Mr. rodriguez identified the thief from a photograph.
4. On monday, Lee polished the chrome on her bike.
5. The firefighters and police were on strike in new york.

Nouns Used in Sentences Decide how each italicized noun is used in each sentence. Write the word and label it *Subject, Direct Object, Indirect Object,* or *Predicate Noun.*

6. Jody received a *telegram* on her birthday.
7. Bill showed his *friends* the winning lottery ticket.
8. *Kara* took photos at the ceremony.
9. The accident was a head-on *collision*.
10. The *Yankees* tallied four *runs* during the fifth inning.

Forming Plurals Write the plural form of each noun.

11. match
12. life
13. class
14. time
15. rodeo
16. story
17. trout
18. cargo
19. victory
20. ax
21. thief
22. studio
23. pony
24. half
25. joy

Forming Possessives Write the possessive form of each noun.

26. Richard
27. scientists
28. pitcher
29. captain
30. Nicholas
31. drivers
32. critic
33. actress
34. grandchildren
35. companies

Using Pronouns

If you only had nouns to refer to people, places, and things, you would have to express an idea like this:

> Andy strummed Andy's guitar and sang the lyrics that Andy had written.

Luckily, you can avoid such awkward sentences. Instead of nouns, you can use **pronouns.** Then you can say:

> Andy strummed *his* guitar and sang the lyrics that *he* had written.

Notice how the words *his* and *he* take the place of the noun *Andy*. These pronouns convey the same meaning in a direct way.

Part 1 Personal Pronouns

A pronoun is a word used in place of a noun. Pronouns are very helpful words. They may be used in three situations:

1. They may refer to the person speaking.

   I pole-vault. *We* played cards.

2. They may refer to the person spoken to.

   You tune *your* own car, don't *you?*

3. They may refer to other people, places, or things.

   She asked *him* a question. *They* opened *their* mail.

The examples above show that a pronoun often refers to a person. For that reason, the largest group of pronouns is called **personal pronouns.**

There are many variations of personal pronouns. Like nouns, personal pronouns may be singular or plural. In the following chart, see how personal pronouns change from singular to plural.

Singular:	I	me	my, mine
	you	you	your, yours
	he, she, it	him, her, it	his, her, hers, its
Plural:	we	us	our, ours
	you	you	your, yours
	they	them	their, theirs

As the chart shows, most plural pronouns are totally different from their singular forms. Notice these examples:

Singular	Plural
I escaped.	*We* escaped.
Stop *her*!	Stop *them*!
It fell.	*They* fell.

Exercise A Number your paper from 1 to 10. Write the pronouns used in place of nouns in these sentences. After each pronoun, write the noun or nouns it stands for.

1. A crane lifted the boulder and loaded it onto a truck.
2. Beth and George parked their motorcycles.
3. The hailstones bounced as they landed.
4. The politician repeated his promises.
5. "I have hay fever," complained Jason.
6. Marietta uses her hands when she talks.
7. The dancers rehearsed for their performance.
8. The paramedics arrived. They took charge.
9. The mirror shattered when it dropped.
10. Susan, did you get a checking account?

Exercise B Follow the directions for Exercise A.

1. Joel and Christina held a garage sale in their driveway.
2. The doctor made her rounds.
3. Barry took the wreck and made it run.
4. Kate met Steve and walked home with him.
5. The little girl stuck out her tongue.
6. The passengers had their luggage searched.
7. Sonia and Brett brought popcorn with them to the movies.
8. An usher directed Ellen to her seat.
9. "Have you ever tasted anchovies?" Laurel asked Richard.
10. Alison bought a Pepsi and drank it with her lunch.

Part 2 The Forms of Pronouns

Pronouns can be used in all the ways that nouns are used. Personal pronouns can be subjects, objects, predicate words, and possessives.

However, a personal pronoun changes forms as its use in a sentence changes. Look at these sentences:

He pitched. (*He* is the subject.)
Riley tagged *him*. (*Him* is the direct object.)
His pitch was wild. (*His* shows possession.)

The three pronouns in these examples all refer to the same person. The forms, though, are different.

The three forms of a personal pronoun are **subject form, object form,** and **possessive form.** Here are the forms for all the personal pronouns:

	Subject	Object	Possessive
Singular:	I	me	my, mine
	you	you	your, yours
	he, she, it	her, him, it	his, her, hers, its
Plural:	we	us	our, ours
	you	you	your, yours
	they	them	their, theirs

Exercise The following sentences use different forms of pronouns correctly. Read each sentence aloud.

1. *We* reported the accident.
2. A blizzard halted *us*.
3. Did *you* endorse *your* check?
4. Wendy and *she* showed *their* identification.
5. The editorial convinced *me*.
6. That was *he*.
7. *They* served on a jury.
8. The camera is *his*.
9. *I* went fishing with Joe and *her*.
10. The dog gnawed *its* bone.
11. *Our* car bumped *her* bike.
12. Sandy makes candles and sells *them*.

13. The next dance is *yours*.
14. The pleasure was *mine*.
15. The car dealer sold *him* a Fiesta.

The Subject Form of Pronouns

Subject Pronouns

I	we
you	you
he, she, it	they

For the subject of a sentence, the subject form of the personal pronoun is used. These sentences use the subject form for the subject:

They laughed and sang. *He* punted the ball.
She carried the boxes. *I* drew a map.

Using pronouns as subjects usually causes few problems. A more troublesome use, though, is the predicate pronoun. A predicate pronoun is a pronoun that is linked with the subject. It follows a linking verb, just as a predicate noun does.

Look at these examples of predicate pronouns:

That must be *she*. (*She* is a predicate pronoun used after the linking verb *must be*.)

The caller was *he*. (*He* is a predicate pronoun used after the linking verb *was*.)

As you see, the subject forms of pronouns are used for predicate pronouns. That form may not sound natural at first. If you are in doubt about which form to use, try reversing the subject and the predicate pronoun. The sentence should still sound correct.

The singer was *she*.
She was the singer.

Here are more examples of the correct use of the subject form for predicate pronouns:

That was *he* on the phone.
Was it *she* at the door?
The winner was *she*.

Always use the subject form for subjects and predicate pronouns.

The Object Form of Pronouns

Object Pronouns

me	us
you	you
him, her, it	them

When personal pronouns are used as objects, the object form is correct. Any pronoun that is not a subject or a predicate pronoun is an object.

There are three kinds of objects: direct objects, indirect objects, and objects of prepositions.

In these sentences the object form of the pronoun is used for direct objects.

Dennis knows *them*. The manager trained *me*.
Carla followed *us*. The visitors surprised *her*.

These sentences use the object form for indirect objects:

Terry loaned *me* his pen. Carol sent *them* gifts.
The school finds *us* jobs. Mr. Lyle gave *her* some advice.

The third kind of object is the object of a preposition. Prepositions are short connecting words like *to*, *for*, and *with*. The pronouns that follow such words are the objects. For more explanation of prepositions, see Handbook Section 7.

These sentences use the object form for objects of prepositions:

We practiced with *him*.
My friends threw a party for *me*.
Ben sketched a portrait of *her*.
The stagehands prepared the set for *us*.

The Possessive Form of Pronouns

Possessive Pronouns

my, mine	our, ours
your, yours	your, yours
his, her, hers, its	their, theirs

Possessive pronouns show belonging or ownership. Many times, possessive pronouns are used by themselves. Then, like a noun, a possessive pronoun has one of these uses: subject, object, or predicate word. Look at these examples:

That suitcase is *his*. (predicate pronoun)
Hers is much heavier. (subject)
Paul and Maria are carrying *theirs*. (direct object)
Steve gave *his* a shove. (indirect object)
This suitcase looks like *mine*. (object of preposition)

At other times, possessive pronouns are not used alone. Instead, they are used to tell about nouns. Look at these sentences:

Phil trained *his* German shepherd.
Each ethnic group has *its* customs.
The team celebrated *their* victory.
Will you read *your* lines?

Exercise A Choose the correct pronoun from the two given in parentheses. Write it. Read the sentence to yourself.

1. The news shocked (he, him).
2. The waiter spilled spaghetti on (I, me).
3. (They, Them) moved to our neighborhood.

4. The cashier gave (she, her) incorrect change.
5. Was that (he, him)?
6. All of (we, us) are taller than our parents.
7. The idea was (my, mine).
8. The artist sold (her, hers) work at a fair.
9. Joy sent (he, him) a funny birthday card.
10. The security guards stopped (we, us).

Exercise B Follow the directions for Exercise A.

1. A pro team drafted (he, him).
2. Is this makeup (your, yours)?
3. The caller is (she, her).
4. During the summer (I, me) work at a day-care center.
5. Next year, (we, us) will be able to vote.
6. Wasn't it (he, him) at the door?
7. Garbage surrounded (they, them).
8. Aaron handed the earphones to (I, me).
9. Rebecca brought (her, hers) favorite album.
10. All of those drawings are by (he, him).

Exercise C The personal pronouns in the following sentences are in italics. Write each pronoun and label it *Subject Form, Object Form,* or *Possessive Form.*

1. Laura rehearsed the scene with *him*.
2. *She* loaded the film into the camera.
3. The movie bored *us*.
4. It's *they*!
5. Curt's older sister gave *him* a haircut.
6. Last week *I* got my first paycheck.
7. Wendy painted pinstripes on *her* car.
8. The best artwork is *his*.
9. *We* ate all of the tacos.
10. Beth loaned *me* a sweatshirt.

Part 3 Pronouns in Compound Constructions

Compound sentence parts, or **compound constructions,** in a sentence have more than one part. The parts are joined by *and*, *or*, or *nor*, as in *Ben and me*. A pronoun may be one or both of these parts.

You may wonder which pronoun form to use in a compound construction. Here are sentences with pronouns used correctly as compound parts:

> *Laura* and *I* learned a form of self-defense. (*Laura* and *I* are both subjects. The subject form *I* is used.)
>
> Mr. Kim taught *her* and *me* judo. (*Her* and *me* are both indirect objects. The object forms are used.)
>
> Just between *you* and *me*, I'm tired. (*You* and *me* are objects of the preposition *between*. The object forms are used.)

You can avoid problems with compound parts if you think of each part separately. For instance, in the first example above, omit the words *Laura and*. Should the sentence read *I learned a form of self-defense* or *Me learned a form of self-defense?* The pronoun *I* is correct.

Here is another example:

> Gail gave Dennis and (I, me) more coffee.
> Gail gave *me* more coffee.

Exercise A Choose the right pronoun from the two given.

1. Rick and (she, her) are going to the show.
2. Save seats for Lori and (I, me).
3. Ann invited (we, us) for supper.
4. Soap operas don't appeal to Janet and (I, me).
5. The argument was between Jamie and (they, them).
6. The judge fined Pam and (she, her).
7. Scott's best friends are Chris and (he, him).

8. My uncle and (he, him) are business partners.
9. My boss relies on (she, her) and (I, me).
10. Just between you and (I, me), I'm nervous.

Exercise B Follow the directions for Exercise A.

1. The shopkeeper ignored Meg and (she, her).
2. Katy and (he, him) met on a bus.
3. That speeding car headed toward John and (I, me).
4. The clerk gave Phil and (she, her) their money back.
5. A child with a water pistol squirted Britt and (he, him).
6. Someone yelled at (they, them) and (we, us).
7. Bogan and (we, us) both have good teams.
8. Tony and (I, me) may join the Navy.
9. The best dancers are Marshall and (she, her).
10. Leave some chili for Marla and (he, him).

Part 4 Pronouns and Antecedents

A pronoun is defined as a word used in place of a noun. This noun is called the pronoun's **antecedent.** A pronoun refers to its antecedent.

> Anna never answers *her* phone.
> (*Her* takes the place of the noun *Anna*. *Anna* is the antecedent.)
>
> The shop closed *its* doors.
> (*Its* refers to the noun *shop*. *Shop* is the antecedent.)

The antecedent usually appears before the pronoun. The antecedent may appear in the same sentence or in the preceding sentence, as in this example:

> The tractor pushed the stones and bricks. It cleared a path.
> (*It* stands for the antecedent *tractor*.)

Pronouns may be the antecedents of other pronouns:

You missed *your* bus.
(*You* is the antecedent of *your*.)

A pronoun must be like its antecedent in one important way. A pronoun must have the same number as its antecedent. If the antecedent is singular, the pronoun must be singular. If the antecedent is plural, then the pronoun must be plural.

A pronoun must agree with its antecedent in number.

The photographers grabbed *their* cameras.
(*Photographers* is plural; *their* is plural.)

The typist erased *his* error.
(*Typist* is singular; *his* is singular.)

TV fans have *their* favorite shows.
(*Fans* is plural; *their* is plural.)

Exercise A In these sentences the personal pronouns are italicized. Write each pronoun and its antecedent.

1. The window washers saw the street far below *them*.
2. The girl carried a radio on *her* shoulder.
3. Jim looked at the gift and knew *it* was an album.
4. Don't wear those shoes if *they* hurt.
5. Tony made a pizza and topped *it* with salami.
6. Mrs. Barclay quit *her* job.
7. Lee gave the boys *their* dinner.
8. Frieda and I studied *our* menus.
9. Ali regained *his* balance.
10. Erik Estrada had an accident during the filming of *his* TV show.

Exercise B Follow the directions for Exercise A.

1. Some people hide *their* feelings.
2. The ship veered from *its* course.

3. I have lost *my* voice.
4. Mr. Monroe moved to *his* new apartment.
5. Gayle opened the battery and filled *it* with water.
6. Some gas caps have locks on *them*.
7. Linda planned the route for *her* next trip.
8. Rod and I split the cheesecake between the two of *us*.
9. Do you need *your* pen back?
10. Adam didn't see the car behind *him*.

Part 5 Compound Personal Pronouns

A **compound personal pronoun** is a pronoun with *-self* or *-selves* added.

myself	ourselves
yourself	yourselves
himself, herself, itself	themselves

Notice how compound personal pronouns are used for emphasis:

Maggie *herself* opened the vault.
The manager *himself* handled the sale.
I planned the reunion *myself*.
They called the police *themselves*.

Exercise A Number your paper from 1 to 10. Beside each number write the correct compound personal pronoun for each of the following sentences. After it, write its antecedent.

Example: The actor thinks of (pronoun) as a star.
himself, actor

1. Dana and I wrote the lyrics (pronoun).
2. Amy gave (pronoun) a permanent.

3. The workers (pronoun) choose their hours.
4. The governor (pronoun) pardoned the prisoner.
5. The members (pronoun) set the club rules.
6. I cooked this meal by (pronoun).
7. The cheerleaders yelled (pronoun) hoarse.
8. The special effects were good, but the movie (pronoun) was dull.
9. Make (pronoun) comfortable, Elliot.
10. We watched (pronoun) on TV.

Exercise B Follow the directions for Exercise A.

1. The general (pronoun) issued the orders.
2. Brian and Bob found (pronoun) in trouble.
3. The doctor (pronoun) became very sick.
4. Sarah drove (pronoun) to the hospital.
5. Give (pronoun) enough time, Debbie.
6. JoAnn tuned the engine (pronoun).
7. Carlos went camping by (pronoun).
8. The problem will work (pronoun) out.
9. Chris wanted the engine but not the car (pronoun).
10. Vic and I made (pronoun) sick by eating too much candy.

Part 6 Demonstrative Pronouns

The pronouns *this*, *that*, *these*, and *those* point out people or things. They are called **demonstrative pronouns.**

This and *these* point to people or things that are near in space or time. *That* or *those* point to people or things that are farther away in space or time.

> *This* makes a good dessert. *These* are leather boots.
> *That* was our first date. *Those* were great times.

Exercise Number your paper from 1 to 10. Write the correct demonstrative pronoun for the blank space in each sentence.

1. ______ are your gloves, not these.
2. ______ are terrific tacos we're eating.
3. ______ is better than that.
4. ______ was a good concert last night.
5. ______ is my bike beside me.
6. ______ must be our bus over there.
7. ______ is my counselor in the principal's office.
8. ______ is beautiful weather today.
9. ______ is the canyon out there.
10. ______ were our happiest years.

Part 7 Interrogative Pronouns

Certain pronouns are used to ask questions. They are called **interrogative pronouns.** The interrogative pronouns are *who*, *whom*, *whose*, *which*, and *what*.

Who won an Emmy award?
Whom did Gloria call?
Whose is this parka?
Which is your favorite?
What started the fire?

Exercise Number your paper from 1 to 10. Write all the pronouns in these sentences. After each pronoun, write *Demonstrative* or *Interrogative* to show what kind it is.

Example: Is that the law?
That—demonstrative pronoun

1. Who knows the old man's age?
2. That makes sense.
3. Which is Carlos's suitcase?
4. These are strange lights.
5. Is that Rob's handwriting?
6. Whom does Cal trust with the money?

7. These are the latest fashions.
8. Are those the house keys?
9. What makes Ramona so lucky?
10. Whose are these?

Part 8 Indefinite Pronouns

Some pronouns do not refer to a definite person or thing. Such pronouns are called **indefinite pronouns.**

The following are indefinite pronouns. They are singular.

another	each	everything	one
anybody	either	neither	somebody
anyone	everybody	nobody	someone
anything	everyone	no one	

Because they are singular, the above pronouns are used with the singular possessive pronouns *his*, *her*, and *its*.

Each of the stores has *its* own hours.
Somebody forgot *his* ski cap.
Somebody forgot *his or her* ski cap.

The final example uses the phrase *his or her* instead of simply *his*. That phrase shows that the indefinite pronoun may refer to a male or female. Many people prefer such a phrase.

Although most indefinite pronouns are singular, some are plural. They refer to more than one person or thing. The following indefinite pronouns are plural. They are used with the plural possessive *their*. Study these examples.

both many few several

Both of the swimmers timed *their* sprints.
Few of the passengers left *their* seats.
Many of our neighbors grow *their* own vegetables.
Several of the racers overturned *their* cars.

A few indefinite pronouns can be either singular or plural, depending on their meaning in a sentence. Read these examples:

all none some

All of the water has chemicals in *it*.
All of the drivers loaded *their* trucks.

None of the medicine has lost *its* strength.
None of these comedians use *their* own material.

Some of the fire burned *itself* out.
Some of the workers took *their* breaks.

Exercise A Number your paper from 1 to 10. For each sentence write the indefinite pronoun.

1. None of us caught a fish.
2. Did someone call me?
3. Anyone can win the sweepstakes.
4. What is everybody waiting for?
5. Only one of the headlights works.
6. Several of the players signed contracts.
7. Many of the starting players fouled out.
8. Kelly made both of the free throws.
9. Why is everyone cheering?
10. Brady got all of the rebounds.

Exercise B Choose the right pronoun from the two given.

1. One of the actresses missed (her, their) cue.
2. Many of the stores have lowered (its, their) prices.
3. Somebody left (his or her, their) checkbook here.
4. Everyone listed (his or her, their) address.
5. If anyone calls, tell (him or her, them) I'll be right back.
6. Neither of our wrestlers pinned (his, their) opponent.
7. Some of the runners wore out (her, their) shoes.

8. Each of these sundaes has (its, their) own special sauce.

9. All of the passengers in the boat wore (his or her, their) lifejackets.

10. Did anybody go out of (his or her, their) way to help?

Exercise C Number your paper from 1 to 10. For each sentence write the indefinite pronoun and the correct verb from the two in parentheses.

1. Nobody (looks, look) very interested in the game.
2. Everyone (makes, make) mistakes.
3. Neither of the teams (has, have) a strong defense.
4. Very few of these foods (is, are) high in calories.
5. One of my sisters (has, have) the flu.
6. All of the big-city newspapers (is, are) sold here.
7. Each of the drivers (races, race) his or her own car.
8. Some of the Packers' games (is, are) televised.
9. Some of the jewelry (is, are) missing.
10. Many of the cases (is, are) settled out of court.

Part 9 Special Problems with Pronouns

Contractions and Possessive Pronouns

Certain contractions are sometimes confused with possessive pronouns.

Contractions are formed by joining two words and omitting one or more letters. An apostrophe shows where letters are left out.

it's = it + is	they're = they + are
you're = you + are	who's = who + is

The above contractions are sometimes confused with the possessive pronouns *its*, *your*, *their*, and *whose*. The words sound alike but are spelled differently.

Incorrect: The plant lost it's leaves.
Correct: The plant lost its leaves.

If you can't decide which word is correct, substitute the words the contraction stands for. If the sentence sounds right, then the contraction is correct.

Incorrect: Their enjoying they're trip.
Correct: They're (They are) enjoying their trip.

Exercise A Choose the right word from the two in parentheses.

1. The movers parked (their, they're) van in front of the building.
2. (Your, You're) expecting a call, aren't you?
3. Wax gives the car (its, it's) shine.
4. (Whose, Who's) signature is this?
5. Is that (your, you're) camera?
6. (Their, They're) trapped in the mine.
7. (Whose, Who's) taking the ball out of bounds?
8. (Its, It's) half time now.
9. (Whose, Who's) the woman with the microphone?
10. (Your, You're) friends are waiting at the station.

Exercise B Write the words each contraction below stands for.

1. They're appealing to a higher court.
2. I'd like to ride the rapids.
3. Soon we'll be on our own.
4. You're spilling your tea!
5. She's ready for a change.
6. They've scouted all the teams.
7. Who's offered you a job?

8. What's wrong with the picture tube?
9. I'm playing third base.
10. We'd like longer weekends.

Who and Whom

Many people have problems with the pronouns *who* and *whom*.

Who sounds natural in most questions. Use *who* as the subject of a sentence.

Who tuned the piano? *Who* is there?

Whom is harder to get used to. *Whom* is used as an object.

Whom did the Regans adopt?
(direct object of the verb *did adopt*)

To *whom* are tax forms sent?
(object of the preposition *to*)

Exercise A Choose the right pronoun from the two given in parentheses.

1. (Who, Whom) can predict weather?
2. (Who, Whom) insulted your friend?
3. (Who, Whom) did you tape record?
4. (Who, Whom) were you watching on TV?
5. (Who, Whom) is the sportscaster?
6. (Who, Whom) towed your car?
7. (Who, Whom) runs the drill press?
8. (Who, Whom) will you stay with?
9. (Who, Whom) do these running shorts belong to?
10. (Who, Whom) did you visit in St. Louis?

Exercise B Follow the directions for Exercise A.

1. (Who, Whom) works the switchboard?
2. (Who, Whom) did the lifeguard rescue?

3. (Who, Whom) did the noise awaken?
4. To (who, whom) is the telegram addressed?
5. (Who, Whom) did your mother hire?
6. (Who, Whom) showered in the locker room?
7. For (who, whom) was the school named?
8. (Who, Whom) polluted the canal?
9. (Who, Whom) do you compete with?
10. (Who, Whom) needs a yearly physical exam?

We and *Us* with Nouns

The pronouns *we* and *us* are often used with nouns, as in the phrases *we boys* or *us students.* Sometimes such phrases cause problems.

To decide whether to use *we* or *us*, omit the noun. Say the sentence with *we* and then with *us*. You will then probably be able to choose the correct pronoun.

Problem: (We, Us) linemen do the blocking.
Correct: We do the blocking.
Correct: We linemen do the blocking.

Problem: Nothing stops (we, us) campers.
Correct: Nothing stops us.
Correct: Nothing stops us campers.

Them and *Those*

Them and *those* are sometimes confused. To use the words correctly, remember that *them* is always a pronoun. It takes the place of a noun.

A search party found *them*. (In this sentence, *them* is used as the direct object.)

Them is never used to tell about or describe a noun. *Those* should be used.

Incorrect: Have you ever worn them clogs?
Correct: Have you ever worn those clogs?

Exercise A Choose the correct pronoun from the two given in parentheses.

1. (We, Us) girls hooked up the antenna.
2. (We, Us) officers have special quarters.
3. Did you see (them, those) state troopers?
4. Can you take advantage of (them, those) new airfares?
5. (Them, Those) greeting cards are funny.
6. The flag signaled (we, us) drivers.
7. (We, Us) athletes are often tense before games.
8. Micki King tried one of (them, those) back dives.
9. When will (we, us) Americans host the Olympics?
10. The ball nearly hit (we, us) spectators.

Exercise B Follow the directions for Exercise A.

1. The Army Reserve wants to talk to (we, us) students.
2. Will (them, those) additives improve gas mileage?
3. (We, Us) boys pushed the stalled car.
4. Can any of (them, those) computers translate languages?
5. Braille is used by (we, us) blind people.
6. There is a lounge for (we, us) employees.
7. Did you eat all of (them, those) strawberries?
8. Yesterday (we, us) campers hiked up a mountain.
9. The hospital treats (we, us) patients well.
10. (Them, Those) stakes hold the tent in place.

REVIEW Using Pronouns

Using Pronouns Correctly Number your paper from 1 to 20. Choose the correct pronoun from those given in parentheses.

1. (They, Them) put new shingles on the roof.
2. Does (she, her) work in a lab?
3. The alderman asked (she, her) for help.
4. Jackson tossed the ball to (she, her) for the third out.
5. A chunk of plaster landed on (him, his) head.
6. Julia and (he, him) work in a sporting goods shop.
7. Alec took Nancy and (I, me) to a roller derby.
8. Todd and (I, me) dug holes for the fenceposts.
9. Don't hurt (himself, yourself) on the blade, Mike.
10. Some men shave (himself, themself, themselves) without using a mirror.
11. (This, That, Those) is Mt. Ranier off in the distance.
12. Has anyone had (his or her, their) fortune told?
13. Some of the gymnasts have (her, their) own warm-up exercises.
14. Each of the parking lots has (its, their) own rates.
15. The bikers loaded (their, they're) backpacks with food for the trip.
16. Does (your, you're) car use unleaded fuel?
17. (Who, Whom) did you sign a contract with?
18. (Who, Whom) brought the FM radio?
19. (We, Us) city dwellers are used to noise.
20. Have you tried one of (them, those) egg rolls?

Using Verbs

The verb is the key part of a sentence. It brings a sentence to life. Without a verb, there would be no sentence.

You have already learned to recognize this special class of word. In this section you will find out more about verbs and how they are used.

Part 1 What Is a Verb?

A verb tells of an action or a state of being.

Action Verbs

One kind of verb may indicate action, even if the action is unseen.

Sarah *smiled.*	Bill *expects* a raise.
A plane *landed.*	Sue *has* many new friends.

An **action verb** tells that something is happening, has happened, or will happen.

Linking Verbs

Some verbs simply tell that something exists. Such verbs express a state of being rather than action.

The election *is* Tuesday.	Spencer *was* ready.
Rita *seems* happy.	The cake *tastes* moist.

These verbs are called **linking verbs.** They link the subject with some other word or words in the sentence.

Here are the most common linking verbs:

be (am, are, is, was, were, been, being)	look	smell	seem
	appear	taste	sound
become	feel	grow	

Some linking verbs can also be used as action verbs.

Linking Verb	Action Verb
The T-shirt *looked* dirty.	Kim *looked* at the painting.
The meal *grew* cold.	The gardener *grew* zinnias.

When you look at the verb in a sentence, see how it is used. Decide whether it expresses action or simply links the subject with a word in the predicate.

Transitive and Intransitive Verbs

In many sentences an action verb expresses an idea by itself. In other sentences a direct object completes the action of the verb. The direct object, as you have learned, answers *whom* or *what* about the verb.

Verbs that have direct objects are **transitive verbs.**

Dave *met* the mayor.
(The direct object *mayor* completes the meaning of the verb *met.*)

The officer *wore* several medals.
(The direct object *medals* completes the meaning of the verb *wore.*)

Verbs that do not have direct objects are another kind of verb. They are called **intransitive verbs.**

The winners *rejoiced.*
(The verb *rejoiced* has no direct object.)

Steve *rested* under a tree.
(The verb *rested* has no object.)

Some action verbs are always transitive or always intransitive. Other verbs change. The same verb may be transitive in one sentence and intransitive in another. Compare these examples.

Transitive Verb	Intransitive Verb
The artist *sketched* the model.	The artist *sketched* by the sea.
The girls *swam* a mile.	The girls *swam* in the pool.
Keith *drove* a taxi.	Keith *drove* slowly.

Exercise A Write the verb in each sentence. After each verb write *Action* or *Linking* to show what kind it is.

1. The Congress cut taxes.
2. Our nation's supply of oil is low.

3. The Senator campaigned for reelection.
4. That old building is dangerous.
5. Diane programmed the computer.
6. The flight seemed very smooth.
7. The ranch was high in the Rockies.
8. Water became scarce during the summer.
9. We saw an old-fashioned rodeo.
10. The company drills for oil.

Exercise B Follow the directions for Exercise A.

1. The state government operates several large parks.
2. A hurricane swept the island.
3. Everyone ran for shelter.
4. Many people were homeless.
5. This armchair feels comfortable.
6. Do those big cars guzzle gas?
7. The Omni is a front-wheel drive car.
8. Meyers was an All-American from U.C.L.A.
9. Reporters uncovered a scandal.
10. A special task force studied crime.

Exercise C Write the action verb in each sentence. After it write *Transitive* or *Intransitive* to show what kind it is.

1. Those trucks have diesel engines.
2. Each fall, many new TV series begin.
3. The networks show recent movies.
4. The spacecraft explored Saturn.
5. Joggers ran by the lake.
6. The train from Washington finally arrived.
7. Tom often cooks dinner.
8. During the storm the airport closed.
9. Sarah reads *Time* and *Newsweek*.
10. All night, the stereo blared.

Part 2 The Parts of a Verb

Many verbs are made up of a **main verb** plus one or more **helping verbs.**

The most common helping verbs are forms of *be*, *have*, and *do*. They may also be used as main verbs. Here are their forms:

be—am, is, are, was, were, been, be
have—has, have, had
do—does, do, did

Used as Main Verb	Used as Helping Verb
I *was* lucky.	I *was eating* lunch.
Jill *has* a cold.	Jill *has finished* her report.
We *did* our chores.	We *did like* the movie.

Here are other frequently used helping verbs:

can	will	shall	may	must
could	would	should	might	

Helping verbs combine with the main verb to become parts of the verb.

Helping Verb(s) +	Main Verb =	Verb
will	stay	will stay
had	stayed	had stayed
should have	stayed	should have stayed
must	join	must join
has	joined	has joined

Sometimes the parts of the verb are separated. The words that come between them are not part of the verb. Study these examples.

Chinese food *has* always *seemed* tasty.
The team *was* barely *paying* attention.
When *will* the President *hold* a press conference?
Did the press secretary *speak*?

Exercise A Make two columns. Label them *Helping Verb* and *Main Verb.* Find the parts of the verb in each sentence. Write them in the proper columns.

1. The glider was soaring.
2. A new snack shop has opened.
3. This train does not stop at Webster Avenue.
4. A computer will prepare the payroll.
5. Has the movie been banned?
6. No fuel should be wasted.
7. Do you use sugar in your coffee?
8. No one had ever climbed that mountain.
9. Construction workers on a job site must often wear hardhats.
10. A smoke alarm could have alerted us to the fire.

Exercise B Follow the directions for Exercise A.

1. The ice rink has been closed for repairs.
2. Greg is expecting a call.
3. The guard had warned us several times.
4. Will the Buckeyes receive the kickoff?
5. Jonas should have tried these barbells.
6. Did Melissa run for office?
7. The temperature has already climbed to 98°.
8. Have you ever worked in a boiler room?
9. Diaz will surely pitch in Thursday's game.
10. The flight attendants must often reassure passengers.

Part 3 Verb Tenses

Verbs indicate time. They tell when an action or state of being occurs. Verbs can indicate past time, present time, or future time by changing form.

These changes in form to show time are called **tenses.** The changes are usually made these ways:

1. Change in spelling
   ran→run   try→tried   close→closed
2. Use of helping verbs
   had eaten   will survive   has fallen

This list shows examples of the six main tenses for the verbs *paint* and *watch*.

Present Tense	I paint.	She watches.
Past Tense	I painted.	She watched.
Future Tense	I will paint.	She will watch.
Present Perfect Tense	I have painted.	She has watched.
Past Perfect Tense	I had painted.	She had watched.
Future Perfect Tense	I will have painted.	She will have watched.

Simple Tenses

The **present tense** shows time in the present. The present tense form is usually the same as the name of the verb. For verbs used with most singular subjects, an *-s* is added to the verb.

I *know*.   Cathy *knows*.   My mother *knows*.

The **past tense** shows past time. Most verbs form the past tense by adding *-d* or *-ed*.

Ben raced.   Yvonne called.   I laughed.

Some verbs form the past tense in different ways.

They rode.   Sue went to the game.   Adam swam.

The **future tense** shows time in the future. In this tense, use *shall* or *will* with the verb.

Keith will start.   Donna will guess.   I shall return.

The three tenses just described are called the **simple tenses.**

Perfect Tenses

The **perfect tenses** are used when we have to speak of two different times, one earlier than the other. The perfect tenses are formed by using the helping verbs *has*, *have*, and *had*.

The **present perfect tense** tells of an action or state of being in some indefinite time before the present. The helping verb *has* or *have* is used.

Dean *has practiced* often. Maggie *has chosen*.
They *have arrived*.

The **past perfect tense** tells of a time before another time in the past. The helping verb *had* is used.

They *had been* lonely until we *came*.
Marie *had waited* for the bus for hours, but it never *arrived*.
We *had* just *gone* into the house when the storm *hit*.

The **future perfect tense** tells of a time in the future *before* some other time in the future.

By this time tomorrow, *you will have met* the Governor.
When the hike is over, *we will have walked* ten miles.

Exercise A Find the verbs in the following sentences. Tell the tense of each.

1. Keith spotted a dog in the alley.
2. A self-serve gas station has opened nearby.
3. The Packers have accepted the penalty.
4. Bernstein kicks most of the field goals.
5. An overtime will decide the game.
6. Each suspect will take a lie detector test.
7. Helmets protect motorcycle riders.
8. By 1990 the birth rate will have risen.
9. Police searched the hideout.
10. The mobsters had already fled.

Exercise B Write a sentence for each of the verbs below. Use the tense indicated.

1. judge (past)
2. try (present perfect)
3. notice (past perfect)
4. live (present)
5. pile (past)
6. drive (present)
7. show (future)
8. prepare (future perfect)
9. work (present perfect)
10. jump (future)

Part 4 The Principal Parts of a Verb

The **principal parts** of a verb are its basic forms. By combining these forms with helping verbs, you can make all tenses.

The principal parts of a verb are the **present tense,** the **past tense,** and the **past participle.** They are usually written in that order.

Most verbs form the past tense and past participle by adding *-d* or *-ed* to present form. These verbs are called **regular verbs.** They are called regular verbs because they form the past tense and past participle in regular ways.

Present	Past	Past Participle
trust	trusted	(have) trusted
want	wanted	(have) wanted
move	moved	(have) moved
change	changed	(have) changed

Some regular verbs change their spelling when the *-d* or *-ed* is added. Study the examples on the next page.

Present	Past	Past Participle
try	tried	(have) tried
trot	trotted	(have) trotted
say	said	(have) said
slip	slipped	(have) slipped

The past participle is used for perfect tenses. It must have a helping verb.

They have changed.	We had tried.
Mark must have known.	Beth has slipped.

Exercise Make three columns on your paper. Label them *Present, Past,* and *Past Participle.* List the principal parts of these verbs in the proper columns.

1. cook	6. copy	11. follow
2. marry	7. happen	12. open
3. seem	8. lift	13. claim
4. belong	9. act	14. trip
5. pull	10. toss	15. drag

Part 5 Irregular Verbs

You have learned the principal parts for regular verbs. Many verbs, though, do not follow the regular pattern. They do not add *-d* or *-ed* to form the past tense and past participle. They are called irregular verbs. Here are some examples:

Present	Past	Past Participle
throw	threw	(have) thrown
feel	felt	(have) felt
spring	sprang	(have) sprung
tell	told	(have) told
cut	cut	(have) cut

You will notice that some of the verbs have one or two different forms. Others have three different forms.

If you do not know the principal parts of a verb, look up the verb in a dictionary. If no parts are listed, the verb is regular. If the verb is irregular, the dictionary will list the irregular forms. It will give two forms if both the past and past participle are the same, as in *catch, caught,* for example. It will give three forms if all principal parts are different, as in *ring, rang, rung,* for example.

Using Irregular Verbs

There are two ways to be sure of the forms of irregular verbs. One way is to look up the verbs in the dictionary. The other way is to learn the principal parts of commonly used irregular verbs.

Once you know the principal parts, keep these ideas in mind: Use the past participle with *have* and *be* helping verbs. The past participle is used for present perfect and past perfect tenses. The past form is not used with helping verbs.

The principal parts of irregular verbs can be confusing. They may seem simpler if you learn the following five patterns.

Group 1 Some irregular verbs keep the same form for all three principal parts. These are easy to remember.

Present	Past	Past Participle
burst	burst	(have) burst
cost	cost	(have) cost
cut	cut	(have) cut
let	let	(have) let
put	put	(have) put
set	set	(have) set

Here are some sentences using verbs from this group:

Some license plates *cost* twenty dollars. (present)
I *put* my signature on the contract. (past)
Matt *has set* up the scenery. (past participle)

Group 2 Another group of irregular verbs changes form only once. The past and the past participle are the same.

Present	Past	Past Participle
bring	brought	(have) brought
catch	caught	(have) caught
lead	led	(have) led
lend	lent	(have) lent
lose	lost	(have) lost
say	said	(have) said
sit	sat	(have) sat

These sentences use irregular verbs from Group 2:

I *sit* in the lifeguard station. (present)
Tyrone *led* the league in R.B.I.'s. (past)
Garrett and Lynn *have caught* three salmon. (past participle)

Exercise A Choose the correct form of the verb.

1. The convention (brang, brought) out-of-towners to Chicago.
2. The infielder has (catched, caught) the foul ball.
3. Rent (costed, cost) half of Tim's pay.
4. Estelle (put, putted) a tape deck in the car.
5. Lauren (lent, lended) me a special wrench.
6. The stage crew (set, setted) up the props and scenery.
7. No one has ever (sayed, said) that before.
8. A hose in the engine (burst, bursted).
9. Duncan has (sat, sitted) on the bench all season.
10. Kris (leaded, led) in scoring for the Wildcats.

Exercise B Follow the directions for Exercise A.

1. All the workers (lost, losed) track of the time.
2. The reward was (setted, set) at $1,000.
3. Suddenly, Jane (burst, bursted) into the room.
4. Jim has (put, putted) a coffeepot on the camping stove.

5. Deena (caught, catched) the flu.
6. The fishermen have not (brang, brought) enough bait.
7. In 1978 gas (cost, costed) less than a dollar a gallon.
8. The soldiers (sat, sitted) in their barracks.
9. Porter (led, leaded) in the primary election.
10. The lawyer has (said, sayed) little about the case.

Group 3 Verbs in this group add *-n* or *-en* to the past tense to form the past participle.

Present	Past	Past Participle
break	broke	(have) broken
choose	chose	(have) chosen
freeze	froze	(have) frozen
speak	spoke	(have) spoken
steal	stole	(have) stolen
wear	wore	(have) worn

Here are three sentences using Group 3 verbs:

Speak into the microphone. (present)
Everyone *wore* strange costumes. (past)
Joan and Bill *have chosen* their teams. (past participle)

Exercise A Choose the correct form of the verb from the two forms given.

1. Ms. Gomez has (chose, chosen) a blue interior for her car.
2. The group has (spoke, spoken) of a plot.
3. Money had been (stole, stolen) from the cash register.
4. The rock group (wore, worn) gold and glitter.
5. Evans (broke, broken) a land-speed record.
6. Tires squealed as the cars (tore, torn) around the track.
7. The side of beef was (froze, frozen).
8. A rock (broke, broken) the display window.
9. The country has (chose, chosen) a new leader.
10. The astronauts (wore, worn) special suits.

Exercise B Follow the directions for Exercise A.

1. A pickpocket (stole, stolen) Ken's wallet.
2. The sign read, "Spanish is (spoke, spoken) here."
3. The sailors (wore, worn) their dress uniforms.
4. The lawyers have (chose, chosen) a jury.
5. Rain (froze, frozen) on the windshield.
6. Lori accidentally (tore, torn) up a dollar bill.
7. The relay team has (broke, broken) a world record.
8. The mourners have (wore, worn) black clothing.
9. Some top-secret papers have been (stole, stolen).
10. The social worker (spoke, spoken) about conflicts.

Group 4 The irregular verbs in this group change their final vowels. The vowel changes from *i* in the present tense to *a* in the past tense and *u* in the past participle.

Present	Past	Past Participle
begin	began	(have) begun
drink	drank	(have) drunk
ring	rang	(have) rung
sing	sang	(have) sung
swim	swam	(have) swum

Here are examples of irregular verbs from Group 4:

I *sing* off-key. (present)
The chimes *rang* softly. (past)
The police *have begun* a crackdown. (past participle)

Exercise A Choose the correct verb form.

1. Ellie (began, begun) a new job.
2. Someone must have (drank, drunk) my Pepsi.
3. Bill (rang, rung) for the flight attendant.
4. Donna Summer (sang, sung) "Last Dance."
5. The telephone had (rang, rung) all day.
6. The church choir (sang, sung) hymns.

7. Construction work on the highway has (began, begun).
8. The hikers (drank, drunk) from canteens.
9. The hospital has (began, begun) a blood drive.
10. Stevie Wonder (sang, sung) his latest hit single.

Exercise B Follow the directions for Exercise A.

1. The loud noises (rang, rung) in my ears.
2. Leslie (swam, swum) in the icy water.
3. The team (began, begun) to rally in the fourth quarter.
4. The boys have (drank, drunk) all of the coffee.
5. Tropical fish (swam, swum) in the huge tank.
6. The candidates have (began, begun) to campaign.
7. After the wedding, bells (rang, rung).
8. Some soups may be (drank, drunk).
9. Many operas are (sang, sung) in Italian.
10. Diana Nyad has (swam, swum) great distances.

Group 5 For some irregular verbs the past participle is formed from the present tense. The past participle looks more like the present tense than the past tense.

Present	Past	Past Participle
come	came	(have) come
do	did	(have) done
eat	ate	(have) eaten
fall	fell	(have) fallen
give	gave	(have) given
go	went	(have) gone
grow	grew	(have) grown
know	knew	(have) known
ride	rode	(have) ridden
run	ran	(have) run
see	saw	(have) seen
take	took	(have) taken
throw	threw	(have) thrown
write	wrote	(have) written

Here are sentences using Group 5 verbs:

I *eat* only vegetables and grains. (present)
Marcy *knew* a shortcut to the station. (past)
Suzanne *has taken* inventory of the stock. (past participle)

Exercise A Choose the correct verb form from the two given.

1. The jogger (ran, run) along a lakefront path.
2. Cary (threw, thrown) a terrific party.
3. A passenger has (fell, fallen) overboard!
4. Vera (ate, eaten) raw fish at a Japanese restaurant.
5. Ken (grew, grown) a beard and a moustache.
6. Charles Kuralt has (went, gone) to all corners of America.
7. Jory had (saw, seen) hundreds of horror films.
8. Chicago is (knew, known) for its pizza.
9. Sterling and Darrell (took, taken) a Greyhound bus to Arizona.
10. Samantha has (rode, ridden) a bike across the state.

Exercise B Follow the directions for Exercise A.

1. The dictator has (fell, fallen) from power.
2. The job had (came, come) along just in time.
3. A gymnast (did, done) handsprings across the mat.
4. George Gallup has (took, taken) polls of public opinion.
5. Dennis (saw, seen) a strange object flying in the night sky.
6. Has everyone (gave, given) up on this project?
7. Anne (went, gone) to City Hall to see the mayor.
8. The candidate has (ran, run) her campaign honestly.
9. *The Outsiders* was (wrote, written) by S. E. Hinton.
10. The escaped prisoners were last (saw, seen) in an Oklahoma town.

Part 6 Active and Passive Verbs

You have seen how the tenses of verbs indicate *time*. There is another way that verbs help you say exactly what you mean.

Suppose that a window has been broken. If you know who broke it, you can say:

My brother broke the window yesterday.

However, suppose you don't know who broke the window. Then you might say:

The window was broken yesterday.

In the first sentence, the subject tells who performed the action. When the subject performs the action, the verb is said to be **active.**

In the second sentence, the subject tells what received the action. When the subject tells the receiver or the result of the action, the verb is said to be **passive.** The word *passive* means "acted upon."

Forming the Passive

The passive form of the verb is made with the past participle. A form of *be* is the helping verb.

Active	Passive
Meg *has finished* the project.	The project *has been finished* by Meg.
Chris *has shown* the slides.	The slides *have been shown* by Chris.
The store *will add* the tax.	The tax *will be added* by the store.
Max *washed* the floor.	The floor *was washed* by Max.

Find the direct objects in the sentences in the first column above. In the sentences in the second column, the direct objects have become the subjects. Only verbs that have objects (transitive verbs) can be changed from active to passive.

A verb is active when its subject performs the action stated by the verb.

A verb is passive when its subject names the receiver or result of the action stated by the verb.

Exercise A Write the verb in each sentence. After each, write *Active* or *Passive* to tell what kind it is.

1. One of the boys baked bread.
2. The weather service predicted a record snowfall.
3. A citizens' group patrolled the streets.
4. The local merchants held a street fair.
5. Ms. O'Brien read the class an interesting article.
6. A meeting had been planned by the workers' union.
7. Several sites were considered by the builder.
8. The Potter's Wheel also sells ceramic supplies.
9. The S.W.A.T. unit was called to the scene.
10. Liz's plans were affected by inflation.

Exercise B Change the verbs in the following sentences from passive to active. Rewrite the sentences.

1. The rug was cleaned by Mr. Harvey.
2. The scores are given by the sportscaster.
3. A new comedian was introduced by Johnny Carson.
4. Paintings are sold to the museum by the Art Club.
5. The trophy had been won by our team once before.
6. Five buildings were destroyed by the fire.
7. Mr. Walters is known by everybody.
8. The error has been found by Bret.
9. The judge's decision will be appealed by the lawyer.
10. Letters had been sent to the President by our class.

REVIEW Using Verbs

Recognizing Verbs Write the verb in each of these sentences.

1. We climbed into the rowboat.
2. The Navy plane patrolled the North Pacific.
3. These rapids seem furious.
4. The helicopter was out of control.
5. Are mouthpieces optional in football?
6. The pilot should have radioed the tower.
7. Nancy must be practicing for the play.
8. The countdown will soon begin.
9. Poisonous gases had leaked into the air.
10. By tomorrow the fog will have cleared.
11. The flight to Miami was canceled.
12. Residents have been told about the danger.
13. A penalty was called on that play.
14. Orr will be removed from the game.
15. The divers have thoroughly searched the river.

Irregular Verbs Write the correct verb form from the two given.

16. Jon had (put, putted) the maps in the car.
17. Medical care has never (costed, cost) more.
18. The raft (brang, brought) us to safety.
19. The Celtics (lost, losed) by one point.
20. The mob (tore, torn) down the goalposts.
21. Has anyone (spoke, spoken) to the career counselor?
22. Stephanie has (broke, broken) her glasses.
23. The actress had (began, begun) with only bit parts.
24. The hikers (drank, drunk) from the stony brook.
25. That bakery has (went, gone) out of business.
26. Eliza (saw, seen) the filming of a movie.

Using Modifiers

Try to tell someone about your best friend, your favorite song, or your new shirt. You'll need more than nouns, verbs, and pronouns.

Nouns and pronouns name. Verbs show action or state-of-being. You also need words, though, to describe the sights, sounds, and smells around you.

Look at these two sentences:

> Water seeped into the room.
> *Brown, murky* water seeped into the room.

The **modifiers** make the difference. **Modifiers are words that modify, or change, other words.**

Besides describing, modifiers can also help you explain and express feeling. Read these two sentences.

Rod Stewart sings.
Rod Stewart *always* sings *powerfully*.

Without modifiers, your writing would seem incomplete and dull. Modifiers help you to express precise ideas. In this section you will learn to identify and use modifiers.

Part 1 Using Adjectives

One kind of modifier is an **adjective.**

An adjective is a word that modifies a noun or pronoun.

Adjectives can tell three different kinds of things about nouns or pronouns.

Which one or ones?

this step, *that* hall, *these* bills, *those* glasses

What kind?

yellow line, *shiny* boots, *happy* mood, *ugly* alley

How many or how much?

three months, *several* visitors, *less* pain, *little* snow

Proper Adjectives

One special kind of adjective is the proper adjective.

A **proper adjective** is formed from a proper noun. Therefore, it refers to a specific person, place, or thing. This kind of adjective is always capitalized. Here are some examples:

Italian food	an Olympic medal
a British accent	a Pacific island
a Japanese car	an American outpost

Predicate Adjectives

Another special kind of adjective is the predicate adjective. Most adjectives come before the words they modify:

The cars collided with a *dull*, *solid* thud.
(*Dull* and *solid* modify *thud*.)

The predicate adjective, though, comes after the word it modifies. A **predicate adjective** follows a linking verb and modifies the subject of the sentence.

Nothing seemed *clear* anymore.
(*Clear* modifies the subject, *nothing*.)

The fight was *brutal*.
(*Brutal* modifies the subject, *fight*.)

As you can see, *clear* and *brutal* are predicate adjectives. They follow linking verbs, *seemed* and *was*. Each one also modifies the subject of the sentence.

Articles

The adjectives *a*, *an*, and *the* are called **articles.**

The is the **definite article.** It points out a specific person, place, or thing.

Keep *the* ball in play. (a particular ball)

A and *an* are **indefinite articles.**

Did you find *a* ball? (any ball)
I would like *an* ice-cream cone. (any ice-cream cone)

Notice that *a* is used before a consonant sound (*a* rest, *a* school, *a* trip). *An* is used before a vowel sound (*an* elbow, *an* oboe, *an* urge).

Pay attention to the sound, not the spelling. We say *a* helper, but *an* honor, for instance.

Diagraming Adjectives

In a sentence diagram, an adjective appears below the word it modifies. It is placed on a slanted line.

This team has a quick backfield.

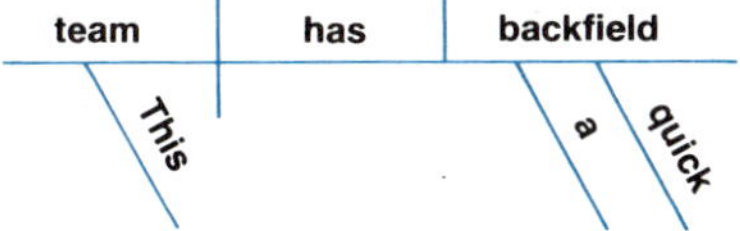

Predicate adjectives are diagramed differently. Like predicate nouns and pronouns, they are placed on the main line. A slanted line goes between the verb and the predicate adjective.

These opponents are tough.

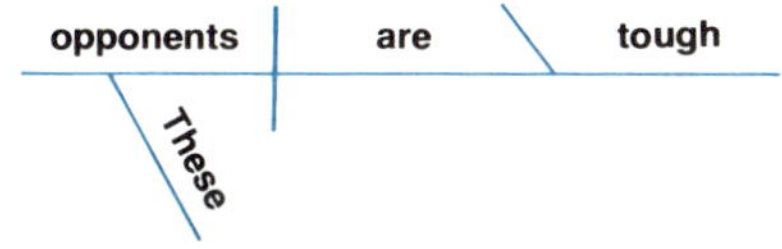

A compound predicate adjective appears on a split line.

The stereo sounds rich and full.

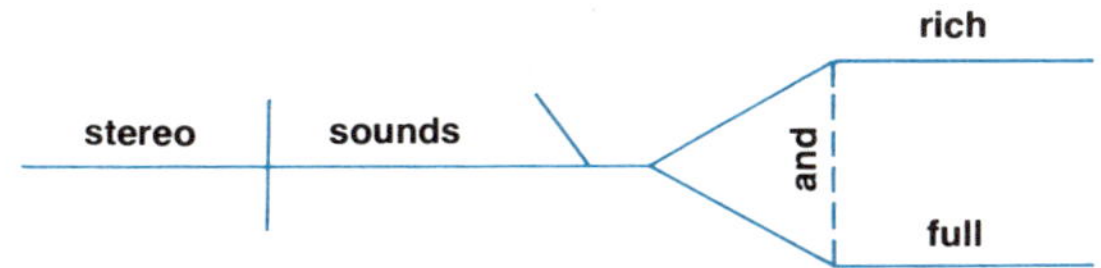

Exercise A Number your paper from 1 to 10. Write the adjectives in each sentence. After each adjective, write the word it modifies. Do not include articles.

1. The tiny shop sells old books, unusual games, and strange costumes.
2. Two small jeeps rumbled down the steep road to the wide beach.

3. Ellie spilled purple paint on that new yellow shirt.

4. Chuck wears flashy clothes and drives a red Camaro.

5. Several foreign leaders had a private meeting with the President.

6. Many experts stress the need for solar heat.

7. Ten people rode in the back of the dirty, rusty truck.

8. Most workers at that site wear yellow helmets.

9. Janice drank more water with the salty fish and tangy peppers.

10. In a sudden surge, the red car inched in front of the other twelve cars.

Exercise B Number your paper from 1 to 10. Write the predicate adjectives in these sentences.

1. The new President seems forceful.
2. Small cars are becoming popular.
3. The team feels confident about the game.
4. The jury felt sure of the decision.
5. The gash looked deep.
6. Safety precautions are necessary.
7. My supervisor is young and bright.
8. Nearly half of the work force is female.
9. How many people are happy with their work?
10. The unemployment rate is high.

Part 2 Adjectives in Comparisons

You often learn about new things by making comparisons. You compare new things with things you already know. You might describe a restaurant's food, for example, as "*better* than homemade food." Or you might explain that cream is *lighter* than milk.

Adjectives help you to make such comparisons.

The Comparative

Adjectives have special forms for making comparisons. When you compare one person or thing with another, you use the **comparative** form of an adjective. Here are some examples:

Evans is a *stronger* pitcher than Richardson.
This quilt looks *prettier* than that one.
Loretta is *more patient* than I am.

The comparative is made in two ways:

1. Add *-er* to short adjectives like *big* and *bright*.

wide + er = wider   young + er = younger
fancy + er = fancier   dark + er = darker

Notice that the spelling of some adjectives changes in the comparative form.

2. Use *more* for longer adjectives like *unusual*.

more energetic   more sensitive

Most adjectives ending in *-ful* or *-ous* form the comparative with *more*.

more powerful   more courageous

The Superlative

When you compare a person or thing with all others in its class, you use the **superlative** form of the adjective. In addition, use the superlative when you compare a person or thing with two or more others.

Here are some examples:

Kevin has the *smallest* part in the play.
Carmen is the *friendliest* person I know.
Football is the *most enjoyable* sport on TV.

The superlative form of an adjective is made by adding *-est* or by using *most*. If an adjective adds *-er* for the comparative, it adds *-est* for the superlative. If an adjective uses *more* for the comparative, it uses *most* for the superlative.

Adjective	Comparative	Superlative
smooth	smoother	smoothest
bright	brighter	brightest
helpful	more helpful	most helpful
difficult	more difficult	most difficult
capable	more capable	most capable

Remember these three points about using adjectives in comparison:

1. To compare two people or things, use the comparative. To compare more than two, use the superlative.

This old coin is *more valuable* than that one.
Joe makes the *tastiest* tacos I've ever had.

2. Use the word *other* when you compare something with everything else of its kind.

Wrong: Tim is faster than any runner.
(This sentence says that Tim is not a runner.)
Right: Tim is faster than any *other* runner.

Wrong: This chair is more solid than any piece of furniture.
(This sentence says that the chair is not a piece of furniture.)
Right: This chair is more solid than any *other* piece of furniture.

3. Do not use *-er* with *more*, or *-est* with *most*.

Wrong: Sue is much more taller than her sister.
Right: Sue is much *taller* than her sister.

Wrong: This is the most thickest book in the library.
Right: This is the *thickest* book in the library.

Irregular Comparisons

Some comparatives and superlatives are formed in unusual ways:

Adjective	Comparative	Superlative
good	better	best
well	better	best
bad	worse	worst
little	less or lesser	least
much	more	most
many	more	most
far	farther	farthest

Exercise A Number your paper from 1 to 10. Two of the following comparisons are correct, but the rest are wrong. If a sentence is correct, write *Correct*. If it is incorrect, write it correctly.

1. Gas mileage has become importanter to car owners.
2. Gasoline is more expensive this month than last.
3. A standard-size car is the bigger size that is made.
4. A mid-size car is more big than a compact.
5. The new cars are made with a lighter frame.
6. Front-wheel drive cars are more better than other cars for getting through snow.
7. Of all the gas stations, Jake's gives the goodest service.
8. This car makes fastest stops than that one.
9. A station wagon is the most roomiest car of all.
10. Of the three cars, this one has the rougher ride.

Exercise B Follow the directions for Exercise A. Three of the comparisons are correct.

1. It's easiest to get parts for American cars than for foreign cars.
2. This car is more expensive than that one.
3. Small cars have a bumpiest ride than big cars.

4. Big cars are often comfortabler.
5. However, big cars get worser gas mileage.
6. Which of these two cars is easiest to handle?
7. Foreign cars often get higher ratings by experts.
8. Which of these two cars sounds quietest?
9. Cars nowadays have more better insulation.
10. The fuel tank is larger in a big car than in a small one.

Part 3 Using Adverbs

An **adverb** is another kind of modifier. Adverbs help you to express yourself clearly and vividly. They tell *how*, *when*, *where*, or *to what extent* about something.

Adverbs are words that modify verbs, adjectives, and other adverbs.

Using Adverbs with Verbs

Adverbs frequently modify verbs. Adverbs tell *how*, *when*, *where*, or *to what extent* something happened.

Adverbs are used with verbs to tell *how*:

Pat *proudly* displayed her sculpture.

This computer works *accurately*.

Adverbs also tell *when* about verbs:

Small car sales have soared *recently*.

The new license plates are required *soon*.

Adverbs can tell *where* about verbs:

A phone booth is located *nearby*.

We sat *there* in the lobby for hours.

In addition, adverbs can tell *to what extent:*

Vanessa *nearly* choked on the soup.

Study the following list of adverbs:

How?	When?	Where?	To What Extent?
quickly	now	here	never
sorrowfully	then	there	often
hurriedly	later	nearby	not
steadily	finally	underground	seldom

Using Adverbs with Adjectives and Other Adverbs

Besides modifying verbs, adverbs also modify adjectives and other adverbs. Look at these sentences:

Some people are *partially* blind.
(*Partially* tells to what extent. It is an adverb modifying the adjective *blind.*)

The assembly line moved *very* quickly.
(*Very* tells to what extent. It is an adverb modifying the adverb *quickly.*)

Here are other adverbs that often modify adjectives or other adverbs:

too	quite	rather	most	more	extremely
just	nearly	so	really	truly	somewhat

The above adverbs tell *to what extent* something is true.

Forming Adverbs

Many adverbs are formed by adding *-ly* to an adjective.

weak + ly = weakly
obvious + ly = obviously
formal + ly = formally
slight + ly = slightly

At times, the addition of *-ly* causes a spelling change in the adjective.

possible + ly = possibly
happy + ly = happily
dull + ly = dully

Some adverbs are not formed from adjectives. *Quite, so, rather,* and *somewhat* are examples.

The switchboard had never been *so* busy before.

Job-sharing is a *rather* new idea.

Some words can be either adverbs or adjectives. *Late* and *high* are examples of such words.

The doctor arrived too *late.*
(*Late* is an adverb, modifying the verb *arrived.*)

Tony took a *late* bus.
(*Late* is an adjective, modifying the noun *bus.*)

The glider soared *high* above the hills.
(*High* is an adverb, modifying the verb *soared.*)

The crew worked on a *high* tower.
(*High* is an adjective, modifying the noun *tower.*)

Diagraming Adverbs

Adverbs are diagramed like adjectives. An adverb is placed on a slanted line attached to the word it modifies. This diagram shows an adverb modifying a verb:

The fire spread rapidly.

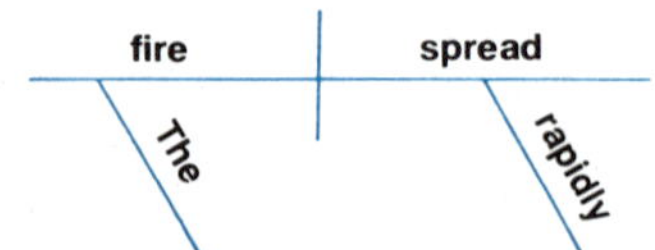

Adverbs that modify adjectives or other adverbs are diagramed like this:

Too many jobs pay very poorly.

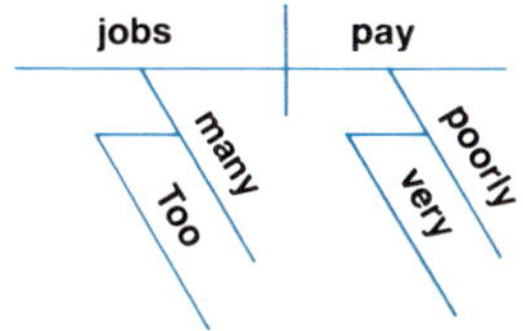

Exercise A Number your paper from 1 to 10. Write the adverbs in these sentences. After each adverb write the word it modifies. Be ready to explain what the adverb tells.

Example: A new family moved here recently.
recently modifies *moved* (tells when)
here modifies *moved* (tells where)

1. The tornado approached slowly.
2. Laura stood dangerously close to the fire.
3. We left early for the ABBA concert.
4. The glider swayed gently from side to side.
5. The pilot immediately controlled the fall.
6. Some spectators had become extremely nervous.
7. Many states have recently lowered their speed limits.
8. Lower speeds are much safer.
9. Our dress rehearsal went quite smoothly.
10. The lead singer moved wildly with the music.

Exercise B Follow the directions for Exercise A.

1. That movie was recently advertised on TV.
2. The movie ads sounded very eerie.
3. The movie itself was less scary.
4. We went to the theater early.
5. The film began slowly but soon improved.
6. Later the action moved very quickly.

7. Stunt people very often replace the real actors.
8. This theater still charges very low prices for tickets.
9. Do movies usually end happily?
10. Adventure films frequently play here.

Exercise C Change the following adjectives into adverbs by adding *-ly*. Check your spelling in a dictionary.

careless	proper	natural	exact
open	joyful	noisy	actual
ready	honest	sincere	real
easy	immediate	serious	safe

Part 4 Adverbs in Comparisons

You can use adverbs to compare actions. For example, you might say, "This team wins often but that team wins *more often*." Or you might say, "Of all the players, Erica practices *hardest*." Such comparisons help you to convey ideas clearly. Like adjectives, adverbs have special forms for making comparisons.

The Comparative

The **comparative** form of an adverb compares one action with another. Look at this example:

This storm hit *harder* than the last one.

The comparative is made in two ways:

1. Add *-er* to short adverbs like *long* and *fast*.

   A computer does the job *faster* than a person could.

2. Use *more* with most adverbs ending in *-ly*.

   Some blockers tackle *more roughly* than is necessary.

The Superlative

The **superlative** form of an adverb compares one action with two or more others. Notice these examples:

This flight takes off *earliest* of all.
Of the three boys, Larry spoke the *most bitterly*.

To form the superlative, either add *-est* or use *most*. If an adverb adds *-er* for the comparative, it adds *-est* for the superlative. If an adverb uses *more* for the comparative, it uses *most* for the superlative.

Adverb	Comparative	Superlative
fast	faster	fastest
tightly	more tightly	most tightly

Remember these points about adverbs in comparisons:

1. To compare two actions, use the comparative. To compare more than two actions, use the superlative.

Air mail will arrive *sooner* than surface mail.
Special delivery mail will arrive *soonest* of all.

2. Use the word *other* when you compare with every other action of the same kind.

Wrong: The general lives more comfortably than any officer.
Right: The general lives more comfortably than any *other* officer.

3. Do not use *-er* with *more*, or *-est* with *most*.

Wrong: Some tool makers work more faster than others.
Right: Some tool makers work faster than others.

Irregular Comparisons

Some adverbs change completely in the comparative and superlative forms. These are examples:

Adverb	Comparative	Superlative
well	better	best
much	more	most
little	less	least
far	farther	farthest

This saw works well.
That new saw works better.
A table saw would work best of all.

Exercise A Write the comparative and superlative forms.

1. wildly	4. gradually	7. quickly	9. generously
2. loosely	5. deeply	8. intelligently	10. early
3. long	6. soon		

Exercise B If a sentence is correct, write *Correct.* If there is an error in the comparison of adverbs, write the sentence correctly.

1. The gymnasts moved smoothlier after much practice.
2. Foods cook more fast over an open fire.
3. We traveled more frequently when we were younger.
4. Some cars run better on unleaded gas.
5. Of all the machines, this one operates more smoothly.
6. I awaken cheerfulliest on Saturdays.
7. Gardner competes more doggedly than Reese.
8. Apples ripen fastest than pears.
9. Of the four pitchers, James pitches more accurately.
10. Epoxy glue holds bestest of all.

Part 5 Adjective or Adverb?

Read these sentences. Which sentence sounds right to you?

The blast came *sudden*.
The blast came *suddenly*.

If you said the second sentence, you are correct. An adverb (*suddenly*), not an adjective (*sudden*), is needed to modify the verb *came*.

Sometimes you may have trouble deciding whether to use an adjective or an adverb. To decide, ask yourself:

1. What kind of word does the modifier tell about?

   If your answer is an action verb, adjective, or adverb, use the adverb.

   If your answer is a noun or pronoun, use the adjective.

2. What does the modifier tell about the word it goes with?

   If it tells *how*, *when*, *where*, or *to what extent*, use the adverb.

   If it tells *which one*, *what kind*, or *how many*, use the adjective.

An adjective tells	An adverb tells
*Which one *What kind *How many	*How *When *Where *To what extent
About a noun or pronoun	About a verb, adjective, or adverb

Exercise A List each adjective and adverb, together with the word it modifies. Do not list articles.

1. The two motorcycles swerved sharply.
2. Tractors slowly pushed the deep snow aside.
3. Open that window very carefully.

4. Lauren watches television endlessly.
5. Too many shows are reruns.
6. Two favorite programs are "M*A*S*H*" and "Barney Miller."
7. Several series have somewhat similar plots.
8. The screen glows brightly in the dark room.
9. That printer uses heavy machinery.
10. The hikers walked rather quickly.

Exercise B Choose the correct modifier from the two in parentheses. Tell whether it is an adjective or an adverb.

1. We worked (furious, furiously) to halt the flooding.
2. Many houses were destroyed by (heavy, heavily) winds.
3. This battery is (terrible, terribly) weak.
4. You look particularly (nice, nicely) this morning.
5. The truckers drove (slow, slowly) down the steep grade.
6. The new car gleamed (bright, brightly) in the sun.
7. The team felt (awful, awfully) bad about the loss.
8. An (extreme, extremely) hot liquid dripped from the furnace.
9. The two teams battled (fierce, fiercely) at the game.
10. The center turned around so (quick, quickly), she fell.

Adverb or Predicate Adjective?

You have learned that a predicate adjective follows a linking verb and modifies the subject. Besides forms of *be*, other linking verbs are *become*, *seem*, *appear*, *look*, *sound*, *feel*, *taste*, *smell*, and *grow*.

That lunch smells rotten. (*Rotten* modifies *lunch*.)

The parking lot looks full. (*Full* modifies *lot*.)

The prisoner grew violent. (*Violent* modifies *prisoner*.)

Verbs in the sentences above, *smells*, *looks*, and *grew*, can also be action verbs. So can *sound*, *appear*, *feel*, and *taste*. When these verbs are action verbs, they are followed by adverbs instead of predicate adjectives. Adverbs tell *how*, *when*, *where*, or *to what extent* about the action verbs.

Here are sentences using the same words as linking verbs and as action verbs.

Linking Verbs with Adjectives	Action Verbs with Adverbs
The water *looked* clear.	Dave *looked* carefully.
The team *appeared* eager.	Clouds *appeared* suddenly.
The pizza *smells* delicious.	A bloodhound *smells* keenly.
This music *sounds* peaceful.	The fire alarm *sounds* often.

If you can't decide whether to use an adverb or an adjective in a certain sentence, ask these questions:

1. Can you substitute *is* or *was* for the verb? If so, the modifier is probably an adjective.

2. Does the modifier tell *how*, *when*, *where*, or *to what extent*? If so, the modifier is probably an adverb.

Exercise Choose the right modifier for the following sentences.

1. Adam (angry, angrily) returned the trophy.
2. The rhythm sounded (slow, slowly) and gentle.
3. Stained glass looks (brilliant, brilliantly) in bright light.
4. The operator answered our questions (patient, patiently).
5. During the overtime the crowd grew (tense, tensely).
6. The teller sounded the burglar alarm (immediate, immediately).

7. Heather's carpentry appears so (perfect, perfectly).
8. The new father looked (proud, proudly) at his son.
9. Gravel feels (rough, roughly) on my bare feet.
10. Those big dill pickles taste (sour, sourly).

Part 6 Troublesome Modifiers

Certain modifiers are frequently used incorrectly.

Them and *Those*

Those can be used as an adjective.

Where are the controls for *those* power saws?

Them is never an adjective. It cannot substitute for *those*.

Wrong: We framed them photos.
Right: We framed *those* photos.
Right: We framed *them*.

Here and *There*

Sometimes people incorrectly say "this here jacket" or "that there room." "This here" and "that there" repeat ideas. The word *this* includes the idea of *here*. The word *that* includes the idea of *there*. Avoid "this here" and "that there."

Kind and *Sort*

Kind and *sort* are singular. *Kinds* and *sorts* are plural. No matter what words follow, use *this* or *that* with *kind* and *sort*. Use *these* and *those* with *kinds* and *sorts*.

This kind of boot is made of cowhide. (singular)
Those sorts of food are high in calories. (plural)

Good and *Well*

Good and *well* have similar meanings, but the words are not the same. You cannot always substitute one word for the other. Look at the differences in these sentences:

> That is a *good* photo of you. (The adjective *good* modifies the noun *photo*.)
>
> You sing *well*. (The adverb *well* modifies the verb *sing*.)

Good is always an adjective, modifying nouns and pronouns. It is never used to describe an action.

Well can be either an adjective or an adverb. In the sentence above, *well* is used as an adverb modifying an action verb. *Well* can also be used after a linking verb to mean "in good health."

> Tara doesn't look *well*.
> (*Well* is a predicate adjective modifying *Tara*.)
>
> Yvonne dances *well*.
> (*Well* is an adverb modifying the action verb *dances*.)

If you are describing an action, use *well*.

The Double Negative

Two negative words used together when only one is necessary is called a **double negative.** Avoid using double negatives.

Wrong: We didn't take no time-outs.
Right: We did*n't* take *any* time-outs.

Wrong: My out-of-town friends never write no letters.
Right: My out-of-town friends *never* write *any* letters.

Wrong: John couldn't eat nothing all day.
Right: John could*n't* eat *anything* all day.

Contractions like *couldn't* contain a shortened form of the negative *not*. Do not use other negative words after them.

Some common negative words are *no*, *none*, *not*, *nothing*, and *never*. Instead of these words, use *any*, *anything*, or *ever* after negative contractions.

Rod has*n't ever* hit a grand-slam home run.
Michelle could*n't* find *any* bargains.
The new Senator did*n't* change *anything*.

Other negative words are *hardly*, *scarcely*, and *barely*. Don't use them with negative contractions like *hasn't* and *didn't*.

Wrong: Rick couldn't barely control the machine.
Right: Rick could *barely* control the machine.

Wrong: The movers hadn't scarcely begun.
Right: The movers had *scarcely* begun.

Wrong: Lightning hardly never strikes houses.
Right: Lightning *hardly ever* strikes houses.

Exercise A Choose the correct word from the two in parentheses.

1. Have (them, those) funds run out?
2. Each state collects (that, those) kind of tax.
3. How do you steer (them, those) canoes?
4. (That, That there) phone call was for Debbie.
5. The spacelab brought back (this, these) kinds of pictures.
6. Which radio station plays (them, those) pop hits?
7. Chris Evert-Lloyd won (that, that there) title.
8. (This, These) sorts of planes are extremely fast.
9. The airline canceled (this, this here) flight.
10. Is (this, these) sort of convertible still made?

Exercise B Follow the directions for Exercise A.

1. Our coach treats us (good, well).
2. This network has many (good, well) shows.

3. "Lou Grant" did very (good, well) in the ratings.

4. Some gymnasts do not have (good, well) form.

5. Marcy does a (good, well) routine on the balance beam.

6. This coconut cream pie tastes (good, well).

7. Snowplows cleared the streets (good, well).

8. The Colts are doing (good, well) in the standings.

9. Ross understood my worries (good, well).

10. Does Carlotta swim (good, well) enough to make the team?

Exercise C Number your paper from 1 to 10. Correct the double negatives in the following sentences. If a sentence contains no double negative, write *Correct.*

1. Jason hasn't seen no movies lately.
2. Haven't you never been to a disco?
3. One runner couldn't barely clear the hurdles.
4. During the test Amy couldn't remember nothing.
5. The elevator doesn't ever work.
6. This hot dog doesn't have no mustard on it.
7. Pam hardly knows nobody at work yet.
8. Since their argument Ramon and Todd haven't scarcely talked to each other.
9. Chris doesn't expect any reward for finding the purse.
10. The team doesn't have hardly any returning players.

REVIEW Using Modifiers

Recognizing Adjectives Write each adjective in these sentences. Tell which word it modifies. Do not include articles.

1. This film was made on a low budget.
2. Does anyone know the true story?
3. That Italian sportscar has a deluxe interior.
4. Dense, black smoke poured out of the tailpipe.
5. One candidate received illegal funds.
6. Two mysterious strangers appeared at the door.
7. No newspaper can print every bit of news.
8. Everyone likes these new shorter hours.
9. Some Indian food is cooked in a clay oven.
10. Reggae is a kind of music from the lush, tropical island of Jamaica.

Predicate Adjectives Write the predicate adjective.

11. Rebecca seems unusually quiet.
12. That dead tree is hollow.
13. The combat forces are strong.
14. The California sun is intense.
15. That African nation has just become independent.

Adjectives in Comparison Choose the correct adjective.

16. Have you ever tasted (more spicier, spicier) chili?
17. Who was the (younger, youngest) of all the Presidents?
18. This year the business was (more profitable, most profitable) than last year.
19. Jennifer looks (happier, happiest) than her friend.
20. Of all the paperbacks, this one is the (more enjoyable, most enjoyable).

Recognizing Adverbs Write the adverbs and the words they modify.

Example: Ray and I met casually.
casually modifies *met*

21. Cindy Nicholas swam the English Channel twice.
22. My grandparents arrived yesterday.
23. A trap door slowly opened.
24. Two helicopters hovered overhead.
25. Carrie is too busy.
26. The union members very grudgingly signed the pact.
27. The skaters practice here quite frequently.
28. Furious, Seth stomped out.
29. Currently, Congress is seriously considering other energy sources.
30. The painter usually throws paint wildly at the canvas.

Choosing the Right Modifier Write the correct modifier.

31. The storm hit (hardest, most hard) in the tropics.
32. Randy can repair appliances (more skillfully, most skillfully) than his brother.
33. Amanda parked (nearer, nearest) to the curb than Carter did.
34. Washington played (badder, worse, worst) than usual.
35. The flood waters receded (quicklier, more quickly) than expected.
36. The veterans talked (honest, honestly) about their problems.
37. The ice-cold watermelon tasted (sweet, sweetly).
38. Nicole looked (eager, eagerly) at the swimming pool.
39. The health department inspects restaurants (good, well).
40. (This, These) kinds of motor bikes use hardly (no, any) gasoline.

Using Prepositions and Conjunctions

Sometimes you can say what you mean with short sentences like these:

Beth raced.
The class uses paints.

Often, though, you will want to provide more information. Modifiers are useful for that purpose.

Beth raced yesterday.
The art class uses vivid paints.

At times, what you have to say is even more complicated. Suppose you want to say where Beth raced. Suppose you want to add that the art class also uses clay. Then you will need words to show those relationships.

Beth raced yesterday along the lake.
The art class uses vivid paints and clay.

Relationships dealing with people, actions, and things are expressed by words that connect other words. In this section you will learn about two kinds of connecting words: **prepositions** and **conjunctions.**

Part 1 What Are Prepositions?

Words that join other words or word groups are called **connectives.** One important kind of connective is the **preposition.** Prepositions show relationships. Look at the relationships expressed in the following sentences:

Sare leaped *off* her bike.
Sara leaped *onto* her bike.
Sara leaped *over* her bike.

The prepositions *off*, *onto*, and *over* show the relationship between *bike* and the verb *leaped*. In each of the above sentences, *bike* is the **object of the preposition.** Like all prepositions, *off*, *onto*, and *over* connect their objects to another part of the sentence.

Prepositions do not show relationships all by themselves. They begin a *phrase*, a group of words that do not have a subject or verb. The **prepositional phrase** makes the relationship clear. In the above sentences, *off her bike*, *onto her bike*, and *over her bike* are prepositional phrases. Here are some other sentences with prepositional phrases:

Zack politely asked *for a refund*.
In the spring, Darrell returned *to school*.
The box *of books* was too heavy.

A preposition is a word used with a noun or pronoun, called its *object*, to show the relationship between the noun or pronoun and some other word in the sentence.

A prepositional phrase consists of a preposition, its object, and any modifiers of the object.

The list below shows words often used as prepositions. Many of them, like *above, over, in,* and *beside,* help to show location. Others, like *until, after,* and *before,* show a relationship of time. Still others show different kinds of relationships. Look at these prepositions and see if you can tell the relationship each one suggests.

Words Often Used as Prepositions

about	behind	during	off	to
above	below	except	on	toward
across	beneath	for	onto	under
after	beside	from	out	until
against	between	in	outside	up
along	beyond	inside	over	upon
among	but *(except)*	into	past	with
around	by	like	since	within
at	concerning	near	through	without
before	down	of	throughout	

Exercise A Number your paper from 1 to 10. Find the prepositional phrases in the following sentences.

Example: Mac went to the game with Gwen.
to the game, with Gwen

1. Marta works after school.
2. The man slumped against the wall.
3. I waited outside the office for Pam.
4. Rosa vaulted easily over the pole.
5. By all means, talk with Gene about your plans.
6. During this season, Franklin pitched three no-hitters.
7. At first, the bite of a black widow spider may not even be noticed.
8. The designs on totem poles often tell stories.
9. Walter jumped over the fallen halfback.
10. Don't walk through that tunnel after dark.

Exercise B Follow the directions for Exercise A.

1. I heard nothing from Ben until today.
2. During the storm, everyone except Dee stayed inside the bus shelter.
3. Beyond a doubt, someone had been there before us.
4. There is no one else like you in the world.
5. Bright crépe paper was strung across the room.
6. There is a fast-food place near the shoe store.
7. Since last week, Anthony has been under pressure.
8. Cecelia walked off the stage with her award.
9. With little trouble, the Cowboys broke through the Bears' defense.
10. For over a month, that rusty old car has been parked in the alley.

Preposition or Adverb?

Many words used as prepositions may also be used as adverbs. How can you tell the difference?

A preposition is never used alone. It is always followed by a noun or pronoun as part of a phrase. If the word is in a phrase, it is probably a preposition. If the word has no object, it is probably an adverb.

> The visitors walked *around the courtyard.* (preposition)
> The visitors walked *around.* (adverb)
>
> The tuba player lagged *behind the other marchers.* (preposition)
> The tuba player lagged *behind.* (adverb)

Exercise A Decide whether the italicized words in these sentences are adverbs or prepositions. Write *Adverb* or *Preposition* for each sentence.

1. Turn the water *on* now.
2. Terry put her mitt *on* the bench.

3. Mindy accidentally knocked the salt *off* the table.
4. Turn the oven *off*.
5. Dolores left last week, and I have not seen her *since*.
6. That was the Pirates' best game *since* last fall.
7. Ed fell *down* and broke his glasses.
8. I have not seen Juanita *around*.
9. James is always looking somewhere *over* the rainbow for happiness.
10. The ball rumbled *down* the alley.

Exercise B Follow the directions for Exercise A.

1. Suzy does not ride *without* headgear.
2. You forgot to turn your headlights *on*.
3. *Without* a word, Sam handed her the letter.
4. Is that nurse *on* duty now?
5. On weekends, the doctor is rarely *in*.
6. Tony put a quarter *into* the slot.
7. Finally the ball fell *through* the hoop.
8. Finally the ball fell *through*, and the fans breathed again.
9. Do you mind if I go *along?*
10. Caroline inched *along* the narrow ledge.

Part 2 Prepositional Phrases as Modifiers

Single words are often used as modifiers. However, groups of words may also modify. Prepositional phrases may modify various parts of a sentence. They work the same way as single adjectives or adverbs.

An adjective phrase is a prepositional phrase that modifies a noun or pronoun. The phrase always includes the preposition, its object, and any modifiers of the object.

The school needs a new coach *for the track team.*
(*For the track team* is an adjective phrase, modifying the noun *coach.* It tells *what kind* of coach.)

The door *on the left* is the emergency exit.
(*On the left* is an adjective phrase, modifying the noun *door.* It tells *which one.*)

All *of the bank tellers* wear matching uniforms.
(*Of the bank tellers* is an adjective phrase that modifies the pronoun *all.* It tells *what kind.*)

As you can see, adjective phrases, like adjectives, tell *which one* or *what kind.*

Adverbs tell *how, when, where,* and *to what extent* about verbs. Adverb phrases modify verbs in the same way.

Adverb phrases are prepositional phrases that modify verbs.

The bottles are sealed *by a huge machine.*
(*By a huge machine* is an adverb phrase telling *how.* It modifies the verb *are sealed.*)

On Saturday the playoffs will begin.
(*On Saturday* is an adverb phrase. It tells *when* about the verb *will begin.*)

Hendricks sat *on the bench.*
(*On the bench* is an adverb phrase. It tells *where* about the verb *sat.*)

Sometimes one prepositional phrase follows another. Frequently, the second phrase is an adjective phrase modifying the object in the first phrase.

Cecily decided *on a name for her new dog.*
(*On a name* is an adverb phrase modifying the verb *decided. For her new dog* is an adjective phrase modifying the noun *name.*)

Jim topped the salad *with bits of cheese.*
(The adverb phrase *with bits* tells *how* about the verb *topped. Of cheese* is an adjective phrase describing the noun *bits.*)

Diagraming Prepositional Phrases

To diagram a prepositional phrase, place it under the word it modifies.

The guests on the show talked about their new movies.

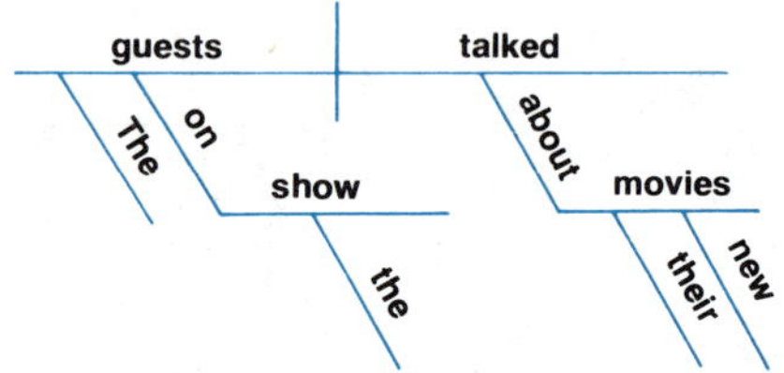

At times a preposition may have two or more nouns or pronouns as objects in the prepositional phrase.

On warm days we fished for trout and bass.

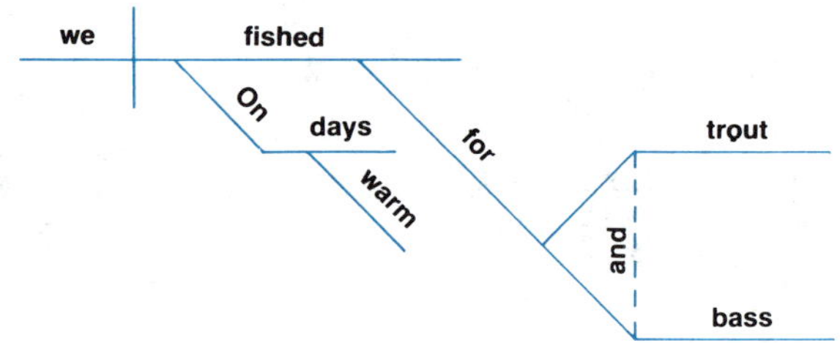

Exercise A Copy these sentences. Circle each prepositional phrase. Draw an arrow from the phrase to the word it modifies. Tell whether the phrase is an adjective phrase or an adverb phrase.

1. Nicole bought a jacket with a hood.
2. The man with a cast on his leg waved to us.
3. Do you work after school?
4. The Navajos and Apaches remained enemies for hundreds of years.
5. Sacramento is the capital of California.
6. We stayed with my aunt from St. Louis.

7. The subways were operating during the blizzard.
8. Did you leave your books at home?
9. We left after lunch and arrived before dinner.
10. During the first half, four of our players fouled out.

Exercise B Follow the directions for Exercise A.

1. Someone is hiding behind the door.
2. The store down the block sells tamales.
3. The autumn trees made a golden arch over the street.
4. Nobody except Vivian knows the answer to that question.
5. The fixture fell from the ceiling and crashed onto the floor.
6. The box under the table contains some sweaters for the clothing drive.
7. With a silly grin, Mick stepped upon the scale.
8. Keith tripped over the rug on the stairs.
9. The tire broke through ice and stuck in a large hole.
10. The girl behind Dana is my sister.

Part 3 Conjunctions

A conjunction is another kind of word that shows relationships.

A conjunction is a word that connects words or groups of words.

Look at the conjunctions in the following sentences:

> Jennie *and* Vanessa will replace the broken window.
> (connects nouns)
>
> The sculptor carves either wood *or* stone.
> (connects nouns)
>
> Kent wrote *and* narrated the skits.
> (connects verbs)

My typing is fast *but* sloppy.
(connects adjectives)

We looked *both* in our rooms *and* at school.
(connects prepositional phrases)

Like prepositions, conjunctions show a relationship between the words they connect. Conjunctions differ from prepositions, however, in two ways. Conjunctions link similar kinds of words, like two nouns or two phrases. In addition, conjunctions do not have objects.

Coordinating Conjunctions

Coordinating conjunctions are used to join single words or groups of words of the same kind. *And*, *but*, and *or* are the most common coordinating conjunctions.

The words joined by coordinating conjunctions are compound constructions. Compound constructions include compound subjects, compound direct objects, and compound verbs, for example.

Cars *and* trucks often have different speed limits.
(*And* links *cars* and *trucks*, making them a compound subject of the verb *have*.)

The skater tripped *and* fell.
(*And* connects *tripped* and *fell*, forming a compound verb.)

Sue looked at the engine *but* couldn't locate the problem.
(*But* connects the two predicates.)

The race cars looked low *and* sleek.
(*And* connects two predicate adjectives.)

The candidate spoke realistically *but* hopefully.
(*But* connects two adverbs.)

Kim added fudge, nuts, *and* marshmallows to her sundae.
(*And* connects the three parts of the compound direct object.)

Tell the coach *or* the assistant your idea.
(*Or* connects the compound indirect object.)

On Monday *or* Tuesday, the cleaning will be ready.
(*Or* connects compound objects of a preposition.)

Correlative Conjunctions

Some conjunctions are used in pairs. They are called **correlative conjunctions.** These are correlative conjunctions:

both . . . and	not only . . . but (also)
either . . . or	whether . . . or
neither . . . nor	

Both oak *and* walnut are used for furniture.
You'll need *either* a coat *or* a warm jacket.
Neither cranes *nor* trucks could lift the marble slabs.
The cafeteria serves *not only* lunch *but also* breakfast.
The team discussed *whether* to kick *or* to run.

Exercise A Find the conjunctions in the following sentences. Tell what words or word groups are connected by the conjunction.

Example: The Honda skidded and swerved.
The verbs *skidded* and *swerved* are connected by the conjunction *and*.

1. Pigeons and sparrows are often seen in cities.
2. Alice moved quietly but quickly to the phone.
3. The blueprints were clear and precise.
4. Simon overslept and missed breakfast.
5. Should I use a fork or a spoon for this soup?
6. Either Anita or Joe will win the award.
7. Linda writes slogans for T-shirts and bumper stickers.
8. Todd not only notices but also remembers.
9. I listen to both Barry Manilow and Kenny Rogers.
10. The team had neither an experienced coach nor a good pitcher.

Exercise B Write the kind of compound construction in each sentence. Write the construction with its conjunction.

1. The gymnasts flipped and turned on the uneven bars.
2. Dallas called time-out but couldn't decide on a new strategy.
3. Bobcats and bears prowl the back woods.
4. A piston moves up and down in its cylinder.
5. The wooden walkway was narrow, shaky, and dangerous.
6. I'll telephone either Jane's mother or her brother immediately.
7. Billie has not only a sore throat but also a bad cough.
8. Is Ellis forgetful or rude?
9. Both the length and the width of my skates need adjusting.
10. The vendor sold us hot dogs, Dr. Pepper, and popcorn.

Exercise C Write two sentences using *and,* two sentences using *but,* and two sentences using *or.* After each sentence, write the words or groups of words that are joined by the conjunctions.

Exercise D Write one sentence for each of the following pairs of correlative conjunctions:

both . . . and   either . . . or   neither . . . nor

REVIEW Using Prepositions and Conjunctions

Recognizing Prepositional Phrases Write the prepositional phrase or phrases in each sentence.

1. Both Sonny Rollins and Miles Davis have played at that club.
2. Mary searched everywhere for the envelope.
3. I enjoy games like Monoply.
4. Ginger woke at dawn to the sound of birds outside her window.
5. The cables ran along the roof.
6. Since yesterday I have changed my mind about the party.
7. The plane passed through the clusters of clouds.
8. Have you looked under the chair for your shoes?
9. Electric cars might be the autos of the future.
10. Bonnie left her bike by the tree near the corner.

Prepositional Phrases as Modifiers Write the prepositional phrase in each sentence. Label each phrase *Adjective* or *Adverb* to tell how it is used.

11. Pat threw the line into the river.
12. Are Volkswagens made in Germany?
13. A movie about a baseball player is playing here.
14. Bert hung his hat carefully on the hook.
15. These gloves are lined with fur.
16. The woman with the briefcase is Dr. Sanchez.
17. A crowd of people swarmed the stage.
18. The young man in the green jacket is Jake Houston.
19. The ball landed in the bleachers.
20. Nobody but Rachel understood the question.

Conjunctions For each sentence, write the compound construction with its conjunction.

21. The Pirates and the Steelers are Pittsburgh teams.
22. Father Hildalgo of Mexico was both a priest and a political leader.
23. Gilda Radner talked and joked with the audience.
24. The speaker's voice was quiet but firm.
25. Andrew was not only hungry but also thirsty.
26. Can you tell whether a computer or a person made the mistake?
27. Rugs, drapes, and pillows muffle the noises in a room.
28. Somebody called for you but left no message.
29. In gym class, we'll play either volleyball or softball.
30. Neither Kelley nor Rivera caught the grounder to left field.

Review of Parts of Speech

Part 1 The Parts of Speech

You have studied nouns, pronouns, verbs, adjectives, adverbs, prepositions, and conjunctions. All of these classes of words are called **parts of speech.** Words are grouped as different parts of speech because of the way they are used in sentences.

There are eight parts of speech. Besides the seven groups listed above, there is one other part of speech. It is called the interjection.

What Is an Interjection?

An interjection is a word or group of words used to express strong feeling.

An interjection may be either a phrase or a word. In any case, the interjection shows strong feeling. Those feelings might be, for example, joy, anger, terror, surprise, disgust, or sadness. Because it conveys strong emotions, an interjection is followed by an exclamation mark.

Notice the following interjections:

Wow! This is fun.
Oh! I didn't see you there.
Ugh! This tastes terrible.

Now you have studied all eight parts of speech:

The Parts of Speech

nouns	**verbs**	**adverbs**	**conjunctions**
pronouns	**adjectives**	**prepositions**	**interjections**

Exercise A Write each italicized word. Next to it, write what part of speech it is.

1. *Fantastic!* The agent likes Vicky's demonstration record.
2. Phillips *dove* for the end zone.
3. Did *anybody* ever thank the Lone Ranger?
4. Anne hung a poster *inside* her locker.
5. Bonnie *or* Earl will adjust the handlebars for you.
6. I should *probably* wake Roger.
7. Your phone is always *busy*.
8. Paula flashed a *cheerful* smile.
9. The *stories* of O. Henry end with a surprise.
10. Lydia *remembered* the friendliness of her old neighborhood.

Exercise B Follow the directions for Exercise A.

1. The truck swerved and *avoided* a collision.
2. Country music has influenced both rock *and* soul music.
3. Some new homes are heated *by* the sun.
4. *Ugh!* There's a worm in this apple.
5. The steel mills in *Gary* reddened the sky.
6. Angie didn't notice the steps in front of *her*.
7. Leslie cleared the hurdles *easily*.
8. The *polite* bus driver waited for the limping man.
9. Traffic should stop for *pedestrians* with white canes.
10. Margaret Bourke-White *became* famous for her war photographs.

Part 2 Using Words as Different Parts of Speech

Very often the same word can be used as different parts of speech. For example, a word might be a noun in one sentence and an adjective in another.

There is only one way to tell what part of speech any word is. You must see how that word is used in a sentence.

Here are some examples of one word used as two different parts of speech:

The artist folded *paper* into unusual shapes.
(*Paper* is used as a noun, the direct object of the verb *folded*.)

At the picnic, we ate on *paper* plates.
(*Paper* is used as an adjective, modifying *plates*.)

The five-dollar *bill* has a picture of Abraham Lincoln.
(*Bill* is used as a noun, the subject of the sentence.)

The store will *bill* us for our purchases.
(*Bill* is used as the main verb.)

Carlotta had a *light* snack of carrot sticks.
(*Light* is used as an adjective, modifying the noun *snack*.)
Light the candle, please.
(*Light* is used as a verb.)

Did you park in the *underground* garage?
(*Underground* is used as an adjective, modifying the noun *garage*.)
After seeing its shadow, the groundhog went *underground*.
(*Underground* is used as an adverb, modifying the verb *went*.)

What is your favorite song?
(*What* is used as a pronoun, the subject of the sentence.)
What programs are on TV now?
(*What* is used as an adjective, modifying the noun *programs*.)

A *low* wall surrounded the building.
(*Low* is used as an adjective, modifying the noun *wall*.)
A plane flew *low* over the beach.
(*Low* is used as an adverb, modifying the verb *flew*.)

After her speech, Sally sat *down*.
(*Down* is used as an adverb, modifying the verb *sat*.)
We rowed the boat *down* the river.
(*Down* is used as a preposition.)

Never! I won't try it again.
(*Never* is used as an interjection.)
Mr. Bailey *never* raises his voice.
(*Never* is used as an adverb, modifying the verb *raises*.)

Exercise A Write the italicized word. Next to it, write what part of speech it is in that sentence.

1. *Really!* Do you expect me to believe that?
2. The potato salad was *really* delicious.
3. *Cross* that intersection very carefully.
4. Julie wore a gold *cross* on a chain.
5. The conductor seems *cross* today.
6. *Daydreams* can serve a useful purpose.

7. Paul *daydreams* about sports.
8. Have you ever played *this* game before?
9. *This* is my aunt's house.
10. *Fire* drills are scheduled every month.

Exercise B Follow the directions for Exercise A.

1. Don't turn the television *on* during an electrical storm.
2. Her pay envelope was lying *on* the table.
3. Our mail carrier *growls* back at dogs.
4. The *growls* were getting meaner and deeper.
5. *Park* your bike in those racks.
6. This *park* provides nature walks.
7. The youth center keeps a job *file.*
8. Passengers usually *file* quietly down to the subway.
9. *That* was my idea.
10. Have you already seen *that* movie?

REVIEW Review of Parts of Speech

Identifying Parts of Speech Read each sentence. Then copy the italicized word. Write what part of speech the word is in that sentence.

1. Jim talks too fast *and* too much.
2. That man looks exactly *like* Lou Gossett, Jr.
3. Did the reporter quote *you* accurately?
4. *Ouch!* That really stings.
5. We planned a *visit* to an historic Indian site.
6. It rained every evening *for* a week.
7. Laura *dances* to any kind of music.
8. The police officer examined the skid *marks*.
9. *This* is Randy's birthday.
10. Do you feel better *now*?
11. *Americans* drink more than one-third of the world's coffee.
12. Ghana and Zaire are *African* countries.
13. The President tossed out the *game* ball.
14. The old man *signs* his papers with a flourish.
15. Ben *starches* his shirts.
16. *That* shop specializes in repairs for motorcycles.
17. How did Indian summer get its *name*?
18. The emergency room is *always* crowded.
19. Did *anyone* pour cool water on the burn?
20. Here winter begins *early* and ends late.
21. The *leaves* of ginkgo trees look like small fans.
22. The art class designed and *sold* calendars.
23. Robert takes his *youngest* sister to a day-care center every morning.
24. The California Angels won their first pennant *in* 1979.
25. *Phew!* We got here just in time.

Using Verbals

You have learned about all eight parts of speech. They are the following:

nouns	verbs	adverbs	conjunctions
pronouns	adjectives	prepositions	interjections

Besides those parts of speech, our language also contains three other kinds of words. They are **gerunds, participles,** and **infinitives.** All three are similar to verbs. For that reason, they are called **verbals.** A verbal is a word that is formed from a verb but is never used as a verb. In this section you will learn about using the three kinds of verbals.

Part 1 Gerunds

A gerund is a verb form that is used as a noun. A gerund ends in *-ing*. It may be used in any way that a noun is used.

Like a noun, a gerund may be used as a subject.

Drawing is Alissa's hobby.
(*Drawing* is a gerund, the subject of the verb *is*.)

Like a noun, a gerund may be used as the direct object.

Debbie tried *surfing*.
(*Surfing* is a gerund, the object of the verb *tried*.)

Like a noun, a gerund may be used as the object of a preposition.

The best place for *jogging* is the park.
(*Jogging* is a gerund, the object of the preposition *for*.)

The Gerund Phrase

A gerund is not always used alone. Often a gerund has a modifier or an object or both. Together, they form a **gerund phrase.** The entire gerund phrase is used like a noun.

Because a gerund is formed from a verb, it can have an object.

We won by *scoring a touchdown* in the last minute.
(*Scoring* is a gerund; *touchdown* is the object of *scoring*. The phrase *scoring a touchdown* is the object of the preposition *by*.)

Because a gerund is formed from a verb, it can be modified by adverbs.

Elliot started *laughing again*.
(*Laughing* is a gerund; *again* is an adverb modifying *laughing*. The phrase *laughing again* is the object of the verb *started*.)

Because a gerund is used as a noun, it can be modified by adjectives.

Quick thinking saved us.
(*Thinking* is a gerund; *quick* is an adjective modifying *thinking*. The phrase *quick thinking* is the subject of the verb *saved*.)

Gerunds can also be modified by prepositional phrases.

Sitting on these benches is uncomfortable.
(*Sitting* is a gerund; *on these benches* is a prepositional phrase modifying *sitting*. The entire gerund phrase is the subject of *is*.)

In all of these examples you can see that gerunds are used as nouns, even though they look like verbs. *Drawing, surfing, jogging, scoring, laughing, thinking,* and *sitting* all look like verbs but are not used as verbs. Because they are used as nouns, they are gerunds. Modifiers and objects that are used with them form gerund phrases.

Diagraming Gerunds

A gerund or gerund phrase used as a subject or direct object is diagramed on a line above the main line.The gerund belongs on a line drawn as a step. Its modifiers are placed on slanted lines below it. Its object is shown on the horizontal line following the gerund.

Telling jokes will cheer us up.

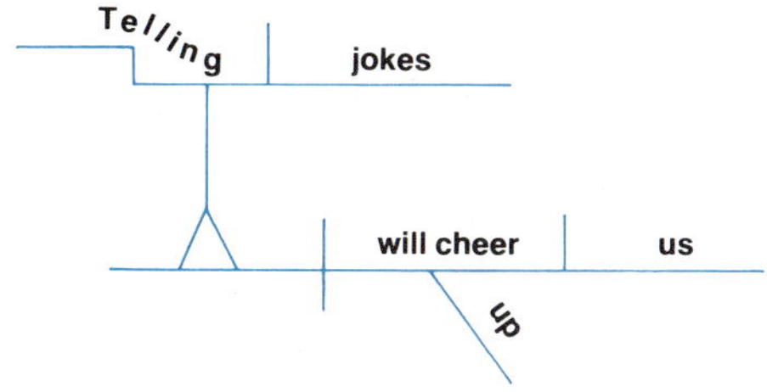

This job requires fast, accurate typing.

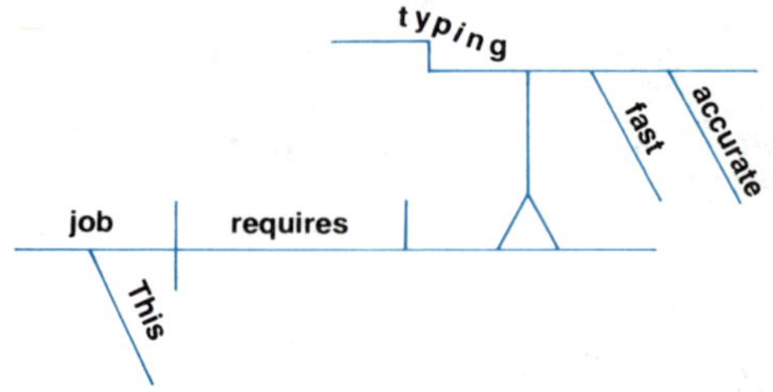

A gerund or gerund phrase used as the object of a preposition is diagramed below the main line. The preposition belongs on a slanted line going down from the word modified. Again, the gerund appears on a stepped line.

We thanked Valerie for helping us.

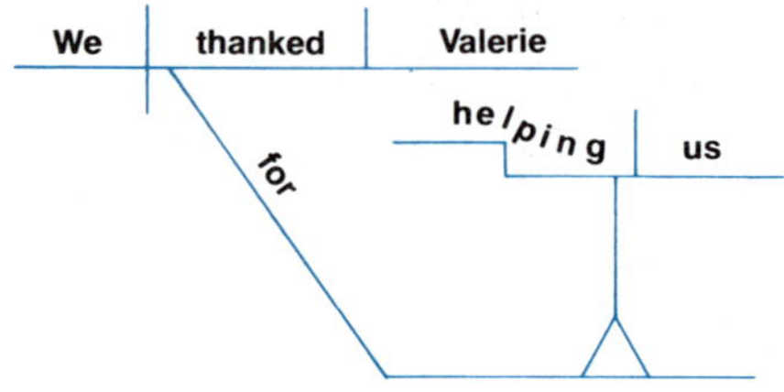

Exercise A Find the gerunds or gerund phrases in these sentences. As your teacher directs, show how each is used.

1. Smiling improves everyone's appearance.
2. Faulty wiring caused the fire.
3. Flooding the engine is usually a beginner's mistake.
4. We were tired from running so far.
5. There is no time for arguing.
6. Washing the windows of skyscrapers is hazardous.
7. Nearly everybody dislikes dieting.
8. Hanging the picture was not easy.
9. Logical thinking can be learned.
10. Colette has always enjoyed singing in the choir.

Exercise B Follow the directions for Exercise A.

1. Sharpening pencils with a knife is tricky.
2. Will hemming the skirt take long?
3. My grandmother enjoys braiding rugs from scraps of cloth.
4. Yawning can be contagious.
5. Painting a dragon on the van was Sonya's idea.
6. Elena practiced skating on one foot.
7. Making the decision was difficult.
8. Scratching mosquito bites only makes them worse.
9. How many calories does an hour of walking burn?
10. The fire department warns against keeping the oven on for warmth.

Part 2 Participles

A participle is a verb form that is used as an adjective.

You learned about the **past participle** as one of the principal parts of a verb. It is formed by adding *-d* or *-ed* to the present tense, as in *dance—danced* or *dress—dressed*. The past participles of irregular verbs are formed differently and must be learned separately: *tear—torn, sing—sung*.

There is another kind of participle besides the past participle. It is called the **present participle.** The present participle is always formed by adding *-ing* to the present tense: *dance—dancing, dress—dressing, tear—tearing, sing—singing*.

Here are more examples of participles:

Verb	Past Participle	Present Participle
look	looked	looking
bring	brought	bringing
cry	cried	crying

As verbals, participles are always used as adjectives. A participle modifies either a noun or a pronoun.

Exhausted, Martina sat down with a sigh.
(*Exhausted* is a past participle modifying the noun *Martina.*)

Whistling, he made his way home through the snow.
(*Whistling* is a present participle modifying the pronoun *he.*)

A *fallen* tree blocked the street.
(*Fallen* is a past participle modifying the noun *tree.*)

The *flying* object had four headlights.
(*Flying* is a present participle modifying the noun *object.*)

The Participial Phrase

A participle is not always used alone. Often a participle has a modifier or an object or both. Together, they form a **participial phrase.** The entire participial phrase is used as an adjective.

Because a participle is formed from a verb, it may have an object.

The person *taking shorthand* is Ms. Baldrini's secretary.
(*Taking shorthand* is a participial phrase modifying *person. Shorthand* is the object of the participle *taking.*)

Because a participle comes from a verb, it may be modified by adverbs.

Racing madly, Carla beat the throw to home plate.
(*Racing madly* is a participial phrase modifying *Carla. Madly* is an adverb modifying the participle *racing.*)

A participle may also be modified by prepositional phrases.

We heard the foghorn *moaning in the distance.*
(*Moaning in the distance* is a participial phrase modifying *foghorn. In the distance* is a prepositional phrase modifying the participle *moaning.*)

In all of these examples you can see that the participles are used as adjectives, even though they look like verbs. *Exhausted, whistling, fallen, taking, racing,* and *moaning* all look like verbs but are not used as verbs. Because they are used as adjectives, they are called participles. Modifiers and objects used with them form participial phrases.

Diagraming Participles

To diagram a participle, place it below the noun or pronoun it modifies. Place the participle on an angled line. Put modifiers of the participle on lines slanted down from it. An object follows the participle on a horizontal line.

Reading carefully, Erin studied the contract.

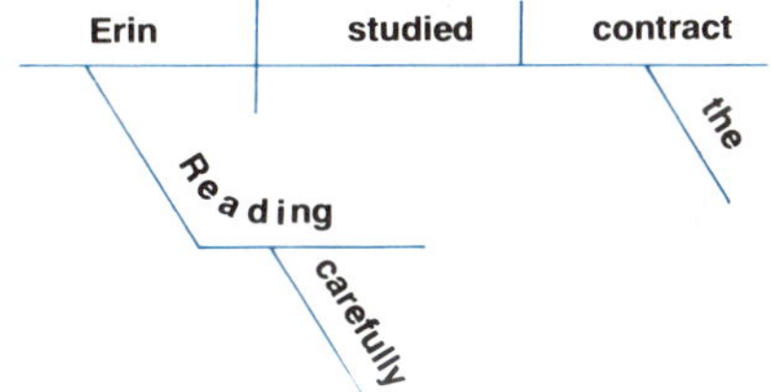

Exercise A Write the participles or participial phrases in these sentences. Show which word the participle or phrase modifies.

Example: Raising her eyebrows, Regina stared at the conductor.
Raising her eyebrows (participial phrase, modifying *Regina*)

1. Working hard, the firefighters controlled the blaze.
2. The glittering snow blinded him for a minute.
3. Fried chicken is a popular food.
4. Cheryl scraped the peeling paint.
5. Frightened, I turned off the horror movie on TV.

6. Harris slipped on the freshly waxed floor.
7. Someone wearing high heels made these footprints.
8. The pie cooling on the table is for dessert.
9. Still snapping her fingers, Lynn left the dance floor.
10. The man with the hat pulled down over his eyes was once a famous boxer.

Exercise B Follow the directions for Exercise A.

1. Shaking her head, the patient refused the medicine.
2. That is a widely known fact.
3. There was no hope of a seat on the packed bus.
4. Opening the door of the laundromat, Mark accidentally bumped into Mr. Rodriguez.
5. Bits of shattered glass in the street told the story.
6. Take gloves off frostbitten hands slowly and carefully.
7. Falling softly on the roof, the rain sounded peaceful.
8. Most of our scattered relatives got together for the reunion.
9. I was trapped inside the revolving door for an hour.
10. Payton, leaping into the air, caught the ball.

Gerund or Participle?

The two kinds of verbals you have studied, gerunds and participles, often look the same. Gerunds and present participles are both formed by adding *-ing* to the present tense of verbs. How can you avoid confusing them?

To tell whether a word is a gerund or a present participle, look at how it is used. If it is used as a modifier, it is a participle. If it is used as a noun, it is a gerund.

Look at the following sentences.

> *Hiking along the nature trail* takes two hours.
> (The gerund phrase *hiking along the nature trail* is the subject of the verb *takes.*)

Hiking along the nature trail, we saw several deer.
(The participial phrase *hiking along the nature trail* modifies the pronoun *we.*)

Exercise For each sentence, write the gerund or participle and say which each is. Be prepared to explain your answer.

1. Diving from the high board requires control.
2. Diving from the high board, Jeff felt free and happy.
3. Tuning the old piano will improve its sound.
4. Tuning the old piano, Mrs. Arthur listened carefully to each tone.
5. Climbing the hill wore us out.
6. Climbing the hill, Sandy spotted a waterfall.
7. Dusting for fingerprints may give the police clues.
8. Using a newspaper, Lynn chased the bee outside.
9. The people sitting in the front row get the best view.
10. Steve calmed the dog by patting it gently.

Part 3 Infinitives

The third kind of verbal is the **infinitive. An infinitive is a verbal form that usually begins with the word *to*.** *To* is called the **sign of the infinitive.**

to write	to shout	to find	to forget
to say	to like	to join	to remind

Note: You have learned that the word *to* is used as a preposition. *To* is a preposition when it is followed by a noun or pronoun as its object. However, when *to* is followed by a verb, it is the sign of the infinitive. Compare these examples:

Prepositional Phrases	Infinitives
We went to the youth center.	We tried to remember.
Justin listened to the music.	Kristin wants to rollerskate.

The Infinitive Phrase

Like gerunds and participles, infinitives are not always used alone.

An infinitive can have modifiers and objects. The infinitive with its modifiers and objects forms an **infinitive phrase.**

Because an infinitive is formed from a verb, it is like a verb in some ways. Like a verb, an infinitive may have an object.

> Megan planned *to have a party.*
> (*Party* is the direct object of the infinitive *to have.*)
>
> The coach wanted *to give the team a good workout.*
> (*Team* is the indirect object and *workout* is the direct object of the infinitive *to give.*)

Because an infinitive is formed from a verb, it may be modified by adverbs.

> The choir tried *to sing together.*
> (*Together* is an adverb modifying the infinitive *to sing.*)
>
> A tape recording asked me *to call again later.*
> (*Again* and *later* are adverbs modifying the infinitive *to call.*)

Infinitives may also be modified by prepositional phrases.

> One customer demanded *to talk to the manager.*
> (*To the manager* is a prepositional phrase modifying the infinitive *to talk.*)
>
> Many people like *to picnic in the park.*
> (*In the park* is a prepositional phrase modifying the infinitive *to picnic.*)

Uses of the Infinitive Phrase

Unlike gerunds and participles, infinitives can be used as more than one part of speech. An infinitive or infinitive phrase can be used as one of the following: a noun, an adjective, or an adverb.

Infinitives and infinitive phrases can be used in ways that nouns are used. As you know, nouns may be subjects or direct objects.

Subject: *To learn a new language* takes time.
(*To learn a new language* is the subject.)
Direct Object: Diane forgot *to send a birthday card.*
(*To send a birthday card* is the direct object.)

Infinitives and infinitive phrases can also be used as adjectives or adverbs. The infinitive or infinitive phrase is used as an adjective if it modifies a noun or pronoun. It is used as an adverb if it modifies a verb, adjective, or adverb.

Adjective: These are the logs *to burn in the fireplace.*
(*To burn in the fireplace* modifies the noun *logs.*)
Adjective: Shelly needs someone *to advise her.*
(*To advise her* modifies the pronoun *someone.*)
Adverb: Everyone came *to celebrate New Year's Eve.*
(*To celebrate New Year's Eve* modifies the verb *came.*)
Adverb: Greg is afraid *to talk to Jessica.*
(*To talk to Jessica* modifies the adjective *afraid.*)
Adverb: The ball flew too high *to catch.*
(*To catch* modifies the adverb *high.*)

From all of the examples, you can see that infinitives look like verbs but are not used as verbs. Infinitives and their phrases are used as nouns, adjectives, and adverbs.

The Split Infinitive

Sometimes a modifier is placed between the word *to* and the verb of an infinitive. A modifier in that position is said to split the infinitive. Usually, a split infinitive sounds awkward and should be avoided.

Awkward: Marietta tried to *patiently* wait.
Better: Marietta tried to wait *patiently.*

Diagraming Infinitives

To diagram an infinitive or infinitive phrase used as a noun, place it on a bridge above the main line. *To*, the sign of the infinitive, belongs on a slanted line. The infinitive is shown on a horizontal line. Modifiers appear on lines slanted down from the infinitive. An object is shown on a horizontal line following the infinitive.

Dale tried to answer the questions correctly.

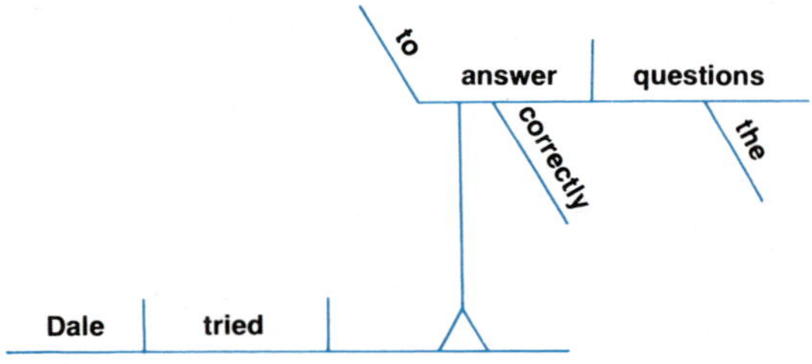

To diagram an infinitive or infinitive phrase used as a modifier, place it below the word modified. Modifiers and objects of the infinitive appear as explained above.

Sandpaper is used to smooth the wood.

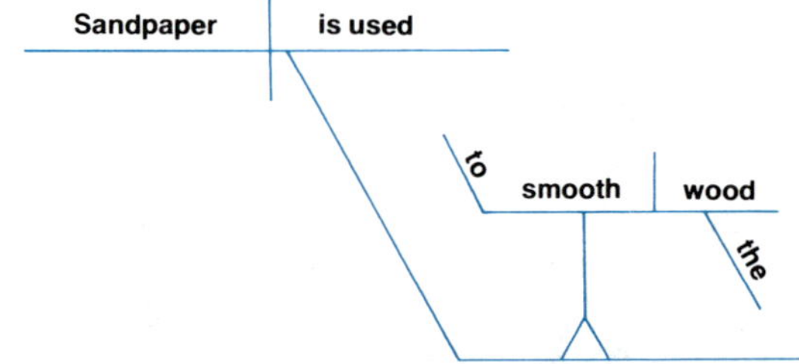

Exercise A Write each infinitive or infinitive phrase. Be prepared to tell how it is used in the sentence.

Example: Deborah wants to tell her side of the story.
to tell her side of the story (infinitive phrase, used as direct object)

1. Don neglected to mention a few important facts.
2. The coat was too expensive to buy.

3. Ruth is too intelligent to believe that.

4. Chief Joseph had hoped to lead his people to Canada.

5. To own a Renegade jeep is Sheila's dream.

6. Egypt intends to report the incident to the UN Security Council.

7. All the candidates promised to find people jobs.

8. Has anyone come to check the furnace?

9. Did Cynthia manage to find her way there without a map?

10. To draw better is Carrie's goal in art class.

Exercise B Follow the directions for Exercise A.

1. I never got a chance to thank Quentin.

2. The counselor is the person to ask about a job.

3. Do you want to borrow my eraser?

4. The manager told Sally to keep a record of her hours.

5. To end the season with an injury is no fun.

6. The pigeons tried to avoid the spray of water from the fountain.

7. A good rock music station is hard to find.

8. To walk to the stadium would take two hours.

9. Bob always tries to please everybody.

10. The boss asked her workers to work overtime.

A Review of Verbals

Although verbals are verb forms, they are never used as verbs. They are used as other parts of speech.

The three kinds of verbals are gerunds, participles, and infinitives. All three kinds of verbals may be used alone. At times, though, they are used in phrases. These phrases are called gerund phrases, participial phrases, and infinitive phrases. Because they are like verbs, all three kinds of verbals may take objects or modifiers.

Gerunds are the verb forms used as nouns. Gerunds, which end in *-ing*, may be used in all the ways nouns are used.

> *Marching* tired us out. (subject)
> The troops began *marching along*. (direct object)
> The parade featured *precise marching*. (direct object)
> The band makes designs by *marching in formation*. (object of preposition)

Participles are verb forms used as adjectives. Like adjectives, participles modify nouns and pronouns. Present participles end in *-ing*. Past participles of regular verbs end in *-d* or *ed*.

> *Turning*, Richard skated back to his friends.
> The girl *turning sideways* is Nancy.
> *Turning the car just in time*, Wendy avoided an accident.
> We saw someone *turning somersaults*.

Infinitives are the verbals that begin with the word *to*. Infinitives may be used as three different parts of speech. They may be nouns, adjectives, or adverbs.

> *To say his lines right* was a challenge for Eric. (noun, subject)
> The president asked us *to say our names*. (noun, direct object)
> Ms. Fields has a few words *to say*. (adjective)
> Everyone rose *to say the pledge*. (adverb)
> This tongue-twister is not easy *to say*. (adverb)

Exercise A Find the verbal in each sentence. Write the verbal or verbal phrase. Tell whether the verbal is a gerund, a participle, or an infinitive.

1. We were invited backstage to meet the cast.
2. The burglar entered through an unlocked basement window.
3. Jeans made in America are popular all over the world.
4. Where did you learn to speak Spanish?

5. Rita lugged the broken TV to the repair shop.
6. Keeping secrets is hard for Frank.
7. Lining the coat with flannel will make it warmer.
8. Martin woke to the smell of frying bacon.
9. The nurse is responsible for sterilizing the instruments.
10. It is too early to tell the outcome of the game.

Exercise B Follow the directions for Exercise A.

1. The defeated candidate accused the winner of vote fraud.
2. Try to understand Peggy's position.
3. Talking quietly is impossible for Dan.
4. Turning on the siren, the police officer drove her squad car through the busy intersection.
5. The wastebasket was filled to the brim with crumpled paper.
6. Separating Mexico from the United States, the Rio Grande flows to the Gulf of Mexico.
7. Reading a newspaper every day is a good habit.
8. Martha has saved enough money to buy a ticket to the concert.
9. Diving for the ball, the third baseman brought the fans to their feet.
10. Understanding the rules makes the game more enjoyable.

REVIEW Using Verbals

Recognizing Gerunds Write the gerund phrase.

1. Rabbits survive by running away.
2. Washing clothes in hot water might shrink them.
3. Gluing the pieces together took several hours.
4. There is an observation deck for viewing the city.
5. Nora suggested returning the carton of sour milk.

Recognizing Participles Write the participle or participial phrase in each sentence.

6. Watch out for hidden rocks.
7. Discouraged, the team retreated to the locker room at half-time.
8. Adjusting the wheels, Lee discovered a new problem.
9. The wildflowers growing in the park are goldenrod.
10. Thrusting itself up out of the water, the dolphin sailed through the hoop.

Recognizing Infinitives Write the infinitive or infinitive phrase.

11. Julie trained to work as a waitress.
12. I expect to see Mel this afternoon.
13. The government attempts to warn us of health hazards.
14. Did you try to talk to Lena first?
15. This Xerox copy is too faint to read.

Recognizing Verbals Write the verbal or verbal phrase in each sentence. Label it *Gerund, Participle*, or *Infinitive.*

16. Moving West solved many problems in earlier times.
17. We had almost persuaded Judy to stay.
18. Forced out of their native country, the refugees sought protection in the United States.
19. Has tapdancing become popular again?
20. The crowd waiting for the bus grew impatient.

Making Subjects and Verbs Agree

When two people have similar ideas, they agree. The subject and the verb of a sentence can also be alike in certain ways. Then they are said to agree. In this section you will find out how to make subjects and verbs agree.

Part 1 Making Subjects and Verbs Agree in Number

The **number** of a word refers to whether the word is singular or plural. A word is **singular** when it refers to one thing. A word is **plural** when it refers to more than one thing. If a subject and verb are the same in number, they agree.

A verb must agree in number with its subject.

If a subject is singular, its verb must be singular. If a subject is plural, then its verb must be plural.

Singular	Plural
She *watches.*	They *watch.*
It *rolls.*	They *roll.*
He *dances.*	They *dance.*
Marcy *adds.*	Machines *add.*

You can see that in the examples, the singular of each verb ends in *-s.* In each plural verb, there is no *-s.*

Subject and verb agreement usually seems natural. Problems arise, though, when you are not sure which word is the subject of the sentence. Remember that to find the subject, first find the verb. Then ask *who?* or *what?* before it.

The papers in this folder are important.
Verb: are
What are? papers
The subject is *papers.*

The subject of the verb is never found in a prepositional phrase.

When you are trying to make subjects and verbs agree, watch out for phrases. Often a phrase appears between the subject and the verb.

The *keys* on the dashboard *are* mine.
That *book* of poems *has* many pictures.
The *words* to that song *are* catchy.
One of the trains *is* late.

Phrases beginning with the words *with, together with, including, as well as,* and *in addition to* are not part of the subject.

A fire *truck,* in addition to the police car, *is* here.
Honesty, as well as courage, *is* a virtue.
The *meal,* including dessert, *costs* two dollars.

Exercise A Choose the verb that agrees with the subject.

1. Those photographs, including the one of Jake, (is, are) in the album.
2. The radio, as well as the flashlights, (needs, need) batteries.
3. The mission of those pilots (was, were) accomplished.
4. The bag of Fritos (is, are) almost empty.
5. Two of the bones in her foot (is, are) broken.
6. The oil on the waves (was, were) from the tanker.
7. Homes near the river (has, have) to be evacuated.
8. The woman in the red sandals (works, work) at the clinic.
9. The walls, as well as the floor, (has, have) been scrubbed.
10. Even the best players (try, tries) to improve.

Exercise B Follow the directions for Exercise A.

1. Leslie, as well as many other students, (takes, take) the subway to school.
2. A person with third-degree burns (requires, require) immediate medical help.
3. The dog with brown spots (leads, lead) that pack.
4. That suitcase without handles (belongs, belong) to Jerry.
5. The sounds of summer (includes, include) the music of ice cream trucks.
6. The keys on that piano (is, are) loose.
7. Two theaters in town (shows, show) first-run movies.
8. Hamburgers at that stand (costs, cost) a dollar.
9. All the students in that class (joins, join) in class discussions.
10. The battery, together with the spark plugs, (is, are) new.

Part 2 Compound Subjects

A compound subject is two or more subjects used with the same verb.

A compound subject joined by *and* is plural. Therefore, it requires a plural verb.

The *radio* and the *stereo* **are playing** the same song.
Steve and *Marcella* **write** for the newspaper.

When the parts of a compound subject are joined by *or* or *nor,* the verb should agree with the subject nearer to the verb.

Neither Jan nor her *friends stay* for lunch.
Either cookies or *cake is* a good dessert.

Exercise A Choose the verb that agrees with the subject.

1. The jacket and the coat (needs, need) to be drycleaned.
2. Janet and Beth (is, are) interested in the job.
3. Ecuador and Colombia (is, are) neighboring countries.
4. Boots and jeans (seems, seem) to be Mike's uniform.
5. Neither the potholes nor the curb (has, have) been repaired.
6. Neither the curb nor the potholes (have, has) been repaired.
7. Either Rhonda or her sister (visits, visit) us often.
8. Either the seat or the handlebars (has, have) to be adjusted.
9. Both Liz and Marilyn (bowls, bowl) at that alley.
10. Neither Joyce nor Pam (bowls, bowl) at that alley.

Exercise B Follow the directions for Exercise A.

1. Neither the drugstore nor the grocery (opens, open) until 8 A.M.
2. Either Ms. McGee or Mr. Baez (teaches, teach) that math class.

3. Neither noise nor crowds (bothers, bother) Patty.

4. Vicks and Kleenex (sells, sell) better in the winter.

5. The ladder and the paint (is, are) behind the garage.

6. Neither the parade nor the fireworks (was, were) as good as usual this year.

7. Cancer and TB (attacks, attack) people of all ages.

8. Either the piano or the singers (is, are) off-key.

9. Neither the Spencers nor Ms. Davis (is, are) home.

10. Glass windows and a wooden floor (was, were) considered luxuries a few centuries ago.

Part 3 Indefinite Pronouns

To make a verb agree with an indefinite pronoun used as the subject, you must know if the pronoun is singular or plural. As you have learned, some indefinite pronouns are singular, and some are plural. Others may be either singular or plural.

The following indefinite pronouns are **singular:**

another	each	everything	one
anybody	either	neither	somebody
anyone	everybody	nobody	someone
anything	everyone	no one	

Nobody here *knows* the answer.
Someone leads the orchestra.
Each of the rooms *has* a TV.

The following indefinite pronouns are **plural:**

both   few   many   several

Several of the candidates *agree* on the issues.
Both of those countries *have* mild climates.

The following indefinite pronouns are **singular** if they refer to one thing. They are **plural** if they refer to several things.

all any most none some

All of the equipment *is* clean and new.
All of the representatives *are* in Washington.

Most of the lake *is* shallow.
Most of the beaches *are* open.

Some of the money *is* Linda's.
Some of the boats *are* at the pier.

Exercise A Choose the verb that agrees with the subject.

1. Most of the batteries (is, are) still good.
2. Each of the coaches (has, have) an even temper.
3. Few of the rumors (seems, seem) likely to be true.
4. (Is, Are) all of the seats taken?
5. Everyone here (has, have) heard that joke before.
6. Somebody upstairs (is, are) playing the piano.
7. Some of Sid's friends (has, have) arrived.
8. Nobody on the block (owns, own) that car.
9. Most of that gossip (is, are) untrue.
10. Some of the spaghetti sauce usually (splatters, splatter).

Exercise B Follow the directions for Exercise A.

1. Most of the track (needs, need) repair.
2. Most of the roads (needs, need) repair.
3. Neither of the pens (has, have) a fine point.
4. Everybody (believes, believe) her.
5. All of the items (was, were) donated.
6. Most of the raffle tickets (has, have) been sold.
7. Many of us (knows, know) that.
8. One of the twins often (pretends, pretend) to be the other.
9. Everybody in the bleachers (was, were) cheering.
10. Each of the nurses (wears, wear) identification.

Part 4 Other Problems of Agreement

Doesn't and *Don't*

The verb *doesn't* is singular. *Doesn't* is used with the subjects *she*, *he*, and *it*. All other personal pronouns are used with *don't*.

It *doesn't* matter to me.
He *doesn't* live near the city.
She *doesn't* speak Spanish.

They *don't* play fairly.
I *don't* work here.
We *don't* watch much TV.

Sentences Beginning with *There*

When sentences begin with *there*, *here*, or *where*, the subject comes after the verb. You must look ahead to find the subject of the sentence. Then you must use the verb that agrees with that subject.

There *are* two *versions* of that song.
Here *is* the beach *towel*.
Where *are* the *peaches*?

Exercise A Choose the verb that agrees with the subject.

1. Michael (doesn't, don't) watch much TV.
2. She (doesn't, don't) often lose her temper.
3. It (doesn't, don't) seem fair to give her both jobs.
4. Where (is, are) the nearest exit?
5. Those names (doesn't, don't) sound familiar to me.
6. (Doesn't, Don't) Lorraine work at Sears?
7. (Doesn't, Don't) the buses run all night?
8. There (is, are) some mail for you on the radiator.
9. There (goes, go) that yellow Thunderbird.
10. There (doesn't, don't) seem to be any soda pop left.

Exercise B Follow the directions for Exercise A.

1. (Doesn't, Don't) Sally and Ken like to dance?
2. Here (is, are) our first customers.
3. (Isn't, Aren't) there any pay phones here?
4. Where (is, are) the outlets?
5. He (doesn't, don't) ever work on weekends.
6. Where (is, are) your new sweatshirt with the hood?
7. Clothes (doesn't, don't) dry as fast in cold weather.
8. Here (is, are) the reference books.
9. I certainly (doesn't, don't) think so.
10. There (is, are) several boxes of powdered milk on the shelf.

REVIEW Making Subjects and Verbs Agree

Making Subjects and Verbs Agree Number your paper from 1 to 20. Write the verb that agrees with the subject.

1. Two pieces of cake (is, are) left.
2. Several people, including Marion, (has, have) a key to that door.
3. Victor, as well as his co-workers, (watches, watch) the clock.
4. Noises from the street (drifts, drift) up to my room.
5. Our chances of winning (is, are) better than theirs.
6. The slices of bread in this loaf (isn't, aren't) moldy.
7. Two rooms in addition to this one (is, are) not in use.
8. Privacy and free time (is, are) not always easy to find.
9. Each of the bikes (has, have) been customized.
10. The suitcase and the totebag (is, are) both stuffed.
11. Each of the books (contains, contain) information on the Olympics.
12. As children, both Thomas Edison and Albert Einstein (was, were) thought to be rather stupid.
13. Farming and ranching (has, have) replaced buffalo hunting for many Plains Indians.
14. Mirrors and water (reflects, reflect) print backwards.
15. Neither white rice nor white bread (provides, provide) as much nutrition as brown rice.
16. Neither Katy nor her sister (looks, look) pleased.
17. Either the manager or one of her assistants (handles, handle) complaints.
18. Some of the injured players (insists, insist) on returning to the field.
19. Some of the fudge (is, are) for the bake sale.
20. Another of those old war movies (is, are) on tonight.

Using Compound and Complex Sentences

In preceding sections, you have learned how the parts of a sentence work together. In this section, you will learn about four different kinds of sentences. They can be studied and compared by their different structures. They are called simple sentences, compound sentences, complex sentences, and compound-complex sentences.

Part 1 Review of the Sentence

The sentence is composed of two basic parts. These key parts are the subject and the predicate.

Subject	Predicate
Lights	flash.
Lights	flash a signal.
Blinking lights at the control panel	flash a signal.

The **subject** of a sentence names the person or thing about which something is said. The **predicate** tells something about the subject.

The **simple predicate** is the verb. The subject of the verb is called the **simple subject.**

Within the subject of the sentence are the simple subject and its modifiers. In the predicate of the sentence are the verb, objects, predicate words, and their modifiers.

Compound Parts in a Sentence

You have learned that all of the parts of the sentence may be **compound.** Each one, in other words, may have more than one part.

Compound subject:	Neither sleep nor dreams are fully understood.
Compound verb:	The audience clapped, rooted, and cheered.
Compound predicate:	Derek cleaned the fish and then fried it on an open fire.
Compound object:	Janelle designed the store decorations and window displays.
Compound object of the preposition:	On holidays and weekends, the store is closed.
Compound predicate word:	That TV studio is large and empty.

The Simple Sentence

Even though sentences may have compound parts, they still express only one main idea. Such sentences, like all of those you have been studying, are called **simple sentences.**

A simple sentence is a sentence with only one subject and one predicate. The subject and the predicate, along with any part of the subject or predicate, may be compound.

Now you are ready to distinguish simple sentences from other types of sentences.

Exercise A Copy each of the following simple sentences. Then draw a line between the subject and the predicate.

1. Teresa and Nat have social security cards.
2. Theodore Roosevelt and Franklin D. Roosevelt were Presidents with strong personalities.
3. Dave found the tuxedo and the top hat in a thrift shop.
4. Stevie Wonder and Brenda Lee both began their singing careers as children.
5. China and Russia border Mongolia.
6. The books on that shelf are quite old and fragile.
7. Maria carefully measured the space for the shelf and then sawed the plywood.
8. The electrician was both quick and careful.
9. The orderly on night duty wears a headband and an Apache necklace.
10. Sharon keeps a flashlight and candles on hand for use during power failures.

Exercise B Write the compound subjects, verbs, and objects you find in these simple sentences.

1. The crew cleared and bulldozed ten acres of wilderness.
2. Vince Evans and Doug Williams are both quarterbacks.

3. First peel and then boil the potatoes.

4. Fireflies gathered in the trees and bushes.

5. South American Indians have unique crafts and customs.

6. Scrooge, Tiny Tim, and Oliver Twist are some of Charles Dickens's characters.

7. Early settlers used ashes, water, and grease to make soap.

8. Don wrote, read, and then rewrote the letter to Marsha.

9. Julia and Sandy left an hour ago and have not returned yet.

10. Did you and Martha finish the peanut butter and jam?

Part 2 The Compound Sentence

Sometimes two simple sentences express related ideas, and they are joined to form one sentence. The resulting sentence has more than one subject and more than one predicate. It is called a **compound sentence.**

A compound sentence consists of two or more simple sentences joined together. The parts of the compound sentence may be joined by a coordinating conjunction (*and*, *or*, *but*) or by a semicolon (;). Look at the following examples.

> The World Series is over, **and** the football season has begun.
>
> This hill is small, **but** it's perfect for sledding.
>
> Return your library books today, **or** you will have to pay a fine.
>
> Special tags on the clothing can set off an alarm**;** they help to prevent shoplifting.

Why are compound sentences used? Why don't writers use only simple sentences? This passage will help you to see why.

Young people receive training in many real-life skills. We take driver education. We have practice for sports. We not only have classes in school. We also have training on the job. We can take courses in everything from first aid to disco dancing. Instruction is important. It is not enough. Real-life experience is the final test.

The series of simple sentences one after another becomes dull and tiresome. Notice how much better the same paragraph sounds with compound sentences.

Young people receive training in many real-life skills. We take driver education, and we have practice for sports. We not only have classes in school, but we also have training on the job. We can take courses in everything from first aid to disco dancing. Instruction is important, but it is not enough. Real-life experience is the final test.

Diagraming Compound Sentences

If you can diagram simple sentences, you can diagram compound ones. The diagram simply shows that a compound sentence is two or more simple sentences joined together. The simple sentences are diagramed one under the other. Then the two sentences are connected with a dotted line. The coordinating conjunction sits on a "step" in the line.

The press secretary spoke first, and then the President held a press conference.

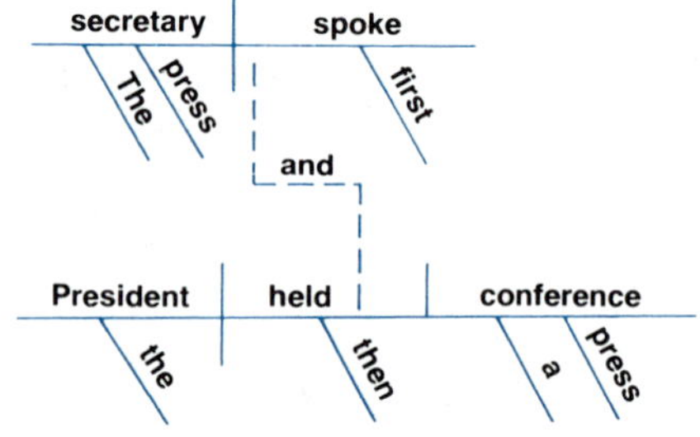

Exercise A Number your paper from 1 to 10. Label three columns *Subject/Verb, Conjunction,* and *Subject/Verb.* For each sentence, fill in the columns.

Example: Nina sings well, but Angie and Ted sing better.

Subject/Verb	Conjunction	Subject/Verb
Nina/sings	but	Angie, Ted/sing

1. Montana is the Treasure State, and California is the Golden State.
2. The instructions confused me, but the nurse explained them.
3. Max led, and the others followed.
4. The first vehicle with a steam engine worked well for a few hours, but then its engine failed.
5. I have lost my pen, or else somebody has borrowed it.
6. The team is very strong this year, and so we are almost sure to win the city championship.
7. Compact cars get good mileage, but they have little cargo space.
8. Do you have a radio, or should I bring one?
9. The cavalry had ridden into Mexico on the trail of Chief Geronimo, but he evaded them.
10. The disc jockey talks to callers first, and then she plays records.

Exercise B Follow the directions for Exercise A.

1. Height is important in basketball, and weight helps in football.
2. Marie wrapped the package, and I mailed it.
3. Ted ran all the way, but he missed the bus anyway.
4. The President ordered the strikers back to work, but they would not return.
5. Some plants eat insects, and the sundew plant is one of them.

6. Will you tell the umpire, or shall I talk to him?

7. The hail and rain slammed against the windows, and the wind banged at the door.

8. Sharon and Janet must share the award, or else nobody will receive it.

9. Levi-Strauss designed the first denim jeans in 1853, and the style has been popular ever since.

10. For the past hour Saul has been practicing the same tune on his horn, but he has not improved at all.

Compound Sentence or Compound Predicate?

You need to know the difference between a compound sentence and a simple sentence with a **compound predicate.** A compound predicate is two verbs within one predicate. The parts of a compound predicate, like the parts of a compound sentence, are joined by a coordinating conjunction.

Alana *joined the team* and *made the starting lineup.*
(This compound predicate is joined by *and.*)

How will you know if a sentence is compound or if it has a compound predicate? If each verb has its own subject, then the sentence is compound. If the verbs share the same subject, then only the predicate is compound.

s. v. v.
Kyle entered a baking contest and *won* first place.

(This simple sentence has a compound predicate. Both verbs, *entered* and *won,* have the same subject, *Kyle.*)

s. v. s. v.
Kyle entered a baking contest, and his *cheesecake won* first place.

(This is a compound sentence. The verb *entered* has its own subject, *Kyle.* The verb *won* has its own subject, *cheesecake.*)

s. v. v.

A *clerk types* letters and *files* information.

(The conjunction *and* joins the compound predicate of this simple sentence. Both verbs, *types* and *files*, have the same subject, *clerk*.)

s. v. s. v.

A *clerk types* letters, and a *computer files* information.

(This compound sentence is actually two simple sentences joined by the conjunction *and*.)

Exercise A Number your paper from 1 to 10. Decide whether the following sentences are compound sentences or simple sentences with compound predicates. Write *Compound Sentence* or *Compound Predicate*.

1. Gloria sits at the table and reads the newspaper after dinner.
2. Margie locked all the windows and then bolted both doors.
3. Mahatma Gandhi used nonviolent protest in India, and Martin Luther King, Jr. used it here.
4. The sand was getting in Rick's eyes, and he had to remove his contact lenses.
5. The lock on our mailbox is broken, but the janitor will fix it.
6. Which one is Mork, and which one is Mindy?
7. Betsy either swims or plays basketball every day.
8. The mail is late today, or maybe we did not get any.
9. I usually walk to school, but sometimes I take the bus.
10. Has Earl found a job, or is he still looking?

Exercise B Follow the directions for Exercise A.

1. Corrie poured salt on the icy sidewalk and then got her shovel.
2. Jeff raised the car's torsion bar and worked on the engine.

3. Dee was hired as a temporary worker but soon was given a permanent job.

4. Mary put some graphite in the old lock, and then the key turned.

5. Several players were cut from the team after the first season, and Barnes was one of them.

6. Network TV is seen across the country, but this station shows only local programs.

7. Did Ginger paint the walls or only wash them?

8. Joni counted the cash and added the checks correctly, but she forgot about the charge purchases.

9. Can you get to the dentist's office by 2:30, or shall I cancel your appointment?

10. Radio, television, and newspapers can change public opinion, but they can also reflect it.

Punctuating Compound Sentences

One of two punctuation marks is used in a compound sentence. Either a **comma** before a coordinating conjunction or a **semicolon** is needed to separate the two parts of a compound sentence. The punctuation keeps the two parts separate. It also shows where to pause in reading the sentence.

In a compound sentence, a comma is used before a coordinating conjunction. Notice how the comma is used in these compound sentences:

> s. v. s. v.
> The subway car was nearly full, **but** all of us piled in anyway.

> s. v. s. v.
> Sandra talked to her adviser, **and** he helped her with her schedule.

Instead of a comma and a conjunction, a semicolon may be used in a compound sentence.

s. v. s. v.
The young boy climbed the palm tree; he returned with a coconut.

s. v.
Mount McKinley is the highest point in the country;
s. v.
Death Valley is the lowest.

A semicolon may also be used with a **conjunctive adverb.** A conjunctive adverb is an adverb like *therefore, however, moreover, consequently*, or *otherwise*. It helps to join the two parts of a compound sentence. It also shows the relationship between them.

s. v. s. v.
We missed our bus; *however*, we caught a later bus.

s. v.
Heavy rains halted repairs on the highway; therefore, the
s. v.
crew is behind schedule.

As you can see, a conjunctive adverb is used after a semicolon. It is followed by a comma.

The parts of a compound sentence are separated by either a comma or a semicolon. However, no punctuation is used between the two parts of a compound predicate. Notice the difference:

s. v. v.
Stickball is played like baseball and requires a rubber ball with a stick.

s. v. v.
The ranchers herded the cattle and branded them.

In addition, commas are not necessary in very short compound sentences.

Alarms rang and everyone awoke.
Either we're early or you're late.

Exercise A Commas and semicolons have been omitted between the parts of the following compound sentences. For each sentence, write the two words between which punctuation belongs. Put in the comma or semicolon. If a sentence needs no punctuation, write *Correct*.

1. You can make delicious pies from Concord grapes however, you must remove their seeds first.
2. Dr. Jekyll was the kind doctor and Mr. Hyde was Jekyll's evil other self.
3. The clouds parted they revealed a full moon.
4. I met Diana last week and I liked her immediately.
5. Sharon writes the newsletter Jerome distributes it.
6. Jay arrived and Cleo left.
7. Vanilla extract and unsweetened chocolate both smell good but they taste bitter.
8. The planet Mars has an average temperature of $-45°$ and Martian winds can blow at 300 miles per hour.
9. Sal and Joy bought season tickets but they attended only the first and the last games.
10. Basketball players must wear appropriate shoes otherwise, they risk injury to their feet and ankles.

Exercise B Follow the directions for Exercise A.

1. Mark did not see the glass door and he ran right into it.
2. Crocuses bloomed and robins returned.
3. Sheila signaled an S.O.S. with her flashlight however, the people on the beach did not know Morse code.
4. Sailors recognize an upside-down flag as an appeal for help and railroad engineers respond to a red flag by the track.
5. Stories about vampires and monsters are popular they have been told for many centuries.
6. Alligators look slow and clumsy nevertheless, they can move very fast.
7. Ms. Gomez manages the buildings Ms. Allweiss maintains them.

8. Quilts and oak furniture were once used in many homes but now they are too expensive to be common.

9. Students in the work-experience program can get jobs with sponsor companies or they can find jobs themselves.

10. Mother Jones was a union organizer and an activist but earlier she had taught in a convent.

Part 3 The Complex Sentence

You have learned about simple sentences and compound sentences. Another kind of sentence, the **complex sentence,** can also help you to express your thoughts.

Before you can understand the structure of a complex sentence, you must know what a clause is.

A clause is a group of words containing a verb and its subject.

According to this definition, a simple sentence is a clause. It contains a verb and its subject.

s. v.
Keith ran in the marathon race.

s. v.
Many stores have clearance sales.

It will be easier to understand sentences, though, if you think of a clause as a *part of a sentence.* Think of a clause as *a group of words within a sentence.*

Compound sentences contain clauses. Compound sentences have two or more groups of words with a subject and verb. Notice these examples.

s. v. s. v.
Ms. Jackson demonstrated the loom, and she wove fibers for a rug.

s. v. s. v.
Sherlock Holmes is a fictional character, but he has a large fan club.

Clause or Phrase?

Clauses differ from phrases. Like a clause, a phrase is part of a sentence. However, a clause has a subject and a verb. A phrase does not.

Phrases: after the season
before the gold rush

s. v.
Clauses: after the Bengals kicked off

s. v.
before you left

Subordinate Clauses

The clauses of a compound sentence are actually two separate sentences. Each one can stand alone. Each is a **main clause.** A main clause, or **independent clause,** is a clause that can stand by itself as a sentence.

Subordinate clauses, or **dependent clauses,** are clauses that cannot stand alone. A subordinate clause is not a complete sentence. Study these examples:

s. v.
If you sign the contract

s. v.
Before the gates close

Both of the subordinate clauses above contain subjects and verbs. However, neither of them expresses a complete thought. Neither of them can stand alone. Both leave you wondering *then what?*

The words that begin subordinate clauses have an important function. Without *if* and *before,* the clauses above become sentences. Words like *if* and *before* are called **subordinating conjunctions.** We say that they *subordinate,* or make *dependent,* the words they introduce. Many, though not all, subordinate clauses begin with subordinating conjunctions.

Words often used as subordinating conjunctions are shown here:

Words Often Used as Subordinating Conjunctions

after	because	so that	when
although	before	than	whenever
as	if	though	where
as if	in order that	till	wherever
as long as	provided	unless	while
as though	since	until	

Note: The words above are subordinating conjunctions only when they begin clauses. Many of them can be used in other ways.

Furthermore, not all subordinate clauses begin with subordinating conjunctions. Some clauses begin with words like these:

that	who, whom, whose
what, whatever	whoever, whomever
which	why
how	

Exercise Using *if, because, when, after,* and *since,* make subordinate clauses out of these sentences.

1. The bus was late.
2. The muffler is loose.
3. Diane enjoys bowling.
4. There is a pinball machine in the back.
5. The juke box played only old songs.
6. Bacon is a salty food.
7. Flies were buzzing around the table.
8. Keith's glasses are broken.
9. Strawberries are in season.
10. Toby worked at Head Start.

Definition of the Complex Sentence

Now that you know the difference between main clauses and subordinate clauses, you can understand the complex sentence.

A complex sentence is a sentence that contains one main clause and one or more subordinate clauses.

Main Clause	Subordinate Clause
We'll be out of the tournament	unless we win this game.
The real fun begins	when Anthony arrives.
King Kong is a fictional ape	that attacks New York.

Exercise A Find the subordinate clause in these complex sentences. Copy it. Underline the subject once and the verb twice.

1. Margaret asked if she could help us.
2. Summer was over before we knew it.
3. These clothes are on sale because they are unusual sizes.
4. The road freezes after the bridge does.
5. Earl stops by whenever he is in the neighborhood.
6. Claudia looks as if she knows the punchline.
7. Mattie steadied the ladder while Dawn replaced the bulb.
8. The ham will spoil unless you refrigerate it.
9. Unless you can think of a better idea, we will use mine.
10. Although Bobbie disliked buckwheat pancakes, she politely finished hers.

Exercise B Follow the directions for Exercise A.

1. Clyde weighs more now than he has ever weighed.
2. Jill climbed onto the top of a truck so that she could see over the crowd.
3. As the Buick was turning left, the light changed.

4. When John is daydreaming, he ignores everything around him.
5. Wherever there are wars, there are refugees.
6. Vanessa works hard at whatever she does.
7. Maria acted as though she had not heard the news.
8. Can't he remember where the bases are?
9. I don't know why she is angry at us.
10. Tina explained how the controls should be set.

Part 4 Adverb Clauses

Complex sentences contain subordinate clauses. The subordinate clause may be one of three kinds. One type is the **adverb clause.** An adverb clause has the same function as an adverb.

An **adverb** modifies a verb, an adjective, or another adverb. It tells *how*, *when*, *where*, or *to what extent*.

Adverb: Marissa watched *intently*.

An **adverb phrase** is a prepositional phrase used as an adverb.

Adverb phrase: Marissa watched *on the sidelines*.

An adverb clause is a subordinate clause used as an adverb.

Adverb clause: Marissa watched *while the gymnasts practiced*.

When the voters were polled, Griffin was leading.

Adverb clauses, like adverbs and adverb phrases, tell *how*, *when*, *where*, and *to what extent*. They modify verbs, adjectives, and adverbs.

Remember that a clause, unlike a phrase, has a subject and a verb.

Diagraming Adverb Clauses

To diagram an adverb clause, place it on a separate horizontal line below the main line. A dotted line connects the adverb clause to the word it modifies in the main clause. The subordinating conjunction is shown on the dotted line.

When Carlos was twelve, he moved to New York.

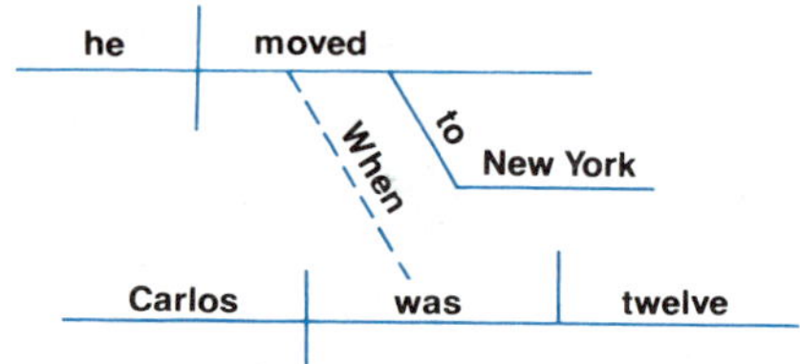

Exercise A Copy the adverb clause from each sentence.

1. We waited until the street was empty.
2. If the treaty is signed, the two nations will be at peace.
3. Although it was December, the weather was warm.
4. The boss calls us when she needs extra workers.
5. The snow was twelve inches deep before the city managers agreed upon a removal plan.
6. Flies should be kept out because they carry diseases.
7. Helmets flashed in the sun as the bikers roared past.
8. Greg stirred the chili with one hand while he answered the phone with the other.
9. Walt Disney made his cartoon animals act as though they were human.
10. The Greys have needed to call the janitor only once since they moved in.

Exercise B Follow the directions for Exercise A.

1. Nurses can usually find jobs wherever they go.
2. Although Rita Gomez has not appeared in movies here, she is a popular movie actress in the Philippines.

3. When the President addressed the United Nations, his speech was translated into many languages.

4. The doctor had to reset Linda's broken arm because she fell on it again.

5. Before electricity became available, many people went to sleep right after sundown.

6. If the newsstand is out of papers, try the drug store.

7. Whenever Jeannie makes a winning basket, she seems amazed.

8. As Sam answered the questions, the computer recorded the answers.

9. Matt must work the second shift until Josie can return to the job.

10. Because Gail had taken a first aid class, she knew immediately what to do.

Part 5 Adjective Clauses

The second kind of subordinate clause is the **adjective clause.** An adjective clause has the same function as an adjective.

An **adjective** modifies a noun or pronoun.

Adjective: Melissa wears *big*, *round* sunglasses.

An **adjective phrase** is a prepositional phrase that modifies a noun or pronoun.

Adjective phrase: We glanced at the list *of sandwiches*.

An adjective clause is a subordinate clause used as an adjective to modify a noun or pronoun.

Adjective clause: A polygraph is a machine *that is used in lie detection*.

Anyone *who tries hard enough* can stay awake.

Adjective clauses, like adjectives and adjective phrases, tell *what kind* or *which one*. They usually come directly after the word they modify. Unlike adjective phrases, adjective clauses have subjects and verbs.

There are several words used to introduce adjective clauses. Two of them are *where* and *when*.

This is the studio *where recordings are made.*

This is the time *when the moon is full.*

Relative Pronouns

Besides *when* and *where*, the words *who*, *whom*, and *whose* are also used to begin adjective clauses. *Who*, *whom*, and *whose* are called **relative pronouns.** They relate a clause, called a **relative clause,** to a noun or pronoun in the sentence. Sometimes *that* and *which* are relative pronouns.

Here are the words used as relative pronouns:

who whom whose that which

Relative pronouns are special because they have three functions:

1. They introduce adjective clauses.
2. They link the clause to a word in the main clause.
3. They have a function within the clause. They act as subject, object, or predicate pronoun of the verb within the adjective clause. They may also be the object of a preposition in the clause. *Whose* functions as an adjective.

Students *who work part-time* are dismissed early.
(*Who* is the subject of *work*.)

The dentist's office plays music *that is soothing.*
(*That* is the subject of is.)

The person *whom we need most* is Anna.
(*Whom* is the direct object of *need*.)

The girl *with whom I chatted* turned out to be a distant cousin.
(*Whom* is the object of the preposition *with*.)

Children *whose parents work here* may attend the day-care center.
(*Whose* modifies *parents*, the subject of the clause.)

Sometimes you may be confused about whether *who* or *whom* is the correct relative pronoun. To decide, see how the pronoun is used within the clause. Keep in mind that *who* is the subject form. *Whom* is the object form.

Diagraming Adjective Clauses

To diagram an adjective clause, use a separate line beneath the main line. A dotted line runs from the relative pronoun to the word in the main clause that the adjective clause modifies.

The people who run the space program are in Houston.

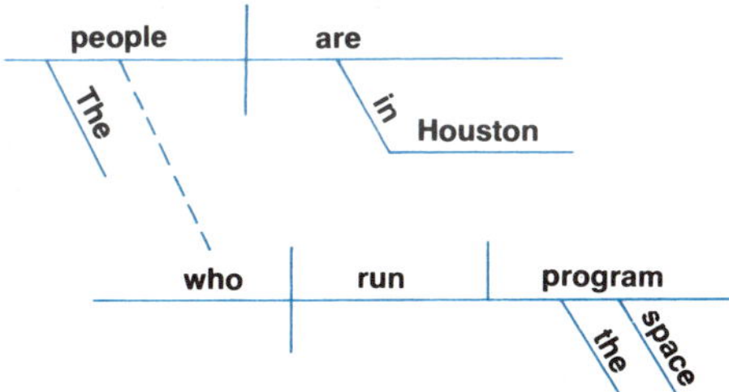

One of the players on whom we depend was injured.

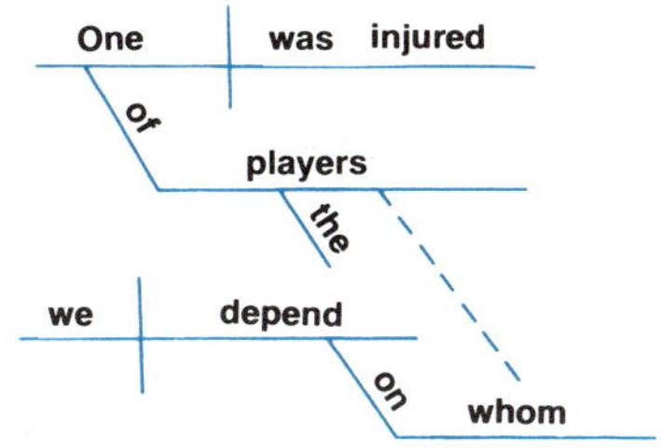

Exercise A Copy the adjective clause from each sentence. Underline the subject once and the verb twice. Before the clause, write the word it modifies.

Example: She is the teacher who wrote our textbook.
teacher—who wrote our textbook

1. It had been the coldest winter that New York had ever had.
2. The movie that is playing at the Varsity is a comedy.
3. Staph germs in the body head for tissue that is damaged.
4. Donna is the cheerleader who also plays baseball.
5. One American writer who lived in Paris was James Baldwin.
6. Students who are on the basketball team usually practice after classes.
7. The mayor is the person to whom the petition should be sent.
8. Fireflies, which are really beetles, produce cold lights.
9. The car that Mr. Sardo bought is an old convertible.
10. This is the time of day that I like best.

Exercise B Follow the directions for Exercise A.

1. One of the boxing tournaments that means the most is the Golden Gloves.
2. The mechanic who gave the estimate no longer works here.
3. In almost every family there is someone who cannot throw anything away.
4. Panama, which joins Central America and South America, is a small but important country.
5. The foster home in which the child was placed was near his old neighborhood.
6. The artist and her husband designed their own home, which was made of steel and glass.

7. The manager gave the reporter a list of the players whose contracts had been renewed.

8. The man whose dog bit me drove me to the hospital.

9. Sunday night is the time when television attracts the most viewers.

10. People for whom we have no current address must be crossed from the list.

Part 6 Noun Clauses

The noun clause is the third kind of subordinate clause.

A noun clause is a clause used as a noun in a sentence. Like a noun, a noun clause can be used as a subject, an object of the verb, a predicate word, or an object of a preposition. It can be used in any of the ways that nouns are used. Unlike adverb and adjective clauses, noun clauses do not modify.

Uses of Noun Clauses

Subject: *Whoever sent the mayday* must need help.
What concerns everyone is inflation.

Direct object: Scientists cannot always predict *when an earthquake will occur.*
The controller radioed *that the runway was clear.*

Object of preposition: Rod was impressed by *whatever Joyce said.* (The clause is the object of the preposition *by*.)
The signs point to *where the trail begins.* (The clause is the object of the preposition *to*.)

Predicate noun: City life is *what he wants.*
The fact was *that the car was missing.*

As you can see from these examples, many noun clauses begin with the words *that* and *what*. The words *whatever*, *who*, *whoever*, and *whomever* can also introduce noun clauses. *Where*, *when*, *how*, and *why* are used, too.

Diagraming Noun Clauses

To diagram a noun clause, extend a bridge from the place where the clause is used in the sentence. The word that introduces the clause belongs on a line over the clause.

1. Noun clause used as subject

What you need is a sense of humor.

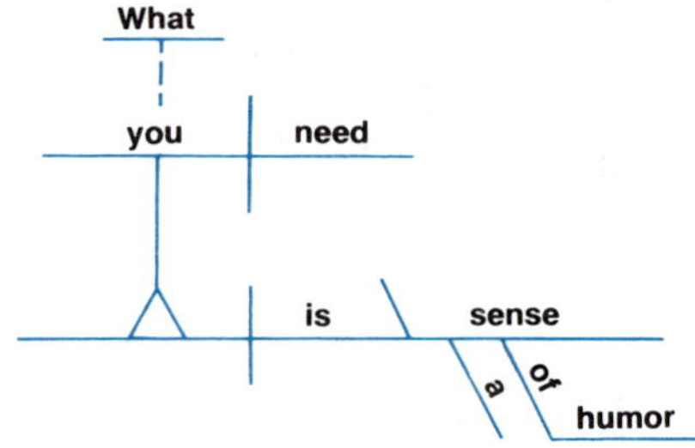

2. Noun clause used as object of the verb

Many people say that good times are ahead.

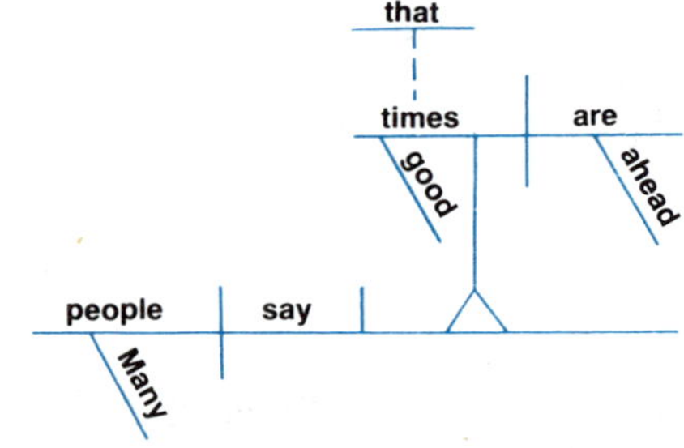

3. Noun clause used as object of a preposition

The candidate talked to whoever would listen.

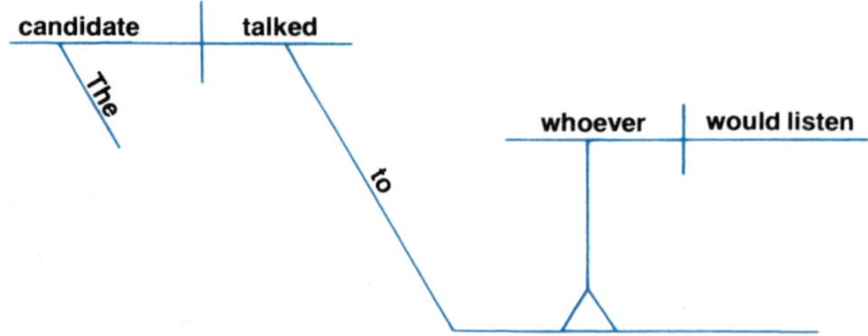

Exercise A Copy the noun clauses in these sentences. Underline the subject once and the verb twice. Tell how the clause is used.

1. Now I understand why you left early.
2. Patrice explained how yogurt is made.
3. Waterloo is where Napoleon was defeated.
4. The reason is that Jake works late.
5. You can make a scarf from whatever fabric is left.
6. Mickie starts a conversation with whoever sits next to her.
7. There will be enough food for whomever you invite.
8. Whoever made that statement does not know the facts.
9. What the audience wanted was another encore.
10. We all worried about where Roland could possibly be.

Exercise B Follow the directions for Exercise A.

1. The manager promised that she would look for my lost roll of film.
2. Hal asked why the game had been delayed.
3. How the pyramids were built is a fascinating story.
4. Alex said that high ozone levels give him headaches.
5. I wonder where the time has gone.
6. When the party is over is up to us.
7. Ken thinks that he has the winning ticket.
8. The only solution is that we raise the funds ourselves.
9. The minister spends her time with whoever needs it.
10. What the neighbors will think bothers him too much.

Part 7 A Review of Subordinate Clauses

You have learned about the three kinds of subordinate clauses. They are the adverb clause, the adjective clause, and the noun clause.

The only way to identify the kind of clause is to look at its use in the sentence. A clause used as a noun is a noun clause. A clause used as a modifier is an adverb or adjective clause, depending on the word modified.

Exercise A Write the subordinate clause in each sentence. If the clause is used as a noun clause, tell how it is used in the sentence. If the clause is used as an adjective or adverb clause, tell what it modifies.

1. Nevada is one state where wild horses still roam.
2. I wonder where I left my backpack.
3. When the movie was over, the audience was silent.
4. Andrew Young, who was once our UN Ambassador, spoke at the assembly.
5. Carol suddenly realized who was on the phone.
6. Tom always worries about what he will say next.
7. The schooldays that were lost during the snowstorm will be made up in June.
8. Ellie remembered that she had a job interview at 3:30.
9. Find a seat wherever you can.
10. Trees that follow day-night cycles may be injured by bright streetlights.

Exercise B Follow the directions for Exercise A.

1. The ring, which had belonged to her grandmother, was Celia's most cherished possession.
2. Call the clinic right away if the pain becomes worse.
3. Neighborhoods that have no parks are rare in Chicago.
4. The census taker who visited our block spoke Spanish.
5. The child could not describe the woman who had left the package.
6. Who will start is the coach's decision.
7. Carl will not answer the phone while he is eating dinner.

8. While Glenda was rehearsing a loud scene from the play, the people next door became worried about her.

9. After Judith wins a game, she sews another tiny smile face on the back of her jacket.

10. The janitor said that he would replace the doorknob tonight.

Part 8 Clauses as Sentence Fragments

You have studied about sentence fragments. You learned about fragments that do not have subjects and verbs.

Alone on the lake. Played the jukebox.

The subordinate clause can be a sentence fragment, too, even though it does have a subject and verb. It still does not express a complete thought. For that reason, it is a sentence fragment. It is only part of a sentence. It is not meant to stand alone.

Notice the difference between these word groups:

The TV was on
While the TV was on

The first word group is a sentence. The subordinating conjunction *while*, though, makes the second word group a sentence fragment. The subordinate clause should be used as part of a sentence.

A subordinate clause must not be written as a complete sentence. It must always be joined to a main clause.

Fragment: When we have winter.
Sentence: When we have winter, Australia has summer.

Fragment: How the gadget worked.
Sentence: No one understood how the gadget worked.

Exercise A Number your paper from 1 to 10. Decide whether the groups of words below are sentences or fragments. Write *S* for *Sentence* and *F* for *Fragment*. Add words to make each fragment a complete sentence. Punctuate and capitalize where necessary.

1. What did the announcer say
2. When is the playoff game
3. What the instructions said
4. After the rain stops
5. After a while everyone returned
6. That showroom is filled with new cars
7. The book that you needed
8. Before the dance started
9. Why is the flag at half-mast
10. Why the dogs are barking

Exercise B Follow the directions for Exercise A.

1. Why the movie ended that way
2. Winter seems longer than summer
3. Whose notebook is this
4. The team practices after school
5. Before breakfast Julie exercises
6. Before the morning was over
7. Crime increases during a full moon
8. That is the signal
9. Because the building is seventy-five years old
10. If the bicycle tire cannot be patched

Part 9 Compound-Complex Sentences

You have already been introduced to simple, compound, and complex sentences. The fourth and final kind of sentence is the **compound-complex sentence.**

A compound-complex sentence consists of two or more main clauses and one or more subordinate clauses.

It may help you to think of a compound-complex sentence as a compound sentence plus a subordinate clause. Actually, the compound-complex sentence joins two sentences, at least one of which has a subordinate clause. The clause may be an adjective, adverb, or noun clause. The main clauses are joined by either a coordinating conjunction or a semicolon.

These are examples of compound-complex sentences:

Main Clause | Main Clause | Subordinate Clause

Yogurt is nutritious, and some say *that it brings good health*.

Subordinate Clause | Main Clause | Main Clause

When Dan called, he was angry; however, he soon calmed down.

Exercise Identify the two main clauses and the subordinate clause in these compound-complex sentences.

1. A bola is a rope that has weights at the end; it is used to catch cattle.
2. Larry tried the disco steps that we demonstrated, but he couldn't quite master them.
3. The instructor told us how we could revive a heart attack victim, and she demonstrated on a dummy.
4. Blair House is located across the street from the White House, and foreign leaders who visit Washington often stay there.
5. Hiawatha was the hero of a poem; moreover, he was a Mohawk chief who organized tribes into the Five Nations.
6. The election judges distribute the ballots, and then they count them after the polls close.
7. In earlier times, infants were wrapped with strips of cloth; people thought that the bindings made babies feel secure.
8. Al drives a snow-removal truck, and whenever a heavy snow falls, he is called to work.

9. Some television sets have tubes; however, newer models, which are usually smaller, are solid state.

10. I've just learned that Congress has set a new minimum wage; consequently, my pay will increase.

Part 10 A Review of Sentences

There are four basic kinds of sentences.

A **simple sentence** contains one subject and one predicate. Parts of the simple sentence, however, may be compound. A simple sentence tells one idea.

s. v.
The tower transmits radio signals.

s. v. v.
Alexis was born in Alaska but grew up in Texas.

A **compound sentence** is made up of two simple sentences. These simple sentences are connected by a comma and coordinating conjunction or by a semicolon. Sometimes a conjunctive adverb follow the semicolon. A compound sentence expresses two related ideas.

s. v. s. v.
The tower is 300 feet tall, and it transmits radio signals.

s. v. s. v.
Alexis was born in Alaska; however, she grew up in Texas.

A **complex sentence** contains one main clause and one or more subordinate clauses. The subordinate clauses may be used as adverbs, adjectives, or nouns. A complex sentence expresses one main idea and one or more dependent ideas.

s. v. s. v.
Because the tower is the tallest structure in the city, it is used to transmit radio signals.

s. v. s. v.
Although Alexis was born in Alaska, she grew up in Texas.

A **compound-complex sentence** contains two main clauses and one or more subordinate clauses. The subordinate clauses may be adverb, adjective, or noun clauses. A compound-complex sentence expresses two main ideas, as well as one dependent idea.

s. v. s. v.
The tower is the tallest structure in the city, and it transmits
s. v.
radio signals *that are heard throughout the Midwest.*

s. v. s. v.
Although Alexis was born in Alaska, she grew up in Texas;
s. v.
now she is living in New York.

Exercise A Number your paper from 1 to 10. For each sentence, write *Simple, Compound, Complex,* or *Compound-Complex* to show what kind it is.

1. Why did the governor veto that bill?
2. Ron asked why everyone was laughing, and Sylvia explained.
3. The helicopter can carry thirty-three armed soldiers, a truck, and supplies.
4. The members of the Drama Club not only produce plays but also write them.
5. When Cortez arrived in Mexico, the Aztecs mistook him for the god of the morning star.
6. What a costly mistake that was!
7. Juanita hopes that one day she will become a chef.
8. Deep in space is a cloud of comets that are made of dust, rock fragments, and frozen gases.
9. Because the planet Pluto is very small and very far away, it was not discovered until 1930.
10. How does the discovery of a new planet influence astrology?

Exercise B Follow the directions for Exercise A.

1. Tracy sings while she plays.

2. Tim ran to the field as fast as he could, but the coach had already left.

3. The planner interviewed the neighborhood residents, and then she wrote her recommendations.

4. After I wrote the report, I proofread it.

5. After this exercise you should flex your shoulders and stretch.

6. The man in the pinstriped, three-piece suit looked odd with the wet dog in his arms.

7. Did you invite Vanessa, or did she just stop by?

8. Do you drink diet drinks, which might contain a harmful substance, or do you drink sugared drinks, which are fattening?

9. General MacArthur said that he would return.

10. The airlines know that some passengers will not show up; therefore, extra tickets are sold for each flight.

REVIEW Using Compound and Complex Sentences

Simple Sentences Write the subject and verb.

1. During the strike Jan borrowed money from her aunt.
2. The hubcap fell off and clattered down the highway.
3. The emergency room is always open and always full.
4. The Orioles and the Angels have solid pitching staffs.
5. Superman and Batman have amazed children for years.

Compound Sentences Copy each sentence. In each part, underline the subject once and the verb twice. Then add punctuation if it is needed.

6. Some Islamic women wear veils but others do not.
7. A marshmallow is a gooey candy but a marsh mallow is a flowering plant.
8. Many players dislike artificial turf nevertheless, they must play on it.
9. The beanbag chair had a small rip in its cover and the filling was leaking out.
10. We must catch that train that's the last one today.
11. The fare increased and service improved.
12. The bus fare increased but service did not improve.
13. Will you choose an album or shall I pick one?
14. The snow has melted and soon the trees will bud.
15. Ernie will use the bonus for a vacation or maybe he will buy a car.
16. The truck weighs three tons it cannot stop very fast.
17. After the explosion the plant was closed moreover, the area around it was evacuated.
18. Rafael is shy but he has a good sense of humor.
19. Debra applied for a job at I.B.M. and she got it.
20. The map is old but it will serve as a general guide.

Complex Sentences Write each subordinate clause.

21. Rosa said that she would be here before dinner.
22. Alice knew who would get the credit.
23. Because Ed works after school, he values his free time.
24. Ms. Simmons and Mr. Moore are the only choir members who can do justice to that spiritual.
25. The cabinet where the supplies are kept is in here.
26. Taharga, who ruled the biggest empire in ancient Africa, led his armies into battle when he was sixteen.
27. In the fog, Liz could hardly see where she was going.
28. Since Ian had been benched, Cal got a chance to play.
29. Where did Karen put the card that I brought?
30. How do you know what happened?
31. The priest comforted the people whose relatives had been hurt.
32. Nicole explained how an electric car operates.
33. After the other guests had left, Danny stayed and helped with the dishwashing.
34. After the wrestling match, we looked for a restaurant that was still open.
35. After her defeat, Natalie trained harder than she ever had before.

A Review of Sentences For each sentence, write *Simple, Compound, Complex,* or *Compound-Complex.*

36. Pauline and Laura gathered the pages together, and Matt stapled them.
37. Until midnight Jerome rehearsed his speech.
38. Jane steered the jeep down the muddy road to the river, and then she discovered that the bridge had collapsed.
39. The callouses on her hands are not from work; they are from climbing the rope in gym.
40. Long ago, soldiers bit on bullets while they were having surgery.

The Right Word

You have studied how to use the sentence and its parts correctly. In this section you will learn to use specific problem words correctly.

Part 1 Standard and Nonstandard English

The language that is presented in this textbook is appropriate at all times and in all places. It is called **standard English.** Standard English is the language of educated people. It is the language that would be judged correct by people in all situations.

In many situations, if you do not use standard English, some people may think of you as less careful or less intelligent. **Nonstandard English** is language that is not generally accepted by all people in all situations.

Here are some examples of standard and nonstandard English:

Nonstandard	Standard
Al should of brung the wood hisself.	Al should have brought the wood himself.
Me and Jody set in the shade.	Jody and I sat in the shade.
He don't know there ain't no difference.	He doesn't know there isn't any difference.

Part 2 Formal and Informal English

Even if you always use standard English, you will use different kinds of language at different times. You wouldn't use the same words, for example, in a letter asking for a job as you would on the phone to a friend. Some situations are more formal than others. In the same way, the language is either formal or informal. Read the following examples:

Formal: During the past five years, the rate of migration from the city to rural areas has increased sharply.

Informal: It's time for a change. Let's move out of the city. We'll find a little farm somewhere and raise chickens.

Formal English is marked by longer sentences, longer words, fewer contractions, and a less personal approach. It is used in the writing of some papers, books, and articles. Informal English, on the other hand, is better for speaking and for using in less important writing situations.

Part 3 Other Types of Language

There are other kinds of English, too. **Slang,** for example, includes expressions that are acceptable only in very casual speech. Some slang phrases are "going bananas," "off the wall," and "uptight." Words from the past that are outdated are called **archaic** or **obsolete.** In addition, language relating to sports, music, science, law, and the military often has a special meaning.

Each kind of language is appropriate at certain times. Legal phrases, for example, belong in the courts, and poetic phrases belong in poetry. At the dinner table, you wouldn't say, "Ere we begin, 'tis the sugar I shall request." In the same way, you wouldn't write in a job application, "Hey, man, how's about givin' me a job?"

Using any of these kinds of language in the wrong situation would be inappropriate. Someone wearing a winter coat during a heat wave would seem odd. In the same way, using slang in a report or using formal English in the locker room would stand out. As you gain more and more skill with English, you will learn to gear your language to the appropriate time and place.

The next part of this section will help you to sharpen your skills in using standard English.

Part 4 Words Often Confused

The words listed in this section are often misused. The pairs of words may look alike or have similar meanings. However, they are not alike. One word cannot be used in place of the other. Study the lists of words often confused. Try to use the right word at the right time.

These words are often confused because they look alike. Notice, however, that their meanings differ.

capital means "most important." It also names the city or town that is the official center of government for a state or country.

capitol refers to the building where a state legislature meets.

the Capitol is the building in Washington, D.C., where the United States Congress meets.

The *capital* of New York is Albany.
The state *capitol* dome can be seen for miles.
Farmers protested outside the *Capitol* in Washington.

des′ ert means "a dry, barren region."

de sert′ means "to abandon."

des sert′ (note the difference in spelling) is a sweet food at the end of a meal.

The explorers were stranded in the *desert*.
Did the soldier *desert* his company?
Our *dessert* tonight is banana cake.

hear means "to listen to or to receive sound by the ear."

here refers to this place.

Did you *hear* the screeching brakes?
A new record store will open *here*.

its is a possessive, meaning belonging to *it*.

it's is the contraction for *it is* or *it has*.

The band has *its* own sound system.
It's almost midnight.

loose means either "not tight" or "free and untied."

lose means "to be unable to find or keep." It is also the opposite of *win*.

Several snakes from the zoo are *loose*.
I *lose* my balance when I spin on skates.
Did the wrestlers *lose* the meet?

principal means "leading, chief, or highest in importance."

principle refers to a basic truth, rule, or law.

The *principal* industry here is steel-making.
The basic *principle* of this country is democracy.

stationary means "not moving, fixed."
stationery refers to writing materials like paper and envelopes.

The trailer can move, but right now it's *stationary*.
The drugstore sells boxes of *stationery*.

their shows possession by *them*.
there means "in that place."
they're is the contraction for *they are*.

The steelworkers have *their* own union.
The bus route ends *there*.
They're losing their courage.

to means "toward or as far as."
too means "also or extremely."

Tracy slid *to* home plate.
I read the book, and I saw the movie *too*.

weather refers to the condition of the atmosphere, such as its heat or cold, wetness or dryness.
whether indicates a choice between two things.

The *weather* in Florida is usually pleasant.
Ask Stacy *whether* she is going or staying.

who's is the contraction for *who is* or *who has*.
whose is the possessive form of *who*.

Who's running the duplicating machine?
Whose sandwich is this?

your shows possession by *you*.
you're is the contraction for *you are* or *you were*.

When is *your* birthday?
You're on the team, aren't you?

Exercise A Choose the right word from the words given.

1. From the top of the Washington Monument, we looked down at the white dome of the nation's (capital, capitol, Capitol).

2. The (deserted, desserted) building was a dangerous place to play.

3. Sand dunes in the (desert, dessert) are always shifting due to wind and rain.

4. We could (hear, here) the alarm four blocks away.

5. The computer can correct some of (its, it's) own mistakes.

6. (Its, It's) always cold in the supermarket.

7. Ballet slippers should be tight, not (loose, lose).

8. I don't want to (loose, lose) my place in line.

9. The (principals, principles) stated in the Hippocratic Oath are still important to doctors.

10. The letter was typed on official (stationary, stationery).

Exercise B Follow the directions for Exercise A.

1. Holly arrived at the meeting early, but Hank got (their, there, they're) late.

2. Sometimes the players get careless when (their, there, they're) ahead.

3. All the students in the speech class have heard (their, there, they're) own voices on tape.

4. The bowling ball veered (to, too) far to the left.

5. Josh yielded (to, too) the school bus making a turn.

6. Are you getting off at this stop, (to, too)?

7. I wonder (weather, whether) I should call her or write her a letter.

8. (Who's, Whose) that leaning against the stop sign?

9. (Who's, Whose) story do you believe?

10. (Your, You're) certainly in fine form today.

Part 5 Troublesome Verbs

These pairs of verbs are often confused. Notice how they differ.

Bring and *Take*

Bring refers to movement toward the person speaking. Example: The pipeline *brings* water here to the desert.

Take refers to motion away from the speaker. Example: Did you *take* those books back to the library?

Here are the principal parts of these verbs:

bring, brought, brought

Present:	*Bring* that hammer to me, please.
Past:	We *brought* Janet with us.
Past Participle:	No one *has brought* enough money.

take, took, taken

Present:	When you leave, *take* some cake.
Past:	I *took* my cycle there to be fixed.
Past Participle:	Someone *has taken* my keys.

Learn and *Teach*

Learn means "to gain knowledge or skill." Example: Did you *learn* the words to that song?

Teach means "to help someone learn." Example: Will you *teach* me to dribble?

Here are the principal parts of these verbs:

learn, learned, learned

Present:	*Learn* the metric system.
Past:	Cal *learned* karate.
Past Participle:	We *have learned* Spanish.

teach, taught, taught

Present:	Mrs. Rivera *teaches* music.
Past:	Kelly *taught* me about photography.
Past Participle:	This course *has taught* us about carpentry.

Let and *Leave*

Let means "to allow or permit." Example: *Let* her go.

Leave means "to go away from" or "to allow something to remain." Example: *Leave* us alone.

The principal parts of these verbs are as follows:

let, let, let

Present: *Let* the motor run for a minute.
Past: Dad *let* the dog out.
Past Participle: The landlord *has let* us stay.

leave, left, left

Present: *Leave* your jacket on.
Past: Jennifer *left* in a hurry.
Past Participle: The robbers *had left* with the cash.

Lie and *Lay*

Lie means "to rest in a flat position" or "to be in a certain place." Example: *Lie* still.

Lay means "to place." Example: *Lay* the wreath here.

Here are the principal parts of these verbs:

lie, lay, lain

Present: *Lie* down on this mat.
Past: Jason *lay* in bed all day.
Past Participle: The patient *has lain* very still.

lay, laid, laid

Present: *Lay* the baby in her crib.
Past: The nurse *laid* a bandage on the wound.
Past Participle: Workers *have laid* the foundation.

May and *Can*

May refers to permission. *May* also refers to something that is possible. *Might* is another form of the word.

May we *have* dessert? I *might be* wrong.

Can refers to ability. *Can* means being physically or mentally able to do something. *Could* is another form.

Can you *do* a push-up? We *could* not *remember*.

May and *might* and *can* and *could* have no principal parts. They are used as helping verbs.

Rise and *Raise*

Rise means "to go upward." Example: The sun rises.

Raise means "to lift or to make something go up." Example: *Raise* your right hand.

The principal parts of these verbs are as follows:

rise, rose, risen

Present:	The steam *rises* and disappears.
Past:	The choir *rose* from their seats.
Past Participle:	The drawbridge *has risen*.

raise, raised, raised

Present:	Please *raise* the window shade.
Past:	Kim *raised* the ladder to reach the roof.
Past Participle:	Inflation *has raised* the cost of living.

Sit and *Set*

Sit means "to occupy a seat." Example: *Sit* on this bench.

Set means "to place." Example: *Set* the tools there.

The principal parts of these verbs are as follows:

sit, sat, sat

Present:	*Sit* near me, please.
Past:	We *sat* in the waiting room.
Past Participle:	All of the passengers *have sat* down.

set, set, set

Present:	*Set* your toothbrush on the sink.
Past:	John *set* the books in his new bookcase.
Past Participle:	We *have set* the costumes backstage.

Exercise A Choose the right verb from the two given.

1. We (sat, set) aside some money in a savings account.
2. The sales tax has (raised, risen) to 6 percent.
3. Litter (lay, laid) all over the park.
4. Stranded passengers (sat, set) in the airport.
5. I'll (bring, take) my glasses here to be repaired.
6. The dog (learned, taught) to obey simple commands.
7. Someone (let, left) the blueprints on the table.
8. (May, Can) we use the employees' elevator, please?
9. The photographer (sat, set) the film in a jar to develop.
10. Marlene's boss (raised, rose) her pay.

Exercise B Follow the directions for Exercise A.

1. Many people (may not, cannot) change a flat tire.
2. (Take, Bring) those books to the library, please.
3. The players (lay, laid) their cards on the table.
4. Who (learned, taught) you about self-defense?
5. When (may, can) students (let, leave) the campus?
6. The gymsuit has (lain, laid) in that locker all year.
7. The manager would not (let, leave) the boys in.
8. Ms. Rawls said we (may, can) park in her driveway.
9. As a plumber's aide, Mike (learned, taught) a trade.
10. The factory (raised, rose) its level of production.

Part 6 Usage Problems

The words in this section are often used incorrectly. Notice the standard usages for these problem words.

accept means "to agree to something or to receive something willingly."

except means "to leave out." *Except* also means "not including."

"I *accept* the blame," Todd said.
"We'll *except* you from this rule," the counselor said.
We bought all the supplies *except* glue.

agree on means "to come to an understanding." You and others agree *on* a plan.

agree to means "to consent to." You agree *to* something, such as a plan.

agree with means "to have the same opinion as someone else." You agree *with* somebody. *Agree with* may also refer to something being suitable, as when foods don't *agree with* you.

The Democrats *agreed on* a candidate.
The team *agreed to* stiff training rules.
Mr. Jackson likes people who always *agree with* him.
Chocolate doesn't *agree with* me.

all right is the correct spelling. *Alright* is nonstandard. There are two words.

All right, I'll turn off the TV.
Ariel felt *all right* after her tonsils were removed.

among refers to a group of more than two people or things.
between refers to two people or things.

We divided the food *among* the four of us.
There is a treaty *between* the two countries.

anywhere, nowhere, somewhere, and **anyway** are standard usages. The words *anywheres*, *nowheres*, *somewheres*, and *anyways* are nonstandard. The final *s* should be dropped.

Nonstandard: She wasn't anywheres in sight.
Standard: She wasn't *anywhere* in sight.

Nonstandard: I know that clip is here somewheres.
Standard: I know that clip is here *somewhere*.

between each, followed by a singular noun, is incorrect. *Between* should not be used with a singular noun.

Nonstandard: Between each game, the Bears practiced hard.
Standard: *Between games*, the Bears practiced hard.

Nonstandard: The elevator stopped between every floor.
Standard: The elevator stopped *between floors*.

borrow means "to receive something on loan." Don't confuse it with *lend*, meaning "to give out temporarily."

Nonstandard: Will you borrow me your pen?
Standard: Will you *lend* me your pen?
Standard: May I *borrow* your pen?

Exercise A Look for sentences with nonstandard usage. Rewrite those sentences, using the right words. If a sentence is correct, write *Correct* after that number.

1. Between each quarter of the game, the band plays.
2. Every block accept ours has sidewalks.
3. Will you borrow me your scissors?
4. Scott couldn't find his sister anywheres.
5. We divided the tips among the three of us.
6. Did you agree on what that columnist wrote?
7. Do you feel all right?
8. The jury agreed on a verdict.
9. My purse has to be around here somewheres.
10. Jane would not except my gift.

Exercise B Follow the directions for Exercise A.

1. Bill borrowed me his radio.
2. The shoe store has every size accept the one I need.
3. Did Jessica and David agree with the best route to take?
4. Alright, tell me what's bothering you.
5. Deena had to choose among the two jobs.
6. The teacher walked between each row of desks.

7. Rachel agrees with me that playing softball is fun.
8. Anyways, I'm heading for home.
9. Ken borrowed my hat for the costume party.
10. The President excepted the resignation of his aide.

fewer refers to numbers or things that can be counted.
less refers to amount or quantity.

Tom makes *fewer* typing errors than Rona.
We hear *less* noise at night.

in means "inside something."
into tells of motion from the outside to the inside of something.

Nonstandard: The performers went in the studio.
Standard: The performers went *into* the studio.

Nonstandard: Joe hit the hockey puck in the goal.
Standard: Joe hit the hockey puck *into* the goal.

kind of a and **sort of a** are nonstandard. The *a* is not necessary.

Nonstandard: What kind of a jacket do you have?
Standard: What *kind of* jacket do you have?

Nonstandard: There is some sort of a problem here.
Standard: There is some *sort of* problem here.

like is a preposition. Using *like* as a conjunction before a clause is not fully accepted. Especially in writing, it is better to use *as* or *as if*.

Nonstandard: *Like* I said, you can depend on Sara.
Standard: *As* I said, you can depend on Sara.

Nonstandard: Ramon talked *like* he was in charge.
Standard: Ramon talked *as if* he was in charge.

of is sometimes incorrectly used in phrases like *could of*, *shouldn't of*, and *must of*. The correct word is *have* or its contraction: *could have, could've, shouldn't have, must have, might have, might've.*

Nonstandard: Darryl should of locked his bike.
Standard: Darryl *should have* locked his bike.

ways does not refer to distance. *Way* is correct.

Nonstandard: We drove a short ways down the road.
Standard: We drove a short *way* down the road.

Exercise A Correct the sentences with nonstandard usage. If a sentence is correct, write *Correct.*

1. Chris acted like the world was ending.
2. This car needs less repairs than I thought.
3. I will have less trouble with this car than with that one.
4. Carolyn stuffed her change in her pocket.
5. Like the President says, we must conserve energy.
6. There are less new TV programs this season.
7. The center should of practiced her lay-up shots.
8. What kind of a penalty did the ref call?
9. The stadium is a ways farther south.
10. The coach sent the players on the bench in the game.

Exercise B Follow the directions for Exercise A.

1. Kate has less lines to memorize in this play.
2. The council must of held some sort of a meeting.
3. The movie ended just like I thought it would.
4. Lauren slipped a message in our mailbox.
5. Fewer radio stations are playing the top ten songs now.
6. The parking garage is quite a ways from here.
7. Less people go to the later show.
8. Jim looks as if he needs more time.
9. What kind of peg goes in this hole?
10. We should of stopped at the park for our picnic.

REVIEW The Right Word

Using Words Correctly Choose the correct word from the words given in parentheses.

1. (Who's, Whose) the passenger in the sidecar?
2. Did you (loose, lose) your ticket stub?
3. Have you cashed (your, you're) check yet?
4. (It's, Its) almost time to leave.
5. The fish had jumped out of (it's, its) bowl.
6. I always keep the Turners' mail for them when (there, they're, their) on vacation.
7. Please (bring, take) me a glass of water.
8. (May, Can) we make a U-turn on this street, officer?
9. The trainer has (learned, taught) the boxer proper footwork.
10. A huge crane (raised, rose) steel beams to the upper stories.
11. The tug-of-war ends when one team (lets, leaves) go of the rope.
12. The test pilot (sat, set) at the controls.
13. Meredith (lay, laid) awake and couldn't sleep.
14. The oil has (raised, risen) to the surface of the sea.
15. Will you (borrow, lend) me some warmer gloves?
16. Our family divides the work (among, between) the five of us.
17. (All right, Alright), operator, we'll (accept, except) the charges.
18. Trisha ran (in, into) the room (as if, like) she was terribly excited.
19. There is some (sort of, sort of a) curb (between, between each) parking spaces.
20. I should (have, of) eaten (fewer, less) pretzels and drunk (fewer, less) 7-Up.

Capitalization

Capital letters make your writing easier to read. They call attention to certain special words and to words that begin sentences.

There are specific rules for capitalizing words. This section will show you the rules. You can refer to this section at any time if you have questions about capitalization.

Proper Nouns and Adjectives

Capitalize proper nouns and proper adjectives.

A **proper noun** is the name of a particular person, place, or thing. In contrast, a **common noun** is the name of a whole group of people, places, or things. A **proper adjective** is an adjective formed from a proper noun.

Common Noun	Proper Noun	Proper Adjective
queen	**V**ictoria	**V**ictorian
country	**I**reland	**I**rish
government	**C**ongress	**C**ongressional

There are many kinds of proper nouns. The following rules will help you to decide whether or not a noun is a proper noun.

Names of People

Capitalize people's names. Also capitalize the initials or abbreviations that stand for names.

F. D. Roosevelt	**F**ranklin **D**elano **R**oosevelt
Susan **B. A**nthony	**S**usan **B**rownell **A**nthony

Capitalize the titles used with people's names. Also capitalize the initials or abbreviations that stand for those titles.

The titles *Miss*, *Ms.*, *Mrs.*, and *Mr.* are always capitalized.

Gov. R. T. Alberg	**M**ajor Edward J. Brooks
Ms. Susan Manzano	**D**r. Evelyn Santucci
Judge Ellen O'Brien	**R**ev. L. K. Jenkins

Do not capitalize a title that is used without a name. It is a common noun.

Barbara Sloan is president of the bank.
The judge in this courtroom is Justice Black.

Capitalize titles of very high importance, even when they are used without names.

the **P**resident of the United States
the **C**hief **J**ustice of the Supreme Court
the **P**rime **M**inister of Canada
a **C**ongresswoman
the **P**ope

Family Relationships

Capitalize such family words as *mother, father, aunt,* and *uncle* when they are used as names. If the noun is preceded by a possessive word or by *a* or *the,* it is not capitalized.

What was **D**ad like when he was sixteen, **G**randma?
Jessica's mother is here, **M**om.
We call our aunt and uncle **U**ncle Hy and **A**unt Lo.
My **m**om's car needs a new battery.

The Pronoun *I*

Capitalize the pronoun *I.*

He and **I** saw a movie. **I** work after school.

The Supreme Being and Sacred Writings

Capitalize all words referring to God, to the Holy Family, and to religious scriptures.

the **A**lmighty	the **B**ible	the **S**on of **G**od
the **L**ord	the **T**almud	the **N**ew **T**estament
the **B**lessed **V**irgin	**A**llah	the **B**ook of **J**ob

Capitalize personal pronouns referring to God.

They asked the Lord for **H**is blessing.

Exercise A Copy the following sentences. Change small letters to capital letters wherever necessary.

1. A hurricane hit the town that dad and i were visiting.
2. My mother's doctor is dr. herrera.
3. If you enjoy being scared, read the horror stories of h. p. lovecraft.

4. The minister read from the new testament.

5. Yesterday ms. turner told me that i could now call her sgt. turner.

6. The pope visited this country in 1979.

7. The director of the hospital is rowine hayes brown.

8. Some religions honor god by not speaking his name.

9. In her lecture, professor bailey explained how laws are made.

10. State sen. dawn clark netsch sponsored the bill.

Exercise B Follow the directions for Exercise A.

1. Can nate tell mr. banzali the best route to memphis?

2. The best-known leader of the dakota tribes was chief sitting bull.

3. Last week reverend williams read to us from the book of job.

4. Did lorene help with the work on your brother's bike?

5. Few people who write to the president of the united states receive a personal answer.

6. Mrs. eppie lederer gives advice under the name of ann landers.

7. My cousin dale and i work at mr. j. j. vernon's downtown office.

8. Did dad make an appointment with dr. case?

9. According to the bible, adam and eve disobeyed god.

10. Will the president meet with governor ray?

Geographical Names

In a geographical name, capitalize the first letter of each word except articles and prepositions.

If the article *the* appears before a place name, it is not part of the name and is therefore not capitalized.

Continents: Africa, North America, Europe, Asia

Bodies of Water: the Atlantic Ocean, the Ohio River, the Gulf of Mexico, the South China Sea, Hudson Bay, the Panama Canal, Lake Michigan

Land Forms: Mount McKinley, Aleutian Islands, Death Valley, Cadillac Mountain, Black Hills, Cape Lookout

Political Units: Florida, Denver, Province of Ontario, Republic of Kenya, State of Israel, Thirteenth Congressional District

Public Areas: Glacier National Park, Fort Sumter, Badlands National Monument, Ford Theater, Dunes State Park, Fallen Timbers Battlefield

Roads and Highways: Route 66, Interstate Highway 610, Hampton Road, Thornwood Avenue, Main Street

Directions and Sections

Capitalize names of sections of the country.

The West has several old trading posts.
The South is sometimes called "Dixie."
The Sorensons moved from New England to the West Coast.

Capitalize proper adjectives that come from names of sections of the country.

a Midwestern town | Western saddle
Southern food | East Coast company

Do not capitalize directions of the compass.

Barrow, Alaska, is north of all other United States cities.
Drive east on Interstate 80 to New York.

Do not capitalize adjectives that come from words showing direction.

The parking lot is on the north side of the building.
The southerly breeze turned into a fierce wind.

Exercise A Number your paper from 1 to 10. Find the words in the following sentences that should be capitalized. Write the words after the proper number, using the necessary capital letters.

1. The tenth congressional district is north of chicago.
2. There is an extinct volcano called mount shasta in california.
3. The yucatan channel connects the gulf of mexico with the caribbean sea.
4. The andes mountains are in south america.
5. The district of columbia's biggest park is rock creek park.
6. Some southern foods are now popular in the north.
7. Hurricanes attacked the southeast, and the tornadoes hit the southwest.
8. Both interstate 90 and route 20 run from albany to buffalo.
9. The north defeated the south in a key battle at gettysburg, pennsylvania.
10. In japan, the cities are extremely crowded.

Exercise B Follow the directions for Exercise A.

1. We live north of daytona beach, florida.
2. Mrs. evans works by her east window in the morning and by her west window in the afternoon.
3. Actually, the trucker bought her western boots in boston.
4. Please meet me on the southeast corner of pearl street and archer road.
5. This new england cookbook has many recipes for fish.

6. The typhoon swept across the bay of bengal.

7. On the frozen midwestern plains, south winds are welcome.

8. How does an eastern accent differ from a southern one?

9. Mount desert island is part of acadia national park in maine.

10. The yukon territory is north of british columbia.

Names of Organizations and Institutions

Capitalize the names of organizations and institutions, including political parties, governmental bodies or agencies, schools, colleges, churches, hospitals, clubs, businesses, and abbreviations of these names.

Republican **P**arty	**C**hildren's **M**emorial **H**ospital
Federal **T**rade **C**ommission	**A**merican **M**edical **A**ssociation
Stevenson **H**igh **S**chool	**N**ational **U**rban **L**eague
St. **J**oseph's **C**hurch	**A.F.L.-C.I.O.**

Do not capitalize such words as *school, company, church,* and *hospital* when they are not used as parts of names.

Several people from our church work at the hospital.

Names of Events, Documents, and Periods of Time

Capitalize the names of historical events, documents, and periods of time.

Battle of **C**oncord	**P**anama **C**anal **T**reaty
Vietnam **W**ar	the **M**iddle **A**ges
United **S**tates **C**onstitution	the **R**eformation

Months, Days, and Holidays

Capitalize names of months, days, and holidays, but not the names of seasons.

July	**T**hursday	winter
Halloween	**T**hanksgiving	summer

Races, Languages, Nationalities, Religions

Capitalize the names of races, languages, nationalities, and religions. Also capitalize any adjectives that come from these names.

Greek	**O**riental	**C**atholicism	**P**rotestant
German	**H**induism	**P**uerto **R**ican	**P**olish

School Subjects

Do not capitalize the names of school subjects, except course titles followed by a number.

history	**R**eading **W**orkshop I
industrial arts	**M**ath 300

Remember that the names of languages are always capitalized.

French **S**panish **J**apanese **E**nglish

Ships, Trains, Airplanes, Automobiles

Capitalize the names of ships, trains, airplanes, and automobiles.

U.S.S. C*onstellation* **C**oncorde **B**uick **S**kyhawk

B.C., A.D.

Capitalize the abbreviations *B.C.* and *A.D.*

The Pyramids of Egypt were begun about 300 **B.C.**
The Middle Ages were from **A.D.** 500 to about 1500.
Mohammed was born in **A.D.** 570.

Exercise A Write the words in each sentence that should be capitalized. Use the necessary capital letters.

1. The national basketball association will hold its playoffs in march.
2. Every june, elizabeth seton high school holds a carnival.
3. The high school is across the street from lakeview hospital.
4. There are many different protestant religions.
5. In the middle ages, people believed that a woman would dream of her future husband on st. agnes' eve, january 20.
6. The battle of antietam was one of the fiercest in the american civil war.
7. Montezuma II, the last aztec ruler of mexico, died in a.d. 1520.
8. Amtrak's *southwest limited* travels over eighty miles per hour on some runs.
9. King tut, the egyptian ruler, was buried in 1344 b.c.
10. Last saturday ms. marzo bought new tires for her plymouth horizon.

Exercise B Follow the directions for Exercise A.

1. The second monday in october is celebrated as columbus day.
2. Both the french and the americans celebrate their independence in july.

3. The democratic party received contributions from many unions.

4. The united mineworkers' union is a member of the a.f.l.-c.i.o.

5. We are reading the declaration of independence in my history class.

6. Cheryl could not sign up for family living 101 because it conflicted with her math class.

7. The national language of the israelis is hebrew.

8. The alaskans make the most of their short summer.

9. After graduating from howard university, judy received job offers from the fbi and general foods corporation.

10. The powells bought a new datsun.

First Words

Sentences and Poetry

Capitalize the first word of every sentence and the first word of most lines of poetry.

> **T**he disc jockey began her program. **S**he played a new album.

> **T**iger, tiger, burning bright
> **I**n the forests of the night, . . .
> —"The Tiger," William Blake

Sometimes, especially in modern poetry, the lines of a poem do not begin with capital letters.

Quotations

Capitalize the first word of a direct quotation.

A **direct quotation** tells the exact words of a speaker or writer.

> Ralph Waldo Emerson said, "**T**he only way to have a friend is to be one."

In a **divided quotation,** a direct quotation is broken into two parts by words like *he said* or *she explained.* Do not capitalize the first word of the second part unless it starts a new sentence.

> "I agree," Tim said, "**t**hat a good friend is rare."
> "I agree," Tim said. "**A** good friend is rare."

Letter Parts

Capitalize the first word in the greeting of a letter. Also capitalize the name of the person addressed, or words like *Sir* and *Madam* that stand for names.

Dear **M**s. **V**aldez **D**ear **M**r. **N**ash **D**ear **S**ir:

In the complimentary close, capitalize only the first word.

Very truly yours, **S**incerely yours,

Outlines

Capitalize the first word of each item in an outline. Also capitalize the letters before each line.

I. **H**olidays
  A. **C**hief legal holidays
    1. **N**ational
    2. **S**tate or local
  B. **R**eligious holidays

Titles

Capitalize the first word and all important words in the titles of chapters, magazine articles, short stories, essays, poems, television programs, radio programs, and songs or short pieces of music.

Chapter title: Chapter 3, "**F**ood and **H**ealth"
Magazine article: "**T**oday's **C**hanging **F**amily"
Short story: "**T**o **B**uild a **F**ire"
Essay: "**F**riendship"
Poem: "**T**he **B**ase **S**tealer"
Television program: "**T**he **M**uppet **S**how"
Song: "**O**h, **W**hat a **B**eautiful **M**orning!"

Capitalize the first word and all important words in titles of books, newspapers, magazines, plays, movies, works of art, and long musical compositions.

Book title: *Where the Lilies Bloom*
Newspaper: *Los Angeles Times*
Magazine: *Ebony*
Play: *You Can't Take It with You*
Movie: *Star Trek*
Work of art: *The Sunflowers*
Long musical composition: *Carmen*

Exercise A Number your paper from 1 to 10. Write the words that should be capitalized. Use the correct capital letter.

1. dear ms. kruger:
   your two tickets to our preview showing of *the empire strikes back* are enclosed. thank you for your order.
   sincerely yours,

2. television shows about hospitals, such as "general hospital," always attract some viewers.

3. the action photography in *sports illustrated* is excellent.

4. I. finding a cure for the common cold
   A. difficulties
      1. more than 200 cold viruses

5. our school library has back issues of several newspapers, including *the washington post*.

6. rachel chose the poem "a dream deferred" to memorize.

7. "dave," joyce called, "how do you like this new fender?"

8. "i keep forgetting my locker combination," said adam. "maybe i should write it down."

9. mary cassatt's painting *the letter* shows a sad woman sealing an envelope.

10. john p. davis and the russian author gogol both wrote stories titled "the overcoat."

Exercise B Follow the directions for Exercise A.

1. all the radios at the beach were playing "summertime."
2. it was many and many a year ago,
    in a kingdom by the sea,
  that a maiden there lived whom you may know
    by the name of annabel lee;
        —Edgar Allan Poe, "Annabel Lee"
3. we discussed the chapter called "two images of the future" from the book *this endangered planet*.
4. "i'm not sure," said gerard, "what we should do now."
5. i read the article "new research in dental care" in *prevention* magazine.
6. megan asked, "have you seen the latest issue of *time*?"
7. george lucas directed *american graffiti* before he made *star wars*.
8. my little sister insisted that i turn to "the muppet show."
9. the song "some enchanted evening" is from the musical *south pacific*.
10. dear sir:
    i would like two tickets to monday night's
  performance of *the messiah*.
          yours truly,

REVIEW Capitalization

Using Capital Letters Correctly Copy each of these sentences. Change small letters to capital letters wherever necessary.

1. reg dwight changed his name to elton john.
2. my sister auditioned for a part in *annie*.
3. students in spanish III can earn extra credit by going to special sessions on thursdays.
4. the okefenokee swamp is in georgia and florida.
5. we drove south through brown county into kentucky.
6. margaret thatcher, a member of the conservative party, became prime minister of england in 1979.
7. students in ms. holden's office machines II class learn to use computers.
8. This passage from the *bible* was written by st. luke.
9. the scanners at many food stores are made by i.b.m.
10. reverend elaine jones, rabbi samuel h. gelman, and father edward kraus teach courses at the new junior college.
11. the television comedy "benson" was a spinoff from "soap."
12. uncle gene converted the '63 chevy into a racing car.
13. my cousin graduated from roberto clemente high school last june.
14. the southwest is very hot in the summer.
15. since 1800, the president of the united states has lived in the white house.
16. the coast of poland is on the baltic sea.
17. who was president during the war of 1812?
18. our history class toured the headquarters of the united nations in new york city.
19. the public schools as well as the catholic schools are closed on good friday.
20. when is the jewish holiday of yom kippur celebrated?

Punctuation

Road signs and traffic lights guide a driver. Likewise, punctuation marks guide a reader. **Punctuation marks** show readers where to stop or slow down or change direction.

When you write, your punctuation signals your reader. It marks groups of words that belong together. It tells how a sentence should be read. All in all, punctuation helps your reader to understand your meaning.

End Marks

End marks are the punctuation marks that indicate the end of a sentence. The three kinds of end marks are the **period,** the **question mark,** and the **exclamation point.**

The Period

Use a period at the end of a declarative sentence.

A **declarative sentence** is a sentence that makes a statement. You use declarative sentences when you tell something.

The streets are covered with ice.

Use a period at the end of most imperative sentences.

An **imperative sentence** is a sentence that orders or requests someone to do something.

Use the revolving door, please.

At times, imperative sentences express strong excitement or emotion. Then an exclamation point, rather than a period, is used at the end of the sentence.

Get away!   Hurry up!

Use a period at the end of an indirect question.

An **indirect question** tells that someone asked a question. However, it does not give the exact words of the question.

The captain asked whether the ship was on course.

Notice how a **direct question** differs:

The captain asked, "Is the ship on course?"

A direct question shows the exact words of the person asking the question. A direct question ends with a question mark.

Use a period at the end of an abbreviation or an initial. An **abbreviation** is a shortened form of a word. An **initial** is a first letter that stands for a word.

Gov. James R. Thomas   4 P.M. on Aug. 4

Lt. Margaret B. Hill   6 lb., 12 oz.

Certain abbreviations do not use periods. To check

whether or not to use a period with an abbreviation, look up the abbreviation in your dictionary.

CIA (*Central Intelligence Agency*)
CB (*Citizens' Band*)
UN (*United Nations*)

Use a period after each number or letter for an item in an outline or a list.

(An Outline)	(A List)
I. Sports	1. nails
A. Contact	2. hammer
1. Football	3. putty

Use a period between dollars and cents and before a decimal.

$13.64   3.14

The Question Mark

Use a question mark at the end of an interrogative sentence.

An **interrogative sentence** is a sentence that asks a question.

What do you want for dinner?

The Exclamation Point

Use an exclamation point at the end of an exclamatory sentence.

An **exclamatory sentence** expresses excitement or other strong emotion.

You're terrific!   How nice you look!

Use an exclamation point after an interjection.

An **interjection** is one or more words that show strong feeling. Sometimes the interjection is a sound.

Nice!   Ouch!   Not again!   Super!

Exercise A Copy the following sentences, adding the necessary punctuation. Be prepared to tell what punctuation marks you used and why you used them.

1. Where is Lt Moseley stationed
2. Vince asked why the car had a fiberglass hood
3. Fantastic Those twenty-dollar shirts have been marked down to $999
4. Did she want me to call at 8:15 A M or P M
5. Say Where have you been
6. I Foods containing calcium
   A Dairy products
      1 Milk
7. The initials WHO stand for the World Health Organization
8. Is your appointment with Dr Sam Williams, Jr or with Dr Sam Williams, Sr
9. Gena's new address is PO Box 12, Altoona, Pennsylvania
10. The *USS Pueblo* was captured by North Korea

Exercise B Follow the directions for Exercise A.

1. Aaron asked if China bordered the USSR
2. Please send all complaints to Brown, Brooks, and Co in New York
3. Is that an AM radio
4. Darryl Fields, RN, helps his patients to keep smiling
5. Oh, no Why did you do that
6. Should I make the check out to Dr Sara Bosco or to Sara Bosco, MD
7. If the amount is $991 or more, round it off to ten dollars
8. The NEA is an educational organization
9. Does the winter sun really set by 3 PM in Alaska
10. Halt Who's there

The Comma

A comma is used to separate words that do not go together. When you are speaking, you can pause. When you are writing, you use commas for breaks in thought. In this way, commas help you to communicate clearly.

Using Commas in a Series

Use a comma after every item in a series except the last one.

A series is three or more items of the same kind. Your writing may contain a series of words, of phrases, or of clauses.

Words: Mel Brooks is a writer, an actor, and a director.

Phrases: We searched under beds, inside drawers, and in closets.

Clauses: The doctor explained how the blood test is made, what it tells, and why it is necessary.

Use commas after *first, second, third,* and so on, when these adverbs introduce a series.

There are four steps to any house-painting job: first, scraping; second, sanding; third, priming; and fourth, painting.

When there are two or more adjectives before a noun, use commas between them.

The vet treated the cold, wet, sick dog.

Exercise A Number your paper from 1 to 10. Copy the following sentences and add commas where necessary.

1. January February and March are cold bitter months here.

2. Football basketball and baseball are all televised in the fall.

3. Nan wanted to know three things about the car: first its gas mileage; second its cruising speed; and third its price.

4. The workers picked grapes in the hot dusty fields.

5. Ron groped for the alarm shut it off and went back to sleep.

6. Mae's radio woke her with news of a fire an airplane crash and a bus strike.

7. Kerry lifted the phonograph needle removed the dust and set the needle back down.

8. Seth has had three part-time jobs: first as a newspaper carrier; second as a cook; and third as an usher.

9. His eyes widened brightened and seemed to smile.

10. Maureen told the class where Libya is when it was founded and how it is governed.

Exercise B Follow the directions for Exercise A.

1. The building inspector listed these problems: first falling plaster; second cracked windows; third peeling paint.

2. Lightning black clouds and blowing leaves streaked across the sky.

3. To make a soda, mix syrup ice cream and soda water.

4. Baking soda and water make a cheap effective toothpaste.

5. Betty climbed the wall gripped the ledge and threw the rope.

6. Tall thin gray lockers lined the halls.

7. Hondas Yamahas Suzukis and Harley-Davidsons glittered in the lot.

8. Denny looked for work at supermarkets theaters restaurants and amusement parks.

9. First I checked the plug; second I looked at the fuse box; third I fiddled with the antennas; fourth I gave up and called the repair shop.

10. The plumber stood up stretched and flexed her fingers.

Using Commas with Introductory Words

Use a comma to separate an introductory word, long phrase, or clause from the rest of the sentence.

No, I'm not leaving yet. (introductory word)

After four rounds with the champ, Diaz was knocked down. (prepositional phrases)

Laughing wildly, Lauren walked offstage. (verbal phrase)

When you pay the toll, the gate goes up. (adverb clause)

As you can see, commas are used after introductory words like *yes* and *no*. They are also used after prepositional phrases, verbal phrases, and adverb clauses that begin sentences.

Sometimes the comma may be left out. When there would be little pause in speaking, no comma is used.

At noon the auction will begin.

Using Commas with Interrupters

Use commas to set off one or more words that interrupt the flow of thought in a sentence.

The judge, in any event, sentenced the man.

William, moreover, made the all-state squad.

The bus lines, I think, have increased the fare.

The cost of some foods, however, has gone down.

The following words are additional examples of interrupters. Set them off with commas.

therefore	I believe	of course
for example	by the way	furthermore
I suppose	in fact	nevertheless

Exercise A Number your paper from 1 to 10. Copy the following sentences. Add commas where necessary.

1. No the Marvin Gaye album is not on sale.
2. After dialing Tony's number Rita had second thoughts.
3. Waiting for her coffee the reporter overheard a startling conversation.
4. Carlos I believe deserves our support.
5. Dazed from lack of sleep the swimmer finally reached the beach.
6. Yes the plane is on schedule.
7. You will be at the party I suppose.
8. To tell the truth this pie could have used more time in the oven.
9. After he talked with the coach Glenn felt better.
10. As other nations get more industry they will share our pollution problems.

Exercise B Follow the directions for Exercise A.

1. Campbell's interception was I think the high point of the game.
2. Brenda on the other hand enjoys her math class.
3. Yes that is the quickest route.
4. The British however do not like iced tea.
5. On the way home from the dentist's office Fran chipped her tooth.
6. Although the street is noisy it is safe.
7. Delighted at the prospect of a summer on the beach Carmen took the job.
8. Whenever a new mail carrier delivers the mail we get somebody else's letters.
9. The rust I am afraid has eaten through the floor of the car.
10. Because the public pool was closed we had no place to swim.

Using Commas with Nouns of Direct Address

Use commas to set off nouns of direct address.

Sometimes when you speak or write to someone, you use the person's name. The name of someone directly spoken to is a **noun of direct address.**

Marsha, call a time-out!

In the hallway, Mark, is a package for you.

Did anybody call, Cynthia?

After you leave, boys, lock the garage.

As in the last example, nouns of direct address may be common nouns.

Using Commas with Appositives

Use commas to set off most appositives.

An **appositive** is one or more words that explain or identify another word. The appositive directly follows the word it explains.

Art Buchwald, a humorous writer, has a column in this newspaper.

Our assistant coach, Mr. Wagner, played with the Jets.

The Superbowl, the biggest game of the year, is Sunday.

As in the final example, an appositive may contain a prepositional phrase.

Nouns used as appositives are called **nouns in apposition.** When the noun in apposition is a single name, it is not usually set off by commas.

My sister Jennifer works here.

Using Commas with Quotations

Use commas to set off the explanatory words of a direct quotation.

The explanatory words are the statements like *he said*, *Greg replied*, or *Sheila asked*. They are not part of the quotation.

Explanatory words often come before the quotation. Use a comma after the explanatory words.

Rich said, "Take the expressway to the third exit."

Now look at this quotation:

"Take the expressway to the third exit," Rich said.

In the sentence above, the explanatory words come after the quotation. Notice that the comma belongs at the end of the quotation inside the quotation marks.

Sometimes a quotation is broken into two parts. The explanatory words separate the two parts. Here is an example of a *divided quotation*:

"Take the expressway," Rich said, "to the third exit."

In a divided quotation, a comma is used within the quotation marks at the end of the first part of the sentence. A comma is also used after the explanatory words.

Indirect quotations do not tell the speaker's exact words. No commas are used.

Rich said that we should take the expressway to the third exit.

Using Commas in Compound Sentences

Use a comma before the conjunction between the two main clauses of a compound sentence.

The Dodgers won the pennant, but they lost the World Series.

The comma is not necessary when the main clauses are very short and are joined by *and*.

We worked and then we relaxed.

Sometimes very short main clauses are joined by *but* or *or*. A comma is used since the words *but* and *or* mark a change in the flow of thought.

Ken works, but he isn't paid much.

Don't confuse compound sentences with compound subjects or compound predicates. There is no comma before the *and* that joins a compound subject or predicate.

Beth dove into the pool *and* retrieved her wallet.

Exercise A Copy these sentences. Add commas as needed.

1. Lincoln Logs the building blocks for children were designed by a famous architect's son.
2. The dentist a kind woman always puts her patients at ease.
3. Ms. Calder this is my cousin James.
4. Use your imagination Cory.
5. Don's sketch a realistic drawing of the park was displayed at the library.
6. Please submit your application to Dr. Vasquez the director of the project.
7. Shawn said "The breakfast will be held in the church."
8. "I was at that show myself" said Vic.
9. "The sun" said the pitcher "was in my eyes."
10. Martin called several times but Nathan's line was busy for hours.

Exercise B Follow the directions for Exercise A.

1. Is Molly still working at Burger King or did she find a new job?

2. Coleman chrome-plated his motorcycle and then he painted a dragon on the fender.

3. Captain William Kidd a well-known pirate buried treasure in New York.

4. Melissa found her information at the library and Ben got his from City Hall.

5. Jackie said "I am in the work-study program."

6. "The tornado broke windows and tore off roofs Cindy" explained Travis.

7. "These recruits already act like professionals" said Sergeant Willis.

8. Gary likes knockwurst a sausage with lots of seasoning.

9. "Your engine" said the mechanic "needs a lot of work."

10. The coach said "Keep up the good work girls."

Using Commas in Dates

In dates, use a comma between the day of the month and the year.

February 22, 1976 May 8, 1945

When a date is part of a sentence, a comma follows the year.

The first talking picture was shown on July 6, 1928, in New York.

Using Commas in Place Names

Use a comma between the name of a city or town and the name of its state or country.

Detroit, Michigan Santiago, Chile

Athens, Greece Houston, Texas

When an address is part of a sentence, use a comma after each item.

For more information, write to the National Wildlife Federation, 1412 Sixteenth Street, Washington, D.C. 20005.

Note that you do not put a comma between the state name and the ZIP code.

Using Commas in Letters

Use a comma after the salutation of a friendly letter. Use a comma after the complimentary close of a friendly letter or a business letter.

Dear Gretchen,   Yours truly,

Using Commas with Nonrestrictive Clauses

Use commas to set off nonrestrictive clauses.

A **nonrestrictive clause** is a clause that merely adds an idea to the sentence. The sentence would be complete without it. The meaning would be definite without it.

A **restrictive clause** is a clause that is essential to the meaning of a sentence. The clause is needed for the sense of the sentence. If a restrictive clause is dropped out of a sentence, the meaning changes.

Nonrestrictive clause: Terry Reese, *who is the center for the Wildcats,* scored the most points.

Terry Reese scored the most points. (The clause can be dropped from the sentence.)

Restrictive clause: Terry Reese is the player *who scored the most points.*

Terry Reese is the player. (The clause cannot be dropped.)

To see if a clause is nonrestrictive, read the sentence without it. If the meaning doesn't change, the clause is nonrestrictive. Use commas before and after it.

Restrictive clauses are often used to identify or to point out the person or thing they modify. Without this identification, the meaning of the sentence would not be clear. Nonrestrictive clauses, on the other hand, add no essential meaning to the sentence.

Restrictive clause: Janice is the girl *who found the money*. (The clause tells which girl.)

Nonrestrictive clause: Janice, *who is very alert*, found the money.

Janice found the money. (The clause is not needed.)

Restrictive clause: This is the book *that has the map*. (The clause tells which book.)

Nonrestrictive clause: This book, *which has pictures*, is my choice.

This book is my choice. (The clause is not needed.)

Using Commas To Avoid Confusion

Use a comma whenever the reader might otherwise be confused. Sometimes no rule applies, but a sentence might be misread without commas.

Without commas, the following sentences could be misunderstood:

Inside everything was a mess.
Whoever called called twice.

With commas, the sentences are clearer.

Inside, everything was a mess.

Whoever called, called twice.

Exercise A Copy the following sentences. Add commas where necessary.

1. The walking catfish was first reported near Clearwater Florida on May 25 1968.

2. Dear Nicole

My summer address will be 205 Linden Street Ladysmith Wisconsin 54848.

I hope to hear from you.

With best wishes

Katy

3. On May 24 1844 the first telegraph message was sent.

4. Duluth Minnesota is one city that produces much iron and steel.

5. The album was made in Nashville a city with many recording studios.

6. On November 1 1835 Texas declared its independence from Mexico.

7. Coins are made in Denver Colorado and Philadelphia Pennsylvania.

8. John Brown's raid on Harper's Ferry West Virginia began on October 16 1859 and was crushed on October 18.

9. Write to Lynn Brown at 665 California Avenue Ames Iowa 50010.

10. Outside the wind blew fiercely.

Exercise B Follow the directions for Exercise A.

1. On December 3 1967 a doctor successfully transplanted a human heart.

2. Dear Caroline

My Aunt Betsy's new address is Rural Route 3 Ridgeway Virginia 62321.

Sincerely

Michael

3. On August 27 1859 Edwin Drake struck oil near Titusville Pennsylvania.

4. The intruder you saw saw you.

5. Martin Luther King, Jr. was assassinated on April 4 1968 in Memphis Tennessee.

6. The school is located at 6900 South Stewart Avenue Chicago Illinois.

7. Do you come from Barcelona Venezuela or Barcelona Spain?

8. He seems to believe the saying, "Whatever is is right."

9. The first American automobile which was called a "gasoline buggy" by some was completed on April 19 1892.

10. Mary's grandmother who lives downstairs left Warsaw Poland in 1935.

The Semicolon

Use a semicolon to join the parts of a compound sentence if no coordinating conjunction is used.

> The operator interrupted the call; our time was up.

When there are several commas in the parts of a compound sentence, separate the clauses with a semicolon.

> On this diet I can eat bread, fruits, and vegetables; but candy, soft drinks, and desserts are forbidden.

When there are commas within parts of a series, use semicolons to separate the parts.

> In the Olympics the winner in first place gets a gold medal; second place, a silver medal; and third place, a bronze medal.

Use a semicolon before a conjunctive adverb that joins the clauses of a compound sentence.

You have learned that the parts of a compound sentence are sometimes joined by such words as *therefore*, *however*, *so*, *consequently*, *besides*, *nevertheless*, *then*, *yet*, and *moreover*. These words, called **conjunctive adverbs,** follow a semicolon.

> The Rams have a fine offense; however, their defense is weak.

The Colon

Use a colon after the greeting of a business letter.

> Dear Ms. Nolan: Dear Sir or Madam:

Use a colon between numerals indicating hours and minutes.

> 4:30 P.M.   8:15 A.M.

Use a colon to introduce a list of items. The colon indicates a pause before the items that follow.

> The FBI investigates the following federal crimes: spying, treason, kidnaping, and counterfeiting.

If there would be no pause in speaking, a colon is not used before a list.

> Secret Service agents guard the President, the Vice-President, Presidential candidates, and former Presidents.

Exercise A Copy the word before and after each missing semicolon or colon. Add the correct punctuation mark.

1. The fullback outran the ball the fans went wild.
2. Some people object to the following clothes made from animal skins leopard furs, sealskin coats, and alligator shoes.
3. Dear Madam

   The item that you ordered is out of stock.
4. Skaters, cyclists, and joggers crowded the path it was not a good place to stroll.
5. From the road, the ocean looked blue however, it was dull brown at the shore.

6. The Community Center requests the following foods dry milk, canned meat, canned soup, and cereals.

7. The flight was scheduled to depart at 7 30 however, we did not even board until 8 15.

8. There were many cars on the road consequently, the smog was thick.

9. The following cities are growing quickly Calcutta, India San Juan, Puerto Rico and Mexico City, Mexico.

10. Willie Nelson was not a typical country and western singer nevertheless, he became quite popular.

Exercise B Follow the directions for Exercise A.

1. The two sides could not reach an agreement therefore, a third party was called in.

2. The picnic tables held bowls of thick, tangy barbecue sauce platters of warm, crisp, fried chicken and big, shiny loaves of fresh-baked bread.

3. Karen built a large, roaring fire and we roasted hot dogs, corn, and marshmallows.

4. Barbara works after school therefore, she will not be home until 6 30.

5. Some popular home remedies for colds include the following fruit juices, chicken soup, garlic cloves, and aspirin.

6. Dear Resident

Would you like to win $500 a week for life?

7. Rafael Septien has an amazing kick besides, he thinks quickly.

8. On Labor Day at 7 30 P.M., the lifeguard closes the pool.

9. Spices are used in cooking for the following reasons they preserve food, they add variety to meals, and they are flavorful.

10. This year, a serious flu is widespread flu shots are being given at the clinic.

The Dash

Using Dashes with Interrupters

You have learned about using commas with words or short phrases, like *however* and *I think*, that interrupt a sentence. A dash is used with a long explanation that interrupts the thought.

An electric car—its battery must be recharged every 1,000 miles—was introduced by one auto maker.

A TV crew—a noise truck, huge cameras, complex sound equipment, and eager reporters—arrived at the scene.

Using the Dash Before a Summary

Use a dash after a series to indicate that a summary statement will follow.

Edsels, Packards, Studebakers, Hudsons—these cars are no longer made.

Chocolate milkshakes, hamburgers, and potato chips—this is the diet of some teen-agers.

Exercise Copy these sentences. Insert dashes as needed.

1. Layoffs a nearby factory cut 100 workers are one way to lower costs.
2. Taxi fares, school busing, and a new shopping district these issues were decided by the city council.
3. The Chicago Hustle a women's professional basketball team is looking for new players.
4. That magazine the new one I told you about is in the library.
5. The coach talked about team work, timing, concentration the keys to any victory.
6. Trains, cars, buses, planes all of them were halted by the snowstorm.

7. The winter of 1978 there were not enough trucks to remove the snow set records for snowfall.

8. We can take the elevator unless it is broken again to the tenth floor.

9. Parks, beaches, shops, interesting sights Toronto has them all.

10. Trumpets, drums, saxophones, trombones the band has all these instruments.

The Hyphen

Use a hyphen if part of a word must be carried over from one line to the next. Words are separated by hyphens only between syllables.

The FBI has about 195,000,000 fingerprints on file.

Only words having two or more syllables can be broken by a hyphen. Never divide one-syllable words, like *growl* or *weight*, at the end of a line. Check your dictionary to learn the syllables of a word.

A single letter should not be left at the end of a line. For instance, this division of *election* would be wrong: *e- lection*. A single letter should not begin a line either. This division of *ordinary* would be incorrect: *ordinar- y*.

Use a hyphen in compound numbers from twenty-one to ninety-nine.

forty-six chairs sixty-five lockers

Use a hyphen in fractions.

a two-thirds majority one-fourth of the votes.

Use a hyphen in certain compound nouns, such as *brother-in-law*, *drive-in*, and *great-grandmother*.

The *editor-in-chief* of the local paper is my *sister-in-law*.

Use a hyphen or hyphens between words that make up a compound adjective used before a noun.

> The radio announcer gives a play-by-play account of the game.
>
> *but:* The radio announcer describes the game play by play.

When compound adjectives are used after a noun, they are not usually hyphenated.

A dictionary will tell you if a word needs a hyphen. These are some examples of compound adjectives:

five-year-old boy	well-oiled machine
beat-up truck	best-selling book
little-used street	long-legged spider
double-edged sword	half-hearted attempt

Exercise Number your paper from 1 to 15. After the proper number, write the word or words that should be hyphenated. Add the necessary hyphens. Use your dictionary if you need to.

1. This out of date map is no help.
2. Have you ever heard a twenty one gun salute?
3. That is a half baked idea.
4. Turn of the century houses lined the street.
5. The old library had built in bookcases.
6. My great grandmother sent me twenty five dollars for my birthday.
7. Only one third of the students at that school have up to date health records.
8. The used paperbacks are forty five cents each, or three for one dollar and twenty five cents.
9. About fifty one out of every 100 babies born each year are boys.
10. Carl prefers his make believe world to the real one.
11. One half of those surveyed were younger than twenty two.

12. Three fourths of the students walk to school.

13. Most of my friends headed for the drive in.

14. The patient had a wild eyed look.

15. The editor in chief of that newspaper writes the editorials himself.

The Apostrophe

The apostrophe is frequently used to form the possessive of nouns. To use the apostrophe correctly, you should know whether a noun is singular or plural.

To form the possessive of a singular noun, add an apostrophe and an *s*.

student + 's = student's   Les + 's = Les's
baby + 's = baby's   Vanessa + 's = Vanessa's

To form the possessive of a plural noun that does not end in *s*, add an apostrophe and an *s*.

women + 's = women's   frogmen + 's = frogmen's

To form the possessive of a plural noun that ends in *s*, add only an apostrophe.

racers + ' = racers'   players + ' = players'
Reeses + ' = Reeses'   sponsors + ' = sponsors'

To form the possessive of indefinite pronouns, use an apostrophe and an *s*.

everybody + 's = everybody's   someone + 's = someone's

Do not use an apostrophe with a personal pronoun to show possession.

hers   ours   yours   its   theirs

The team changed *its* attitude.

Use an apostrophe in a contraction.

In contractions words are joined and letters are left out. An apostrophe replaces one or more letters that are left out.

she's = she is	hasn't = has not
we'll = we will	won't = will not
they're = they are	I'm = I am
it's = it is	shouldn't = should not

Use an apostrophe to show the omission of numbers in a date.

the spring of '79 (the spring of 1979)
a '71 Ford (a 1971 Ford)

Use an apostrophe and *s* to form the plurals of letters, figures, and words used as words.

ABC's   two *n*'s   three *4*'s   *yes*'s and *no*'s

Exercise A Number your paper from 1 to 10. Write the words that need apostrophes. Insert apostrophes where they are needed.

1. Experts cannot tell the difference between a mans handwriting and a womans.
2. Ive already met Russs sister.
3. Its going to rain before we reach the Carlsons porch.
4. The class of 70 is holding its reunion in the gym.
5. Thats Sandras favorite team.
6. Im sure the brakes of most cars are lined with asbestos.
7. Anybodys guess is as good as mine.
8. Theyve admitted that the fault is theirs.
9. DeeAnnes name is spelled with three *e*s.
10. He didnt notice the childrens absence.

Exercise B Follow the directions for Exercise A.

1. Is that Suzys book youre reading?
2. How would you describe the 1970s?

3. His *maybes* arent the same as *yess*.
4. The coachs jacket was a gift from her team.
5. Dont the Reeses dogs ever stop barking?
6. The band lost some of its best musicians when the class of 80 graduated.
7. Arent the clinics hours from 2:00 until 8:00?
8. The two scientists conclusions were the same.
9. This is everyones park, not just yours.
10. The young children havent learned to tell the *d*s from the *b*s.

Quotation Marks

Use quotation marks at the beginning and at the end of a direct quotation.

Quotation marks tell your reader that a speaker's exact words are being given. Here is an example:

Linda said, "Someone is following me."

Quotation marks are *not* used with indirect quotations. An indirect quotation does not tell the speaker's exact words.

Linda said that someone was following her.

At the beginning of a sentence there are often explanatory words. Use a comma directly after these words. Then begin the quotation with quotation marks. A period at the end of a sentence belongs *inside* the quotation marks.

The pilot said, "Fasten your seat belts."

Sometimes explanatory words end the sentence. Then the quoted statement at the beginning of the sentence is followed by a comma. The comma belongs inside the quotation marks.

"Fasten your seat belts," the pilot said.

Using Divided Quotations

Sometimes a quotation is divided into two parts by explanatory words. In that case, each part of the quotation is enclosed by quotation marks.

> "One very healthful food," Pamela said, "is granola."

When the divided quotation is a single sentence, the second part begins with a small letter. Look at the example above. At times, however, the second part begins a new sentence. Then a capital letter is used at the beginning of the second part.

> "There is entertainment at halftime," Toby noted. "**T**he band will play."

The first part of a divided quotation is followed by a comma. Commas always appear inside quotation marks.

> "On the way," Derek said, "we will pick up Kelly."

The explanatory words in the middle of a divided quotation are followed by either a period or a comma. A period is used if the first part completes a sentence. A comma is used if the sentence continues after the explanatory words.

> "At the plant," Eric said, "we work in shifts."
>
> "First, we spread paste on the wallpaper," Ginger explained. "Then we hang the paper and cut it to size."

Exercise Write each of the following sentences three ways as a direct quotation.

Example: I need an honest answer.

a. "I need an honest answer," she said.
b. She said, "I need an honest answer."
c. "I need," she said, "an honest answer."

1. Don't talk to me while I'm working.
2. Yes, Stevie Wonder writes many of his own songs.

3. I'm sorry that I forgot to call you.
4. In the last two minutes, the Cowboys took the lead.
5. Finally, a wrecking crew attacked the vacant building.

Using Punctuation with Quotation Marks

Place question marks and exclamation points inside the quotation marks if they belong to the quotation itself.

Andrew asked, "Who sent you a telegram?"
Andrea screamed, "Move fast!"

Place question marks and exclamation points outside the quotation marks if they do not belong to the quotation.

Did Keith say, "Meet me at school"?
What a surprise it was when the manager said, "You're hired"!

Commas and periods, as you have seen, always appear within quotation marks.

Exercise A Copy the following sentences. Punctuate them correctly with quotation marks, end marks, and commas. (There are three indirect quotations that need only end punctuation.)

1. Go away yelled Pat
2. Do you like that yellow Chevette asked Mindy
3. Oh well said Angie a little glue will fix that
4. Ms. Pappas explained why copper wiring is used
5. I have finally learned to use the brakes on my skates Tisha said
6. Terry announced proudly I knocked down all ten pins
7. Adam said that he was on a diet
8. We locked this door when we left said Harris nervously Why is it open now
9. Did Dr. Korshak say that you should tape your ankle
10. Did the dentist say I think your tooth must be pulled

Exercise B Write each of the following sentences as a direct quotation. In some examples, put the quotation first. In others, put the quotation last. Also, for variety, divide some quotations.

1. Is Costa Rica part of Central America?
2. Don't say that!
3. I called the fire department from a neighbor's house.
4. There's a restaurant by the bowling alley.
5. I never know what Merle will say next.
6. By next June, I should have my driver's license.
7. We swam in the quarry.
8. Stand back!
9. Was that snake a copperhead?
10. This weekend I have to help my cousin.

Using Long Quotations

You may wonder how to use quotation marks for quoting two or more sentences by the same speaker. Look at the following example:

> "When you keep accounts, there are credits and debits," Stacy explained. "Debits are amounts that you owe. Credits are amounts that are paid to you."

Using Quotation Marks for Dialogue

Dialogue is conversation between two or more people. It is punctuated in a special way. Begin a new paragraph each time the speaker changes.

> "What are your favorite TV commercials?" Christy asked.
>
> "I like the commercials for Coca-Cola," replied Ted.
>
> "My favorites are Dr. Pepper and Pepsi commercials," Delia said. "I also like the new ones for Hubba Bubba. Which ones do you like, Christy?"
>
> "I like most of them," Christy answered. "Some of them are better than the TV programs that come in between."

Exercise Rewrite the following conversation. Make correct paragraph divisions, and use the right punctuation.

What kind of job do you want after you graduate Ms. Morales asked. Well answered Shirley I haven't thought much about it. I do know that I'm good at keeping calm in a crisis. James said I know what kind of job I *don't* want. I would hate a job that kept me in one room all day. Marva looked sympathetic. I feel that way, too she said. I want a job that will keep me on the go.

Punctuating Titles

Use quotation marks to enclose the titles of magazine articles, chapters, short stories, essays, poems, television and radio programs, songs, and short pieces of music.

Magazine article:	"On-the-Job Training for You"
Chapter title:	Chapter 2, "The New World"
Short story:	"Clothes Make the Man"
Essay:	"The Dog That Bit People"
Poem:	"The Raven"
Television program:	"Eight Is Enough"
Song:	"Jingle Bells"

Underline the titles of books, newspapers, magazines, plays, movies, works of art, and long musical compositions.

In writing or typing, such titles are underlined, like this: The Chocolate War.

In print, these titles appear in italics instead.

Book title:	*The Pigman*
Newspaper:	*New Haven Register*
Magazine:	*Motor Trend*
Play:	*Annie*
Movie:	*Rocky II*
Work of art:	*Mona Lisa*
Long musical composition:	*Porgy and Bess*

Exercise A Copy the following sentences, adding quotation marks around titles or underlining titles where necessary.

1. The story Requiem was published in Ms. magazine.
2. Old Abe Lincoln Came Out of the Wilderness was a popular marching song during the Civil War.
3. I reported on Althea Gibson's article, I Always Wanted To Be Someone.
4. The article appeared in the book Out of the Bleachers.
5. Our city was featured on the TV show 60 Minutes.
6. Of all the Frankenstein movies, I like Young Frankenstein most.
7. The Daily Defender is a Chicago newspaper.
8. The musical West Side Story is a modern version of Shakespeare's play Romeo and Juliet.
9. Monet's painting Waterlilies has now been reproduced on bedsheets.
10. Many people recognize the eerie notes of the ballet music The Firebird.

Exercise B Follow the directions for Exercise A.

1. Surely you can think of a better title for your essay than What I Did During My Summer Vacation.
2. I like Langston Hughes's poem Dreams.
3. Julia Ward Howe wrote the song The Battle Hymn of the Republic.
4. Please read Chapter 10, The Last Frontier.
5. John Tenniel, who illustrated the book Alice in Wonderland, also drew cartoons for the magazine Punch.
6. The Time Machine was first a novel and then a movie.
7. The Searchers was a famous Western.
8. The first New York newspaper was called the Gazette.
9. The Devil's Dictionary is a book of humorous definitions.
10. Our school play last year was A Raisin in the Sun.

REVIEW Punctuation

End Marks and Commas Rewrite the following sentences, adding the missing punctuation.

1. Skates are becoming more popular and skateboards have almost been forgotten
2. How thin you are
3. How thin are you
4. Carol asked if she should bring her own pliers wrench or hammer
5. Joan of Arc the French heroine was declared a saint in 1920
6. Ms Doyle Dr Antonelli and Mr McCoy are holding a meeting at 8 P M on Saturday September 3
7. On March 13 1852 the first newspaper cartoon of Uncle Sam appeared
8. After Robin bought the tickets she put them in her pocket
9. Yes Mel I remembered to buy Doritos and ginger ale.
10. Georgia looked in her address book rummaged through a stack of old mail and finally found this address: 215 Main Street Carthage Illinois 62321

Semicolons, Colons, Dashes, and Hyphens Add semicolons, colons, dashes, and hyphens as you rewrite these sentences.

11. At eighty six, my great grandmother still has a happy go lucky view of life.
12. Donna can remember everything that she hears furthermore, she has a photographic memory.
13. The commander in chief, the general, and the prime minister these people will arrive at 7 15 P.M.

14. Three fourths of the students listed these long term goals more education, an interesting job, and a happy family life.

15. Dear Madam

We have received your letter, it will be published in next week's column.

Apostrophes, Quotation Marks, and Underlining Write each sentence, putting in necessary apostrophes, quotation marks, and underlining.

16. Rachel said, I like the TR-7s that were made in the early 1970s.

17. The students theme for their dance will be from the movie Grease.

18. The song Ring My Bell reminds me of the summer of 79.

19. Did the teacher say that we would discuss Tillie Olsens story, I Stand Here Ironing?

20. Get out of the way! yelled Lee.

21. Is it true, asked Glorias brother, that the injured player is my sister?

22. Its somebodys problem, but not yours, said Ms. Stranskey.

23. Little Chriss laces are always flapping because he cant tie his shoes.

24. All three teachers classes are reading the novel Ordinary People.

25. I dont see Cheryl Tiegss picture in this copy of People, said Beth. Maybe its in last weeks issue.

Spelling

Good spelling is a skill that is valuable throughout a lifetime. It is a skill that is important in all writing, ranging from school reports to messages, letters, and job applications. On the job, too, you will often need to write. Good spelling is noticed and admired.

Becoming a good speller is not an easy task, though. The spelling of many English words does not seem to make sense. Many words are not spelled the way they sound.

Learning to spell well is not hopeless, however. There are certain patterns of spelling that English words follow. There are general rules that make spelling easier. In addition, there are methods for attacking spelling problems. With such tools, you can avoid many problems and improve spelling. This section will show you some solutions.

How To Improve Your Spelling

1. Locate and conquer your own specific spelling problems. What spelling errors do you make over and over? Study your past written assignments. Make a list of words you misspelled on them. Work on mastering those words.

2. Pronounce words carefully. Are you misspelling words because you aren't pronouncing them right? If you are writing *famly* for *family*, for instance, you are probably mispronouncing the word. Try to pronounce your words more precisely.

3. Try to remember the letters in new words. Do you really look at the spelling of new or difficult words? That habit can help you to remember how to spell words. Write the correct spelling of a new word several times.

4. Always proofread your writing. Are some of your misspellings careless mistakes? By examining your writing, you may catch such errors. Read over your work slowly, word by word.

5. Look up difficult words in a dictionary. Do you reach for the dictionary when you're unsure of a spelling? Get into the habit of letting the dictionary help you to spell well.

6. Learn the few important spelling rules explained in this section.

How To Spell a Particular Word Correctly

1. Look at the word and say it to yourself. Make sure to pronounce it correctly. Say it twice, looking at the syllables as you say them.

2. Look at the letters and say each one. Sound out the word from its spelling. Divide the word into syllables and pronounce each syllable.

3. Write the word without looking at your book or list.

4. Check to see if you spelled the word correctly. Look back at your book or list. If you spelled the word correctly, repeat the process.

5. If you made an error, note what it was. Then repeat steps 3 and 4 until you have written the word correctly three times.

Spelling Rules

Adding Prefixes

When a prefix is added to a word, the spelling of the word remains the same.

im- + perfect = imperfect
re- + entry = reentry
inter- + action = interaction
dis- + agree = disagree
ir- + rational = irrational
mis- + use = misuse
de- + face = deface
il- + legal = illegal

Suffixes with Silent e

When a suffix beginning with a vowel is added to a word ending in a silent *e*, the *e* is usually dropped.

save + ing = saving
style + ish = stylish
grace + ious = gracious
value + able = valuable
rate + ing = rating
imagine + ation = imagination

When a suffix beginning with a consonant is added to a word ending in a silent *e*, the *e* is usually retained.

time + less = timeless
like + ly = likely
same + ness = sameness
strange + ly = strangely
amaze + ment = amazement
hope + ful = hopeful

The following words are **exceptions.** Study them.

truly argument ninth wholly

Exercise A Find the misspelled words. Spell them correctly.

1. Dorothy was gazeing at the graceful skaters.
2. She is leaveing that missmanaged company.
3. The driver of the handsomly painted car made an illegal turn.
4. These arguements are not solveing the problem.
5. We were dissappointed that the sportscaster mistated the facts.
6. That penalty was wholly unecessary.
7. Our district relected that insincere politician.
8. Tim has trouble wakeing up on these freezeing days.
9. A fameous surgeon performed the operateion.
10. Leaving everything to chance is imature.

Exercise B Add the prefixes and suffixes as shown and write the new word.

1. like + ing
2. mis + understand
3. im + mobile
4. note + able
5. ir + regular
6. separate + ion
7. tape + ing
8. un + needed
9. un + wanted
10. mis + spent
11. re + apply
12. dance + ing
13. re + examine
14. place + ment
15. place + ing
16. amuse + ing
17. amuse + ment
18. love + able
19. dis + similar
20. dis + prove

Suffixes and Final *y*

When a suffix is added to a word ending in *y* preceded by a consonant, the *y* is usually changed to *i*.

carry + er = carrier
worry + ed = worried
silly + est = silliest
fury + ous = furious
thirty + eth = thirtieth
holy + ness = holiness

Note the following exception: When *-ing* is added, the *y* does not change:

hurry + ing = hurrying   study + ing = studying
rally + ing = rallying   cry + ing = crying

When a suffix is added to a word ending in *y* preceded by a vowel, the *y* usually does not change.

play + ing = playing   destroy + er = destroyer
decay + ed = decayed   annoy + ing = annoying

Exercise Add the suffixes as shown and write the new word.

1. dizzy + ness
2. carry + ing
3. ready + ness
4. heavy + er
5. witty + est
6. marry + ing
7. marry + age
8. fifty + eth
9. employ + able
10. stay + ed
11. terrify + ing
12. creepy + est
13. relay + ed
14. glory + ous
15. cozy + er
16. history + an
17. joy + ful
18. enjoy + able
19. tiny + ness
20. fry + ed

Adding the Suffixes *-ness* and *-ly*

When the suffix *-ly* is added to a word ending in *l*, both *l's* are kept. When *-ness* is added to a word ending in *n*, both *n's* are kept.

cruel + ly = cruelly   even + ness = evenness
general + ly = generally   lean + ness = leanness

Doubling the Final Consonant

In words of one syllable that end in one consonant preceded by one vowel, double the final consonant before adding *-ing*, *-ed*, or *-er*.

beg + ing = begging   scar + ed = scarred
flap + ed = flapped   grab + ing = grabbing
thin + er = thinner   tap + ed = tapped

In words of one syllable that end in one consonant preceded by two vowels, the final consonant is not doubled.

steer + ing = steering   lead + er = leader
join + ed = joined   fool + ing = fooling

Exercise A Find the misspelled words. Spell them correctly.

1. Lana foolled everyone by speaking truthfuly.
2. Chris spoted the actress and beged for her autograph.
3. I finaly stopped the driping of the water faucet.
4. Something is cloging the exhaust.
5. Dot is hoping on one foot because she stepped on a bee.
6. Reservations are not usualy booked a month in advance.
7. The miser Scrooge is generaly known for his meaness.
8. The days are geting cooler now.
9. The openess of this building makes it especialy comfortable.
10. Are you realy digging a new trench?

Exercise B Add the suffixes as shown and write the new word.

1. green + ness
2. tip + ed
3. boom + ed
4. lag + ed
5. top + ed
6. awful + ly
7. grim + est
8. playful + ly
9. brag + ing
10. plain + ness
11. cook + ed
12. sob + ed
13. run + ing
14. clip + ed
15. stern + ness
16. cheerful + ly
17. groan + ing
18. pat + ed
19. stop + ing
20. stoop + ing

Words with the "Seed" Sound

There is only one English word ending in *sede: supersede*. Three words end in *ceed: exceed, proceed, succeed*. All other words ending with the sound of *seed* are spelled *cede:*

recede   precede   concede   secede

Words with *ie* and *ei*

There is a general rule for words with the long *e* (*ē*) sound. The word is spelled *ie* except after *c*.

I before *E*

piece	fierce	field	grief	chief
believe	relief	niece	reprieve	retrieve

Except after *C*

perceive	deceit	ceiling	receipt
conceive	conceit	receive	deceive

The following words are exceptions to the rule. Study them.

either	weird	leisure
species	seize	neither

Exercise Find the misspelled words in these sentences and spell them correctly.

1. This new law superceeds the old one.
2. South Carolina seceded from the Union in 1860 and siezed Fort Sumter in 1861.
3. My neice Meredith received a wierd surprise.
4. Sally beleives that she can clear that field in her liesure time.
5. The warden conceeded that the prisoner should get a reprieve.
6. Erin succeded in tying the boat to the pier.
7. Niether peice of land is big enough for an apartment building.
8. The forged reciept did not deceive the sales clerk, who proceded to call the detective.
9. In some cultures the period of grieving excedes two years.
10. That species of owl has a peircing shriek.

REVIEW Spelling

Applying Spelling Rules Read each sentence carefully. Find the misspelled words. Write each word correctly.

1. She defended her chief loyaly.
2. The council was disatisfied with the zoneing laws.
3. Some advertisements are meant to decieve us.
4. Pollution levels were continualy rising.
5. Many arguements are completely unecessary.
6. Unbeleivable! Judy is takeing the lead.
7. The fire crew choped down the door of the blazeing apartment.
8. Sam hurryed over to his crying niece.
9. Claire was runing to the bus stop when she heard that the drivers were strikeing.
10. Gus has succeeded in arriveing punctualy every day.
11. The guard had only the slimmest chance of stoping the ball.
12. Kevin looked around fearfuly before makeing a move.
13. We received some especialy good news earlyer today.
14. I'm sneezing because this is the dustyest room I've ever stayed in.
15. Abby grinned happyly as the judges studyed her work.
16. The driver missjudged the distance and ramed into a fence.
17. Varyous foods, includeing fried fish and broiled meat, dissagree with me.
18. Going to that employment agency was wasteing valueable time.
19. Although Kris talked cheerfuly, she was angryer than I have ever seen her.
20. Jeremy's thiness realy made shopping for clothes a problem.

A List of Commonly Misspelled Words

abbreviate
accidentally
achievement
across
address
all right
altogether
always
amateur
analyze
anonymous
answer
apologize
appearance
appreciate
appropriate
argument
arrangement
associate
awkward
balance
bargain
beginning
believe
bicycle
bookkeeper
bulletin
bureau
business
cafeteria
calendar
campaign
candidate
certain
changeable
characteristic
column
committee
courageous
courteous
criticize
curiosity
cylinder
dealt
decision
definitely
despair
desperate
dictionary
dependent
description
desirable
different
disagree
disappear
disappoint
discipline
dissatisfied
efficient
eighth
eligible
eliminate
embarrass
emphasize
environment
enthusiastic
equipped
especially
exaggerate
excellent
exhaust
expense
experience
familiar
fascinating
February
financial
foreign
fourth
fragile
generally
government
grammar
guarantee
guard
gymnasium
handkerchief
height
humorous
imaginary
immediately
incredible
influence
intelligence
interesting
knowledge
laboratory
lightning
literature
loneliness
maintenance
marriage
mathematics
medicine
minimum
mischievous
missile
misspell
mortgage
municipal
necessary
nickel
ninety
noticeable
nuclear
nuisance
obstacle
occasionally
occur
opinion
opportunity
original
outrageous
parallel
particularly
permanent
permissible
persuade
picnicking
pleasant
pneumonia
politics
possess
possibility
practice
prejudice
preparation
privilege
probably
professor
pronunciation
propeller
psychology
quantity
realize
recognize
recommend
reference

referred
rehearse
repetition
representative
restaurant
rhythm
ridiculous
sandwich
schedule
scissors
secretary

separate
sergeant
similar
sincerely
sophomore
souvenir
specifically
strategy
strictly
success
surprise

syllable
sympathy
symptom
temperament
temperature
thorough
throughout
together
tomorrow
traffic
tragedy

transferred
truly
Tuesday
twelfth
undoubtedly
unnecessary
vacuum
vicinity
village
weird
writing

The Correct Form for Writing

Anyone who reads your papers notices the content. What you say is important. You may not realize, though, that a reader also notices the form of your papers. Your writing is judged not only on its content, but also on its form.

Good form is careful, neat, and consistent. Such form will impress any reader. Some schools set their own specific rules for the correct form for written work. In this section you will learn about the kind of form that is accepted by many schools.

Guidelines for Clear Writing

Neatness

A neat, legible paper can be read easily. Neatness also suggests that the writer cares about what he or she is writing. There are several ways to give your papers a neat appearance.

Legible Writing

Typewritten papers are usually more legible than handwritten ones. However, many students do not have typewriters, and few schools require typed papers.

Handwritten papers can be clear and legible, too. They should always be written in ink. Blue or black is easiest to read. Make sure that letters are distinct, since some letters look similar. For example, *a*'s and *o*'s can be confused unless they are formed carefully. So can *e*'s and *i*'s.

The First Draft and the Final Copy

You cannot expect the first draft of a paper to be in perfect form. You write a first draft from your pre-writing notes or an outline. Then you need to correct or revise the first draft. You may need to change words and sentences or rearrange whole sections.

Afterward, you can make your final copy. Proofread this new copy. You may find errors or words left out. To insert a word, write it above the line. Use a caret (ʌ) to show where the word belongs. To change a word, draw a line through it and write the correction above it. If you have made more than about three corrections on a page, you should recopy the page.

Acceptable Form

The correct form for writing means more than a neat appearance. In a paper with acceptable form, the various parts are positioned correctly. Headings, titles, margins, and spacing should be in the correct form.

The Heading

A heading identifies your paper. It is usually placed in the upper right-hand corner of the first page. Place your name on the first line. Write the name of your class on the second line. Write the date on the third line. In a paper with a title page, the heading is placed in the upper right corner of that page.

Each page, except for page one, should be numbered. Beginning with page two, place the page number in the upper right-hand corner. To identify all pages, you might want to put your name under the page number.

Some teachers may require a different form for labeling your paper. Follow any special instructions you are given.

The Title

The title of a paper should appear near the top of the first page. In general, place the title two lines down from the last line of the heading. Begin the first line of your paper two lines below the title.

Correct form for a title also means proper capitalization. The first word and all important words in the title should be capitalized. Use capitals for only the first letters of words, not for every letter. Do not underline your title or place it in quotation marks.

When a paper is more than three pages long, sometimes a title page is used. This page precedes the paper.

Margins and Spacing

Use correct margins and spacing to achieve an attractive appearance. Margins of one inch at the top, bottom, and left side of the paper look pleasing.

Try to keep the right-hand margin fairly even. Do not break too many words with hyphens, though, in order to keep the margin straight. A safe rule is to avoid hyphens in more than two lines in a row.

Double-spacing makes typed papers look neat. Paragraphs are usually indented five spaces. Skip two spaces after the punctuation mark at the end of a sentence.

Writing Numbers

The form for writing numbers should be consistent. Numbers under 100 are usually spelled out. Larger numbers are written in figures.

> I got a raise of *twenty-four* dollars a month.
> The National League consists of *twelve* teams.
> Ticket sales amounted to *$2,125*.
> Over *170* players have made the Baseball Hall of Fame.

A number at the beginning of a sentence is always spelled out.

> *Thirty thousand* people attended the game.
> *One thousand* millimeters make up one meter.
> *Four hundred dollars* was stolen.

Figures rather than spelled-out words are used for these numbers: dates, street and room numbers, telephone numbers, temperatures, page numbers, decimals, and percentages.

> The Battle of Concord took place on April 19, 1775.
> The clinic is at 66 West Schiller.

Our typing class meets in Room 35 today.
Matthew's phone number is 328-6610.
Last night the temperature went down to 10 degrees.
Did you see that article about vans on page 16?
Ann ran the hurdles in 15.8 seconds.
The new sales tax is 4 percent.

In large sums of money or expressions of large quantities, commas are used to separate the figures. Commas are not used in dates, serial numbers, page numbers, addresses, or telephone numbers.

Correct: The Statue of Liberty cost $500,000.
Correct: The Milky Way has 200,000,000,000 stars.
Incorrect: The first World Series was in 1,903.
Correct: The first World Series was in 1903.

Exercise Copy these sentences, correcting any errors in the writing of numbers.

1. A movie shows fourteen hundred forty frames of film per minute.
2. The serial number of the typewriter is 20,002.
3. 1st prize is one thousand two hundred and fifty dollars.
4. About ninety percent of the patients who have this operation recover fully within 6 months.
5. Although the temperature was actually 30 degrees, the wind chill factor lowered it to two degrees.
6. The profit of twelve thousand two hundred and five dollars is ten percent higher than last year's.
7. 3 years ago the Chandlers moved to 1,682 Garfield Street.
8. 1 barrel of oil is equal to 31 gallons.
9. 1000 grams equals a little more than three pounds.
10. On March eighteenth, 1,959, Hawaii became our 50th state.

Using Abbreviations

Abbreviations are shortened forms of words. In formal writing, abbreviations are usually not acceptable.

Abbreviations, however, may be used for most titles before and after names. Abbreviations may also be used for government agencies and for time.

Titles before proper names:	Mrs., Mr., Ms., Gen., Dr., Rev., Sgt., Fr., Sen.
Titles after proper names:	Jr., M.D., D.D.S., Ph.D.
Government agencies:	FBI, VA, EPA, FTC
Dates and times:	A.M., P.M., B.C., A.D.

Notice that periods are not used in the abbreviations of government agencies.

A title is abbreviated only when it is used with a person's name, as in *Dr. Lauren Sherwood*. The following, for example, would not be acceptable: The dr. found a cure for the disease.

Abbreviations are not used for certain titles. *Honorable* and *Reverend* are not abbreviated when preceded by *the: the Reverend Lee Withers*. Abbreviations are not used for the titles of the President and Vice-President of the United States.

In most writing, abbreviations are not acceptable for the following: names of countries and states, months and days of the week, addresses, and firm names.

Incorrect: The Mayans built pyramids in Mex.
Correct: The Mayans built pyramids in Mexico.

Incorrect: Detroit, Mich., is called "Motor City."
Correct: Detroit, Michigan, is called "Motor City."

Incorrect: Tues., Nov. 2, is Election Day.
Correct: Tuesday, November 2, is Election Day.

Incorrect: The Coca-Cola Co. has a plant on Oak Ave.
Correct: The Coca-Cola Company has a plant on Oak Avenue.

In ordinary writing, abbreviations are not acceptable for the following: names of school courses, and the words *page*, *chapter*, and *Christmas*. Abbreviations for measurements, like *ft.*, *in.*, *min.*, *hr.*, *oz.*, *qt.*, *mi.*, are also unacceptable.

Exercise Correct the errors in abbreviation in these sentences.

1. The secy. of H.E.W. is usually not a medical dr.
2. The Pres. met with the Secy. of Defense at Camp David, Md.
3. The Rev. Amelia Gleason gave a sermon about the true meaning of Xmas.
4. McDonald's Corp. has its headquarters on Twenty-second Ave. in Oakbrook, Ill.
5. Mr. Frank Ransom, Jr. is applying for a govt. grant to start a center for sr. citizens.
6. Benito Juarez, a nineteenth-century pres. of Mexico, is described in Ch. 10.
7. Last Fri., our home ec. class visited Mercy Hosp.
8. I lost two lbs. in forty-eight hrs. on the diet Dr. Rossi gave me.
9. Cleopatra ruled Egypt in the first cent. B.C.
10. Pres. Roosevelt closed all banks in the U.S. on Mar. 6, 1933.

A

B

D

E

O

P

Q

R

S

T

U

Y

Z

Acknowledgments

William Collins Publishers, Inc.: For entries appearing on pages 13, 167, 169, 170, 172, 173, 285.

Photographs

James L. Ballard: ii, 30, 42, 52, 96, 130, 183, 214.

Magnum: Bob Adelman, 74, 188; Abigail Heyman, 80; Ernst Haas, 88; Constantine Manos, 114.

Woodfin Camp: Jim Anderson, xiv, 18, 62, 138, 164, 174; Timothy Egan, 68; Marc and Evelyn Bernheim, 106; Sylvia Johnson, 122.

Illustrations

Jeanne Seabright: all handwritten art. Ken Izzi: special mechanical art. Amy Palmer: diagrams. Kathleen A. Langwell: art production.